AF522276

SOCIAL JUSTICE

SOCIAL JUSTICE

Shehzad Ahmad

ANMOL PUBLICATIONS PVT. LTD.
NEW DELHI - 110 002 (INDIA)

ANMOL PUBLICATIONS PVT. LTD.
H.O.: 4374/4B, Ansari Road, Darya Ganj,
New Delhi - 110 002 (India)
Ph.: 23278000, 23261597
B.O.: No. 1015, Ist Main Road, BSK IIIrd Stage,
IIIrd Phase, IIIrd Block,
Bangalore - 560 085 (India)
Visit us at: www.anmolpublications.com

Social Justice

First Published, 2007
ISBN 978-81-261-3223-2

PRINTED IN INDIA

Printed at Mehra Offset Press, Delhi.

CONTENTS

PREFACE

Social Justice is one of the greatest virtues of humanity. In fact, it is a divine attribute given to Man on the earth. Though, one of the toughest jobs, ensuring social justice has, now, become a matter of serious concern. Social injustice is rampant to the extent that only the powerful and wealthy win all the goals in society. In Constitution of India, there are provisions for social justice—with justice of every kind, i.e., economic justice, political justice, and legal justice, etc. India is known for a number of human-friendly provisions in its polity. That's why Indian integrity can never be challenged in spite of myriads of castes, creeds or classes. However, with due course of time, India has fallen prey to some anti-social forces, which have led the country to an obnoxious mesh of unsocial practices.

Unfortunately, some of the high profile socialites and political heavyweight—what to speak of those belonging to the lower rung—and custodians of peace and justice have also joined hands with these elements, which are eating into the grandeur and glory of our nation. They are no more than the black spots on the forehead of the society. All such black sheeps should be meted out their due.

Given the scenario, there was an urgent need to produce such a work, which may focus on the crux of the problem and strike the root. Present book, *Social Justice* fills that room efficiently. It must prove to be useful to scholars, researchers, students, academics, general readers and particularly social activists.

Readers' comments and suggestions are invited and would be appreciated.

—Editor

1

CHANGE BY JUSTICE

Of the two broad types of processes of social change such as the one which sustain the social system and the one which brings about change in the system and change of the system, one will be dealing with the former type of social change. It deals with conformity, status quo, maintenance etc. Parsonian theory on social change thus made a point of departure from his predecessors such as Marx, Comte etc.

Before embarking upon his theory of social change, a brief outline on the theory of the concept of social system is to be highlighted. According to him, social system consists in a plurality of individual actors interacting with each other in a situation having at least a physical or environmental aspect, actors who are motivated in terms of a tendency to the optimization of qualification and who are in relation to their situations is defined and mediated in terms of a system of externally structured and shared symbols. Each of these subsystem interact with each other.

The concept of structure focuses on those elements of the patterning of the system which are independent of short-time fluctuations in the external situation. The structural features may be treated as constants over certain ranges of variation in behaviour. The functional aspect of the social system assumes dynamic aspect of the structure. The giveness of the environing situation external to the system consists of dynamic process and mechanisms that help in the operation of the system and are integrative in nature.

Equilibrium : The concept of equilibrium is the reference point for analysing the processes by which a system either comes to terms with the exigencies imposed by a changing environment, without essential change in its own structure or fails to come to terms.

Hierarchy of Relations of Control in a Social System : The subsystems of any large social system constitute a hierarchical series of agencies of control. At the lowest level, the anatomical features of the physical organism is a regulating factor on the organism. At the societal level, the cultural system of norms and prescriptions of various degrees presents a level of control There are several such systems of control within the social system and they are arranged hierarchically in terms of the degree of control that they can exercise on the entire or part of the organism.

Structural Change : The process of structural change may be regarded the obverse of the equilibrating process. The difference of state between phenomena internal and external to the system, that is, the boundaries of the system, are broken down in the process of change.

This means that the boundaries that separate the social system from other systems like personality system, political system, are no more there. Change according to Parsons is a natural process for bringing about equilibrium to society and such an overance takes place after a process of structural change occurs. Therefore, it is not pathological.

The structural changes could be discussed from different sources of change such as exogenous and endogenous.

The exogenous sources of change is the change from outside agencies. Exogenous cultural exchange, for example, can lead to assimilation of external cultural elements. Exogenous factors can however, have an effect only through the mediation of the internal mechanisms of the social system. Assimilation of exogenous cultural borrowings, for example, can take place only if the internal arrangement of the system in consideration is receptive to it. *e.g.* Westernisation in India.

Changes caused by the internal factors is indigenous *e.g.* Sankritisation the changes in the individual's life due to economic improvement, social welfare programmes etc. This causes individual mobility.

Parsons interpret the aforementioned form of changes in the following ways :

One type of change is that induced by endogenous forces, called 'structural differentiation', and the other as a result of exogenous forces, namely 'changes in the value system.

The first, structural differentiation', refers to the process by which the units of the system whose functions were fused, get differentiated. There is an increasing division of labour and the number of units in the system also multiplies. The transition in the West, from a pre-industrial system to the present industrial set-up is a clear example of structural differentiation. The economic, cultural, societal functions were all performed by the family.

Here the functions are fused in one unit. With structural differentiation, economic functions get separated and become the jurisdiction of industrial and commercial institutions that have emerged to undertake economic activities exclusively. Similarly, socialisation is taken over by the school and institutions such as the state and so on. Thus a simple society gets progressively complex as its structural components proliferate and differentiate, each taking over a distinct function.

The second kind of change induced by exogenous sources is a change in the social value system—Weber's theory of the protestant ethic and the spirit of capitalism in the West. Apart from the factors making for structural differentiation, a corresponding change in value systems effected the transition to an industrial society from a pre-industrial set-up. The protestant ethic that legitimised material acquisition encouraged profit-making.

Parsons' theory of change has always been criticised for its failure to take conflict and change into account and persistent tension within and between systems. As the theory is geared towards the description of structural and functional features of systems, it consciously or unconsciously promotes a static view of social system.

No social system is as smooth as Parsons sees it. Violence, revolutions, unrest have become the order of the day.

Parsons' approach fails to deal with social change satisfactorily. It focuses more on integrative forces. It has ignored the role of social movements, factionalism, emergence of dissent groups, counter culture and terrorism, which are crucial issues which any contemporary theory of society and change should be handling.

Besides, Parsons' theory has been severely criticised for being a historical and thereby antithetical to change. Also, the framework is regarded as being too abstract and general as to be oblivious to important concrete features of process of social change.

But his theory provides us the framework of understanding the operation and the interrelated working system of the social system in a systematic manner.

Sorokin's Theory of Social Change : Sorokin's theory of social change pertains to the processes of cultural change in the following ways : The life and death of cultural system :

According to Sorokin, a cultural system grows in the following ways :

(i) Quantitative increase such as the increase in human agents.

(ii) Qualitative increase such as increase in the quality of such human agents.

Deterioration of system of meanings can occur through the loss of parts. When a system declines to the point that its meanings become unrecognisable or loses all of its vehicles or agents, it dies.

The factors that can cause the loss of human agents in a cultural system are the system itself may not be powerful, useful or satisfying enough to hold the loyalty and enthusiasm of human beings.

The characteristics of the system are not the only factors which influence its survival as a living system. It can be destroyed through the destruction of human agents. The vehicles of a cultural system may be destroyed, such as the curtailing of movies, particular books etc.

Finally, in order to survive, a cultural system must maintain the identity of its system of meanings for meanings are symbols for particular objects. Systems that are relatively free from internal contradictions and congeries and those clearly defined are likely to remain intact over a period of time.

Theory of Cultural Diffusion : Cultural diffusion is the transmission of culture from one place to another. The basic condition for this is that the cultures concerned should have contact and communication. Those in direct contact with the other cultures are likely to get influenced first. Normally the elite and high classes adopt the patterns of other cultures more easily.

The changes in culture that occur due to diffusion can affect almost any single element. But greater the difference between the diffusing culture and the recipient, the greater the extent of change. The more complex and difficult the diffusing culture the more likely it is to be accepted by new groups.

Immanent Change : According to the theory the basic cause of change in a socio-cultural system lies within the system itself. Change can take place by the factors and the consequence of its changes too. The system itself brings the source of its own change and thus moulds its own destiny. The role of the environment consists essentially in retardation or acceleration, facilitation or hindrance, reinforcement or weakening of the realisation of the immanent potentialities of the system. The environment can crush a system or stop its development, but it cannot change the nature of its immanent potentialities. The relative influence of the system's own potentials and of the effects of the environment, however, vary for each individual system.

Thus, according to him other conditions being equal (including the milieu) in similar social and cultural systems, the greater is their integration, the greater is their self-determination in moulding their own destiny.

Other conditions being equal, the greater the power of the system, the greater its self direction.

In the first premise, integration means the extent of causal and meaningful interdependence among the system's components, the degree of solidarity in the relationships among its human agents and the degree of compatibility of its vehicles.

Sorokin's theory of change has been criticised on the grounds that his theory neglects the fact that culture is a component system, *i.e.* an element of a particular dies out, does not imply that the whole external tradition decays.

His theory is more of an abstraction and general that lacks concreteness and specificity.

Social Welfare and Movement

It is related to the concept of development. Therefore directed social change is related to the planning of various policies and programmes in an attempt to bring about various welfare measures of the society. This could differ from society to society, from region to region, from community to community since every society is different from the other and hence planning and social change also differs from society to society.

Communist China and Cuba offer good examples of the success of planned change in peasant societies. Although economic statistics are sparse and not altogether reliable, western social scientists have been generally impressed with the achievements in food production, housing and health care in both countries. Both governments have succeeded in virtually eliminating starvation and in bringing about dramatically improved living conditions, where in the past hunger and poverty perennially plagued large number of their citizens.

Although some of the gains have been a result of redistribution of societal resources, without the substantial economic gains that have been achieved, these improvements would never have been possible. Such achievements might be regarded as particularly noteworthy when we consider the relatively short time in which they have been attained, the extent of China's technological backwardness and its vast population and Cuba's former extreme dependence upon the American economy. However much we may value the democratic approach to change, it is not necessarily the most effective for all cultures, in all situations.

Importance of Planning

Social change is a vast complex phenomenon involving many aspects and areas. Social phenomena are so complex that any change that is introduced with a particular aim, may result in so many other changes which were not anticipated even distantly.

Social planning has to consider two aspects:

(1) changes in the social structure itself bringing about changes in the pattern of social relations, and

(2) changes in the attitudes and motivations or changes in the values themselves.

Planning involves a certain consensus in the whole society or at least in the majority of the people. Especially so in a democratic country like ours where people elect its representatives. People must desire for change and accept it. The basis of acceptance may be different. It may be fear or faith in the dominant minority in totalitarian countries or participation by the people in democratic countries through representative institutions.

The framers of the Indian Constitution set the goals in the Constitution emphasising certain social objectives, namely equality of status and opportunity, social justice, liberty of thought, etc. These objectives provided the framework for the Five-Year Plans.

The model of development which is the basis for the Five-Year Plans is that of a mixed economy, which provides for private ownership of capital for an open market and yet provides for State enterprise and State intervention in regulating the economy. The intervention of the State was expected to ensure that the social justice aspects of development, were not lost sight of in the pursuit of the goals of economic growth. In keeping with socialist objectives the government have also tried to introduce land reforms through enforcing a limit on land ownership and abolition of the system of tenancy under a class of absentee landlords.

A combination of private enterprise, presumably intended

to foster entrepreneurship—through the profit motive and state control—to put a limit to the growth of vested interests, keeping in view an equitable distribution has led to the growth of an enormously complicated system of licenses and permits controlled by the bureaucracy and the politician.

The value systems and roles have also been sought to be changed through the enactment of various legislations. The Hindu Marriage Act of 1955 abolished all caste restrictions as a necessary requirements for a valid marriage. The Hindu Succession Act of 1956 confers for the first time absolute rights over her property to a Hindu woman. Secondly, both the sons and daughters get the right of inheritance from the property of an intestate Hindu. Untouchability has been abolished and dowry has been prohibited by law. Various welfare measures are chalked out for the improvement of women's condition and other minority groups.

The goal of development planning in growth plus change—which means accelerated economic growth and alterations of institutional arrangements which stand as hurdles in providing better living conditions for the citizens of each country. But, economic growth is not enough, it is just one dimension of social development.

Thus, planning also involves periodical review to consider whether targets have been fulfilled or, in other words, progress attained. In India, all the objectives of planning have not been achieved.

In agriculture, production of food crops has increased but this has not kept pace with the increase in population. Efforts to achieve equitable distribution of landholdings have had varied success in different States. In some States like Punjab Haryana, greater use of irrigation, fertilizers and the new hybrid varieties have led to the development of capitalistic methods of farming. Thus, inequalities have not been reduced.

The last but not the least is that planning, development

and social change should take place in a context whereby the involvement of community participation is made desirable by taking into account of their needs and aspirations, their experiences etc. and it should not be state imposed as far as possible plus it should also protect environmental conditions which should be made compatible with social development.

Modernising Attempts

Problems of Role Conflict-youth unrest intergenerational gap changing status of women; Major sources of social change and of resistance to change, impact of West, reform movements, social movements, industrialisation and urbanisation, pressure groups, factors of planned change— sanskritisation, westernisation and modernisation, means of modernisation-mass media and education; problem of change and modernisation-structural contradictions and breakdowns.

Various Sources of Social Mobility

Change is a part of both the individual and the social life. No society can ever exist without bringing changes. But almost always these changes are resisted in every society, India being no exception to that. Every social change in India is vehemently opposed in the beginning because there is a psychological feeling that every change will do more harm than good to the society. There is also a feeling that change will create many other problems, which a traditional society is not prepared to face. But social change does not come by one factor alone. Several factors combine together before a change comes.

Before we discuss social changes and their resistance in India, let us in the first instance understand as to what is a social change and in general why it is resisted. What is Social Change?

In our society changes are bound to come. In some societies these changes are very slow while in others these are rapid and fast. But no society can escape from changes. A sociologist is therefore, required to take these changes into consideration for proper study of society. In our own times we find that changes have been coming rapidly. Stability of family has been shaken and hold as well as grip of religion has considerably weakened. We also find that the joint family system which was the order of the day, is being replaced by single family system. Similarly we also find that rural society is being replaced by urban society and so on. It will however; be wrong to believe that a change in society is in any way an isolated event. On the other hand it is a link in the chain and those events which bring about that change can be seen with clarity. One of the main reasons for social change is dynamic nature of the people.

Definition of Social Change : Change is natural to every society and even if any society makes any attempt to stall social change that shall be an impossible task. According to Jones, "Social change is a term used to describe variations or modifications of any aspect of social processes, social patterns, social interactions or social organisation". According to Gillin and Gillin, "Social changes are variations from the accepted modes of life; whether due to alterations in geographical conditions, in cultural equipment, composition of the population or ideologies and whether brought about by diffusion or invention within the group".

MacIver has given a very simple definition of the term by saying that "Social change is change in social relationship". Merrill and Andres have said that, "Social change means that large number of persons are engaged in activities that differ from those in which they or their immediate forefather engaged in some time before. Society is composed of a vast and complex network of patterned human relationships, in which all men participate, when human behaviour is in the process of modification, that is only another way of indicating that social change is occurring". From the above definitions, it is clear that change is occurring and is a continuous process. As MacIver says, "It is soon apparent that social change is a process responsive to many types of change, to changes in the man-made conditions of living, to changes in the attitudes and beliefs of men, and to changes that go beyond human control to the biological and physical nature of things".

System of Social Mobility

Social change cannot be studied in isolation and as already said each change is only a link in the series of changes which have occurred or are likely to occur. It is therefore essential that a social change should not be taken in its present form or of an incident of the present alone. It is connected with the past and affects the future. The changes are influenced by every social happening. As MacIver and Page say, "To understand how social change takes place and why it follows certain trends it is necessary to investigate its relation to the three great orders—the bio-physical, the cultural and the technological". A social change on the whole change the way of life, pattern of behaviour and the very set up of society.

Elements of Social Mobility

Social change is law of society and also inevitable. In some cases the process may be slow, while in others it may be fast, but the change is always going on. As already pointed out there is difference between social and cultural change and here we are concerned with the former. Some of the major factors which are responsible for social change are as under.

Urbanisation : One of the important causes responsible for social change is the ever increasing trend towards urbanisation. Social values, social behaviour and approach to social problems in the urban areas is quite different than what it is in the rural areas. The more urbanisation there is, the more are the chances of social change.

Factors regarding Biological Needs : An inter-mixture of male and female results in the birth of a new child but the development of the new baby depends on biological conditions. We find that each generation shows bodily variation. Due to biological reasons weaker sections are pushed out and in their place strong emerge. Social changes occur due to this pushing in and pushing out. Biological factors also help in social change in more than one way. We know that in societies where population is on the increase living standard, of the people comes down. Similarly where the birth rate is higher than the death rate the standard of the society on the whole cannot be expected to get up.

In the words of MacIver and Page, "But it is also clear that the changes in the death rate, the birth rate and the marriage rate are both responsive and determinant of changes in social attitudes and in social relationship". Population affects our social, cultural and economic life. In societies where there is more population their way of living and economic standard is different from those where population is less. The institutions of marriage and family are influenced by population and so is the social status of men and women. In societies where female population is more than the male population, the women do not enjoy more respect than the men and *vice-versa.* Thus biological factors go a long way in bringing about social changes.

Industrial Growth : India is gradually industrialising itself. Social system and approach to social problems in urbanised and industrialised society is different from what it is in a rural or agricultural based society. History is a witness that industrialisation has always brought social changes of far reaching importance.

Factors regarding Environment : Environments in which people live and work also bring about social changes. Some of our thinkers believe that geography is the exclusive factor for bringing about social change but that is over estimating the influence of geography on the people. We know that in many societies, both in the East as well as in the West, there have not been many geographical physical changes but at the same time social changes have rapidly come. But at the same time it cannot be denied that the geographical conditions have their influence and effect. Floods, earthquakes, unwanted or untimely rain, drought etc. positively bring social changes.

We built houses and thought of clothes only due to environments which undoubtedly brought about social changes. We also find that distribution of natural resources have also helped in making and raising living standard of the people. We find that due to environments and physical conditions of a place big and small cities emerge and trade and commerce flourishes which is responsible for social change. In the words of MacIver and Page, "Every civilisation is exploitive of resources of its environment. Its continuance depends, among other things, on its ability to conserve or replace these resources to find substitutes for them. Our own civilisation has reached a stage of control where it can almost maintain the fertility of the soil while satisfying its present agricultural needs, but it has as yet found no adequate means of replacing the sources of power which it derives from the inexhaustible supplies of oil and coal nor is there an endless stock of the metals, such as iron and copper, which it finds so necessary".

Factors regarding Technology : There is no dispute over the fact that technology brings far reaching and fundamental changes in our social set up. Our modern society is the outcome and product of modern technology. It is due to technological advancement that we come close to each other and our way of living, thinking and behaving has changed. Technological advancement has helped considerably in urbanising our society. Every technological invention changes the very outlook of our life. Division of labour, trade unionism and specialisations which are quite common these days and are rapidly influencing and changing our social order are the outcome of advancement of technology.

In the words of Ogburn, "Technology changes society by changing our environments to which we in turn adopt. This changing is usually in material environment and the adjustment we make to the changes often modify custom and social institutions". In the words of MacIver and Page, "Certain social consequences are the inevitable results of technological change, such as new organisation of labour, the expansion of the range of social contacts, the specialisation of function, and the encroachment of urban influences on rural life,. Today, there is no aspect of human life which has not been influenced by technology. Therefore, technology is a very important factor of social change.

Factors regarding Culture : One of the most important factors bringing about social change is cultural factor. Cultural variations change our social life. Today, due to rapid and quick means of transportation and communication there is much of cultural crossing. Since there are frequent cultural crossings, therefore society cannot remain uninfluenced by these conflicts. It has rightly been said that cultural changes give both speed and direction to the social changes. Culture is both an influencing factor and also an internal force for bringing social change in our social life, if that appeals to our mind. Religion which is a great cultural force is evidently a powerful instrument for bringing about social change. We have already said that there is close relationship between cultural and social changes. Kingsley Davis has said that, "Of course, no part of culture is totally unrelated to the social order, but it remains true that changes may occur in these branches without noticeably affecting the social system.

Factors regarding Culture : Some of our modern sociologists including Gillin and Gillin believe that psychological factor is most effective in bringing about social change. According to him people of course respect old traditions and customs and do not wish violent changes but at the same time they wish that gradually old order should be replaced by new one. They respect the old but at the same time desire that society should be dynamic. According to them when the society becomes static and does not make room for the new system, revolution is bound to come. It is therefore, this psychological factor which helps bringing changes rather than anything else.

New Ideas : Still another factor responsible for social change is breaking of new ideas. Our social, economic and political leaders give us new ideas and ideologies. The ideas of our social reformers such as Raja Ram Mohan Roy, great political thinkers like Karl Marx, Jawaharlal Nehru and Mahatma Gandhi have given new philosophies to the people which have in turn helped in bringing social changes. Why People Oppose Changes?

Social changes are always opposed in the beginning and that is the reason as to why social reformers find it difficult to carry reforms. Some of the causes are:

Habits and Customs of People : Individuals have habits and societies, some customs and traditions which have been passed on to them from the posterity. It is believed that these are the essence of their wisdom and knowledge and gradually become part of individuals and social life. These become very dear to them and usually people are in no mood to leave them. Social changes try to change these habits and customs and due to this the people, particularly the old and orthodox, oppose them.

Stability Concern : The people love stability primarily because that helps them in deriving their advantages and they get accustomed to their disadvantages, which slowly and gradually they do not mind. Therefore, they prefer stability over instability. It is feared that each social change must bring with it some instability.

Economic Factors : In many cases economic considerations also force the society and the government to bring about social changes, particularly when these cost the society and the state.

In some cases the society prefers to adhere to the past rather than to get in to the present with the help of social or technological inventions.

Absence of Knowledge : Lack of knowledge is one of the contributing factors for opposition to the social changes. Firstly, the people do not come to know of social and technological inventions and even if they come to know, they do not know their full implications and advantages. But the opponents of these changes try to convince them about their disadvantages to which they readily agree and begin to oppose them as well.

Absence of Patience : Usually the people lack patience. As soon as an invention comes to light they wish that it should start giving results. They forget that each invention in the beginning is at experimental stage and its defects are to be remedied only with the passage of time. This requires patience which the people lack with the result that disadvantages are glorified and advantages under-estimated.

Personal Interest : But perhaps the most important reason for opposition to social changes is interests of the vested interests. Those who have been in a position and manage to get power by one way or the other, are not interested to leave that in any way. Thus those who are in political power, will not wish that due to any social change some new element in the political life should be introduced which challenges their supremacy and so is the case with those who are in authority either in the political or religious field.

Endurance to Social Changes in India : Indian society is traditional in nature and that is why social changes have always been resisted. We find that when Raja Ram Mohan Roy raised his voice against the then prevailing *sati* system he had to face tough resistance from the society. He had to seek the assistance of British Government for achieving the purpose.

Similarly when Swami Dayanand Saraswati, Swami Vivekananda, Swami Rama Krishna Paramahansa and many of our social and religious reformers raised their voices against our social evils like caste system, child marriage, dowry system and widow remarriage they had to face very tough time from the society. Some of them had to sacrifice their lives.

In our modern times when Pt. Jawahar Lal Nehru proposed Hindu Code Bill suggesting some changes in Hindu social system, he was bitterly opposed by the orthodox section of the society.

More recently when family planning programme was introduced with some strictness, the people showed their resentment at the time of general elections by throwing the Congress Party out of power. There was perhaps no time in Indian society when changes were welcomed. But a question arises as to why the people always oppose changes and for this not only one but several causes are responsible.

The people in India in majority are still illiterate and thus do not appreciate the value of change. Due to illiteracy they are easily misled by orthodox people. Those who have vested interests bring to the notice of the people all bad points of the change, whereas good points of the change are either ignored or under-estimated. India is spread over a large area and it becomes usually difficult to educate all about the change before it is introduced. The result is that when change actually takes place that is very much resented. The people of India are traditionally in favour of *status quo* and thus do not like changes and wish that the things should continue, as there are.

Social Change : various Sources : As is well known that Indian society is witnessing many social changes and some of these have far reaching consequences. These changes are coming due to several factors combined together namely:

(a) Impact of the West.

(b) Social Reforms movements.

(c) Industrialisation and urbanisation.

Effect of the West : In bringing social changes in India impact of the West can in no way be under-estimated. It was under this impact that *sati* system was considered inhuman and ultimately abolished. Again western impact created an impression that constant struggle should be made till such political changes are brought which make the nation independent.

Western system of education had its own impact. English system of education was introduced and came to stay in India. In addition, through English literature we could study western society and felt that many social changes were needed in our society. These included higher marriage age both for boys and girls or giving up tough resistance to the institution of widow remarriage. Again it was the impact of West that in India social reformers thought of abolishing untouchability, which was deep rooted and was an integral part of Indian society.

India's contacts with the West changed our traditional way of dressing and to a large extent food habits. It was again this impact which created a class of people, the educated ones and the bureaucratic elites, who considered themselves much above the people. They did not mix with them frequently. On the other hand these people considered themselves superior.

Western style of living and thinking created cleavages and differences in our society. It made urban people feel that they were much superior to the rural people, who were illiterate and poor. Similarly it created a feeling in society that complex life was much better that a simple life and thus efforts were made to make the society as complex as it could be.

Western system did not believe in caste system, which is the basis of our social system. It had altogether different outlook towards the institutions of marriage and family. Similarly it had no faith in untouchability. These affected our system as well.

Reformation in Society and Religion

In the 19th century there was political anarchy. Our culture and civilisation was under heavy pressure. On the one hand there were the Britishers and their followers who were trying to disfigure our cultural heritage whereas on the other hand our social evils were proving a blot on our culture. At this critical time it appeared as if the true face of our culture would disappear very shortly. At this time some of our social reformers and religious leaders took upon themselves the responsibility of reforming the society by awakening the people which aimed at introducing social reforms. Some such important religious movements were as under:

The Brahmo Samaj : The Samaj was founded in 1832, by Raja Ram Mohan Roy, who was the most advanced and intelligent social reformer in India. He believed that the Government should interfere in social affairs of the country only when social reformers failed to reform society. In his opinion Indian society now had reached that stage. Idol worship, caste and *sati* system were of recent origin and held no place in true religion. Similarly he believed that the present stage of womanfolk was also without any religious approval. He realised the need and necessity of proper interpretation of our religious books. Thus the Samaj preached that Hindu religion should be properly understood and interpreted. He suggested that religious books of other religions should be studied and their good points and features followed in their true spirit. Thus Brahmo Samaj made an attempt to reform Hindu society. After the death of Raja Ram Mohan Roy in 1834, responsibility fell on the shoulders of Devindra Nath Tagore who infused a new spirit into it. After his death in 1872 the influence of this Samaj gradually decreased. The main effect of the Samaj was that conversion of Hindus into Christianity was checked.

Prarthana Samaj : It was another Samaj which aimed at

reforming Hindu society. The Samaj suggested the worship of one Almighty. In order to end social evils it started many institutions like orphanages etc. It also condemned ban on widow remarriage. With this end in view, it opened widow *ashrams* and supported the cause of widow remarriage. It also started a plan for adult literacy. It also argued that our womenfolk should have their rightful place in society.

One of the main supporters of this Samaj was Justice Ranade who believed that religion and society could not be separated from each other. Religious and social evils were bound to interact and influence each other. Similarly he believed that religion and politics are inseparable. A socially degenerated society could not demand, obtain and enjoy political rights. He therefore suggested that religions and society must be reformed for successful political set up. It was due to his efforts that the Deccan Education Society was founded. Ranade influenced Gokhale and Tilak.

Theosophial Society : The society also played a very leading part in awakening the Indian masses. It was founded in 1875 in USA. In 1879 its founder members visited India and at Adyar founded the society. It was subsequently in 1893 that Dr. Annie Besant joined it, and infused a new spirit into it. Members of the society believed that India had a proud past and Indians could rightly take pleasure and pride in their ancient cultural heritage. If there were evils in Indian society, these could be removed by making some efforts.

The Indians should realise their past and they should demand their rights from those foreigners who had snatched political power from them", In order to create awakening among the masses she spent the whole of her life in serving this cause and even earned the displeasure of the government. She very boldly said that after ending social evils there was no difficulty in getting political rights. She also made it clear that for getting political rights, Indians themselves will have to struggle and that no foreign individual or institution shall be of any help.

Arya Samaj : Arya Samaj has played a very leading and significant part in awakening our masses. It was founded in 1875 by Swami Dayanand. The main object of the Arya Samaj was the spread of ancient Indian culture and civilisation based on our ancient religious books—the *Vedas* and *Shastras*. In his opinion ancient Indian civilisation was one of the most advanced one in the world. He also believed that all Indians were equal and that there was no high or low in the society. In his opinion child marriage and ban on widow remarriage were the product of some selfish people. These have no religious sanctions behind them.

He was of the opinion that due to these social evils our country had been defamed in the world and our rulers are making it an excuse for denying us our political rights. He challenged all existing religions and tried to establish that our Vedic religion was the most ancient religion of the world. He laid stress on female education and expected that all other social reformers will help him in this noble cause. In the political field he declared that our own worst Raja was better than the best alien ruler. Some of the persons who did not approve of his reform programme poisoned him in 1883, but the path which he showed is still being followed honestly by his devoted followers which among others included persons like Mahatma Gandhi, Lala Lajpat Rai, Rabindra Nath Tagore and Mahatma Hans Raj.

Rama Krishna Mission : Rama Krishna Mission also contributed significantly to the cause of Indian awakening. The foundation of the Mission was laid in 1896 by the famous religious and social reformer, Swami Vivekananda in the memory of Rama Krishna Paramhansa. After its establishment its ideas gradually began to spread throughout the country. The followers of this Mission believed in all religions and for them human religion was the best to be followed. Its founder,

Swami Vivekananda, so lucidly and clearly exposed ancient Indian philosophy and doctrines of Hindu religion at the Congress of Religions at Chicago that the whole of the Western world was surprised.

In his opinion there was no religion which did not contain some good points and as such all religions must be appreciated and no religion was superior to the other. For him ancient Indian culture was so comprehensive and glorious that it could be a torch-bearer for our people. He appealed to the Indians that they should realise it themselves and try to come out of their present pitiable conditions. He was of the opinion, that religion and politics could not be separated from each other and as such religion alone could be the basis of our political life. He suggested to the Indians that they should fight, for their freedom. Freedom, he pleaded, is essential both for national and international development.

In his opinion freedom does not mean absence of hindrances but it was a right by which every individual had a right to develop his physique, wisdom and wealth and to get the required type of education. In this way Swamiji infused a new sense and spirit throughout the country. Like other social reformers he also believed that female education should be encouraged and our society should be relieved from such evils as ban on widow remarriage, child marriage and caste system. Through his mission he made an attempt to awaken masses by properly interpreting Indian religion and glorifying ancient Indian culture and civilisation.

Dev Samaj : The Samaj was founded in 1887 by Swami Satyanand Agnihotri. In his opinion the Samaj should try to educate the people and also awaken them. With this end in view the Samaj started propagation of education and opened many schools and colleges in the country. In these institutions such a type of education was imparted through which Indians could understand themselves and take pride in their past.

All these reform movements made the people of India realise about our social evils. They pointed out that unless these evils were removed society could not make any progress. Some of the important social evils which drew the attention of our society were untouchability, caste system, dowry system, ban on child marriage and encouragement to widow remarriage. According to them our society was suffering because it had degenerated itself.

They wanted that untouchables should be treated as an integral part of the society and given human treatment. Doors of temples should be thrown open to them. Women should be treated equal with men and considered as co-sharers with them both in joys and sorrows. They desired that women should be uplifted. Such evil systems as dowry and *purdah* should be ended as soon as possible. Caste should be on the basis of qualifications of a person and not on the basis of the family in which one was born. These reformers were one in so far as rooting out corruption in the society was concerned.

In the Muslim society changes started coming when Sir Syed Ahmed Khan came to the front. He propagated the abolition of *Purdah* system and the education of women. He propagated his views in his magazine entitled *Takzelul Akhalq*. With his efforts many changes came in the society. The other Muslim reformers included Shah Abdul Aziz of Delhi, Saiyed Ahmed of Bareilly, Shiekh Kamat Ali of Jaunpur and Haji Shariat Ullah of Faridpur.

Abdul Aziz wanted that Muslim society should get rid of superstitions. Kamat Ali slowly and gradually brought the Indian Muslims near the western education and ideas. There were also Faraidhi Movement, Puritan Movement and then came Aligarh Movement. In this way social changes were tried to be brought about by these movements. These had far reaching effects on the society. These saved the society from much of degeneration and evils which otherwise would have crept into our social system.

Development of Industry

Many changes came in the society with industrialisation and urbanisation. In fact whole social outlook changes with the growth of industry and urbanisation. India, as already said, is gradually becoming urbanised and industrialised. Migration from villages to the cities is going on and the whole process has become a continuous one. India which was industrially a backward country is today one of the advanced industrial nations of the world. With this changes in society were bound to come and in fact have come.

Industrialisation and urbanisation almost go hand in hand. The more industrialisation there is, the more we think of urbanisation. Some of the important changes which industrialisation and urbanisation bring with it include:

> With industrialisation people begin to migrate from villages to the cities. They try to find jobs in the newly set up industries, where they become wage workers. They cannot afford to live in big houses and as such they live either in shanties or in small houses. They then cannot live in joint family system. Thus joint family system gets replaced by single family system. In addition, every family has little space to live. The guests are not welcome because space is not there to live. No one has time to attend to the guests because every one is required to attend to daily work punctually. In addition, pressure on city resources very much increases. New areas are developed. New constructions take place. The society is required to provide more facilities to the people living in different parts of the city.

This is what is happening in India. In the urban areas population is increasing. In every metropolitan city it is becoming difficult to provide houses, electricity and water as well as transport facilities. Whole outlook towards life has changed. Now due to industrialisation and urbanisation, the people in the cities are less orthodox and superstitious. They have new outlook and scientific outlook to problems.

Education is becoming more widespread. Women are joining more vocations. This has made the women self-sufficient. But at the same time there has arisen the problem of family instability. The woman in employment now does not care much for her husband. The number of divorce cases has increased.

Moreover, in the urban areas outlook is different than what it is in the rural areas. The rigidity of caste system is not so much in these areas. There is inter-caste mixing and marriages, which is a welcome social change. In these areas there is no distinction of man on the basis of castes. The people belonging to different castes travel in the same buses, eat at the same place and in the same hotels and meet on equal footing in the social functions.

Then another social change that urbanisation and industrialisation is bringing is in the size of family. Since there is awakening and consciousness among the urban people and due to various limitations usually there is a desire to have small family size. Thus the people in these areas are more keen to have family planning than the people living in the villages and depending on agriculture.

Urbanisation and industrialisation also bring social changes in another way. In India there was always respect and regard for social customs and traditions. These were always highly regarded and no one dared to violate these. But the hold of customs and traditions in the urban areas is very much relaxed. The people feel like doing the things in the way they like. They scorn some of the customs as outdated and the people who follow them are declared as orthodox. They try to have their own customs which suit their own convenience.

Still another social change which comes with urbanisation

and industrialisation is that there is no face to face contact with each other. The people belonging to different places, castes and creeds who come to cities have no bonds of love with each other. Thus neighbourhood bonds are very weak, which are always strong in the rural area. Thus many changes in society which weak neighbourhood brings are brought in urban society.

Social changes are rapidly coming in India. In spite of India's love for traditions, outlook of the people towards social system and problems are rapidly changing. Dowry system, casteism, child marriage etc. are being reviewed by the educated youth, particularly in the urban areas. The government is using mass media to bring social changes and ensure that the society is freed from social evils.

Social Change and Modernisation Aspect : In the world there is no society in which changes do not come. If there is any such society that is sure to be stagnant and will soon be weeded out. In some societies, the change is fast while in others it is slow. Similarly in some parts and by some sections of the society changes are more quickly accepted than the others. In India, one finds that on the whole the society is traditional and the people by and large are not prepared to accept changes. Whatsoever changes are accepted these are more rapidly and readily accepted in the urban rather than the rural areas. It is wrong to believe that every change is always good and for the health of the society. Sometimes the changes may not be in the interest of the society as well.

Though there are several causes and factors responsible for bringing about social changes, the most important of these are urbanisation, industralisation and modernisation. In India modernisation has changed the whole economic and social life and the process is continuing. It was also the impact of the West and western system of education which has brought many changes in Indian society.

Our present day Indian society is faced with many

problems. It is witnessing changes though at a slow speed. The youth is on the path of revolt because the society is failing in meeting many of its expectations. There is inter-generational gap in thinking between the old of the previous generation and youth of the present generation. The women, under the influence of modernisation and westernisation, are demanding more and more rights.

There are however, many who are opposed to introducing changes and creating their own problems, which weakens the whole process. Resistance in some quarters is very strong. In the society reforms and social movements launched by our social reformers have not brought the desired result and what they say is not seriously but casually listened to and more often ignored, except when that serves personal interests.

Role Conflict Problem : In Indian society today one emerging problem is that of role conflict. The conflict is finding expression in the form of youth unrest, inter-generation gap and through several other ways. The youth of today is not satisfied with what it has been given. The result is that in India he is engaged in destructive rather than constructive activities. In addition, he is engaged in demonstrations and agitations. The youth of today does not think in those terms in which the old generation used to think. The women are not prepared to be the slaves of men alone and to be merely the source of their pleasure. They are now demanding their rights and that too with a force. Several women organisations are now engaged in protecting rights and privileges of the women. The women in Indian society, have become very conscious and careful. But before discussing all these problems let us understand as to what is meant by role and role conflict.

Role and Role Conflict : Our society is getting complicated day by day in which integrating and disintegrating groups are playing their own role. In these groups there are people who have different capacities and capabilities. They have different occupations and jobs to perform. Since all cannot do all jobs therefore, there is division of labour in our society. Thus each individual has some specific role to play in the society.

Meaning of Role

As long as society is simple age, sex or physical strength decides the role of an individual in it but in our complex society, there are various other factors as well. Each individual is therefore required to create a place for himself and as such he is supposed to exert and struggle. His capabilities are therefore, a considerably important factor. Ogburn says that, "A role is a set of socially expected and approved behaviour pattern, consisting of both duties and privileges, associated with a particular position in a group." Similarly Lundberg says that, "A social role is pattern of behaviour expected of an individual in certain group or situation". In simple language it can be said that role indicates what an individual owes to the society and what society expects from him. It also decides the manner in which those obligations should be discharged. It is on efficient performance of social role that smooth working of our society depends and both are directly linked with each other.

Types of Role Differentiation

In a simple society age, sex, physical strength and similar other things decide the role of an individual towards society but today there are many other things which influence role. Age is one of the basis for deciding role differentiation. Infancy, childhood, manhood and old age are linked with capability and efficiency in the performance of social duties. Age is almost considered a qualification in handling certain types of serious and responsible jobs. For quite sometime kinship was also a deciding factor in the social role of an individual. It was believed that those who were related to the people performing important roles were capable of discharging important obligations.

The females, have a different role from the males in our society. Usually women are supposed to take care of the house, leaving outside field to the care of the men. Similarly women are not supposed to perform strenuous and immoral jobs. In some cases they are not allowed to perform certain types of religious ceremonies. Sex thus helps in determining social roles. It also forms the basis of our social role. There are few who are engaged in production while some others are engaged in consumption and distribution. Those who are engaged in more productive labour have definitely better and important role to play than those who are otherwise engaged.

In our modern society political and economic allocations are far more important than any other allocation. Political allocation implies more power and authority which means that those exercising it have definitely to perform very responsible role as compared with those who have to obey and depend on them. Religion also allocates different roles to different people. Thus the priests or Brahmins in India, in the true sense will have to play altogether a different role than the others. Roles can be differentiated on the basis of knowledge. Those who are highly qualified or have acquired knowledge after getting training or have become experts after doing a particular type of work again and again, are required to play different role as compared with those who are lay men and are supposed to depend on others.

Due to geographical conditions different roles may be performed. Thus people may be required to perform different roles under different circumstances. In fact their necessity and importance may be realised only under those geographical conditions and not outside.

Role and Conflict Issue : So long as the structure of the society was simple each individual had very simple and specific role to play but today there are many conflicts in the roles. In industry role of the same individual as a worker and as a trade unionist may come in conflict. Similarly the role of an individual as a member of family or as a judge or doctor may differ. In fact in social, economic and political life the roles of the individuals very much differ and one of the serious problems of our modern complex society is to adjust these conflicting roles in a very smooth and harmonious manner for the smooth running of the society.

Thus as the society grows complex and complicated different agencies and conditions are bound to decide the role of an individual in society and those roles are sure to come in conflict with each other. Unless these are adjusted society is bound to be adversely affected.

Activity of Youths

Youth in Indian society is in a situation of unrest. He finds that in other societies his counterparts are much better placed than what he is in Indian society. He finds that there are no chances for better employment. He is to roam about here and there to find a job, which he cannot get. He also finds that no chances exist for him to channelise his energies in a constructive manner. His energies are being wasted. His sore points increase still more. When he finds that those who are undeserving but are economically, socially or politically influential get high places and position in the society. They soon get themselves settled in life, whereas he remains always unsettled. Socially he is under-estimated and less respected and economically he is hard pressed. Politically he is not encouraged and thus he is not allowed to enter the political forts, which politicians have created around themselves with the help of their political bosses.

Ever coming changes in the world and modernisation and technological advancements are still more responsible for his unrest. The more he comes in contact with the youths of other nations of the world, the more his dissatisfaction increases. He finds that education system in the country is outdated and far away from actual requirements of life. He finds that after coming out of educational institutions and having qualified in university examination, he finds himself at a point where he does not know how to proceed and from where and in which direction.

He is very much agitated over prevailing social, economic and political corruption, which surrounds and follows him everywhere. Not only that its chances of being wiped out are very less, but the agony is that these are more and more getting deep rooted.

Roots of corruption in Indian society to the annoyance of Indian youth have gone so deep that today, these cannot be dug out unless there is violent revolution. The things as they are, he does not know what is right or wrong. He is bewildered about materialism and idealism. His educators are providing him no alternatives or are no guide to him. Economically increasing disparity is a reality for him. Political parties, in order to serve their own interests, create utter dissatisfaction among the youth leading to frustration.

The result of all this is that he wants to play his role to set the society right. Since everywhere he finds himself helpless and unable to do anything, he channelises his energies in the direction in which these can find expression. He then gives outlet to his energies by participating in processions and demonstrations, in destroying public and private property, in brick-batting and stone throwing, in creating stirs in the educational institutions and at public places. Some of them who get more frustrated try to become criminals, dacoits, pick-pockets and indulge in looting and similar other activities. They use intimidating methods for earning money and engage themselves in kidnapping and similar other indecent activities.

The youth in India is in a situation of turmoil. All efforts being made by the authorities to control this unrest have not, as yet, met with absolute success. Both in the campuses, in the streets and at public places, the youth gives vent to his dissatisfaction as and when opportunity arises.

It will be better if proper type of education is given to him. He is made to realise his responsibilities towards the state. Employment opportunities are increased and vocational education is encouraged. Political, (parties') intervention among the youth is discouraged.

Youth Unrest Solving Measures : The means of curing youth unrest can be achieved by following the suggestions made in this regard:

Improvement in the Teacher's Conditions : This comprehends increase in salary, better conditions of work, more just and impartial selections and appointments, reasonable prospects of advancement, etc. If these conditions are met, the educators will be able to live satisfactory lives and thus they will be encouraged to impart some idealism to their adjutants.

Presentation of Right Ideals by the Educator : Since almost all adjutants imitate their educator both consciously and unconsciously it is necessary that the educator must present the correct ideal in every sphere of conduct. He must in this way lead the educand.

Improvements in the System of Education : As far as possible, the defects in the system of education pointed out by various committees and commissions should be removed immediately.

Improvements in the Examination System : Education achieves development of the total personality. The examination, therefore, must test this development, not merely the memory, as it does at present.

Preventing Political Influence in Schools : No political party should be given the chance to penetrate school and college life.

Check of Unwarranted State Interference **:** More often than not, the vice chancellors appointed to the universities are appointed on any consideration except that of merit. These appointments are made by the government, and hence are illustrations of undue state interference in education. It is undesirable for the state to interfere in the working of education in this manner.

Independence of Educational Institutions **:** Of the many incidents of violence and destruction by the students in the recent past, many were inspired by the entry of the police into college compounds, either without the permission or in violation of the express command of the college authorities. All educationists agree that no government employee has the right to enter the premises of educational institutions without the permission of the principal. If this rule is not violated it would be easier to prevent manifestations of youth unrest from becoming violent and destructive.

Educators and Parents Relation **:** Another method of curbing student/youth unrest is to encourage contact between educators and parents so that they may meet and discuss the problems of adjutants and thus remove the causes leading to indiscipline.

Education of Moral Values **:** Most thinkers agree that absence of moral education is responsible for youth unrest and character defects of the adjutants. In any case moral education will definitely curb indiscipline.

Proper Atmosphere in College : The psychological factors which are at the root of the youth unrest can be eliminated by creating the proper atmosphere in schools. As far as possible, this atmosphere should resemble that of a large family in which the relations between boys, girls, educators, students, etc., should be morally and psychologically healthy.

Youth unrest is a complex problem having its social, political and psychological aspects. In order to remove it these aspects must be understood and the cooperation of educators, parents and state must be used to solve this problem.

Complieation among Generations

There is no society in the world in which problem of inter-generational gap does not exist. In some societies, particularly in a traditional society like India, the gap becomes wide. It is because each generation comes up and develops in a different situation and condition. One finds that Indian society of pre-partition days *i.e.* about 4 decades back was tradition ridden. In the society there was illiteracy.

Educational facilities were few and far between and that was more so in the rural areas. Hardly 8 per cent of the people then were educated. The people were superstition ridden. Illiteracy among the women was high and alarming. Living standard of the people was very low. The country was industrially backward and there was neither any industrialisation nor modernisation. The result was that the thinking of those days was narrow.

In those days the people were satisfied with what they got. They did not give vent to their ideas. They always wanted to please their superiors and rulers. There was fear psychology. They believed in child marriage and spent extravagantly on all social and religious ceremonies much beyond their capacity. They always believed that God does everything for the good. They condemned widow remarriage and were opposed to the idea of female education. They did not know the use of latest agricultural equipments. The society presented the look of a primitive society.

Then comes the next generation which was born in free India. Now in free India still another generation is taking birth. This generation is altogether different in its approach to social and economic problems. It is a generation which has altogether different approach and thus the thinking of these two generations clearly indicates inter-generational gap.

Present generation is not prepared to completely subordinate itself to superiors and rulers. It believes that everything should be accepted on the tests of reasoning. All that does not appeal to reasoning should not be accepted. It is in revolt against unjust systems, laws and customs, may those be in the social, economic or political life. It believes that every one has a right to get the right to freedom of expression as a fundamental right and in Indian society he has got that too. In our society he wants to have maximum share in running the country's administration.

In the economic field too the gap is quite visible. He does not wish to be exploited any longer. He has raised his voice that the land should be for the tiller. There should be far reaching land reforms. He wants that there should be some upper ceiling on possession of land and beyond that all surplus land should be distributed. He wants now that means of production and distribution should not be concentrated in few hands but these should be used for social benefit and welfare. In fact today his thinking is that there should be justice—social economic and political.

Inter-generational gap in Indian society today is also visible in social life. The youth of today does not think in terms, of getting dowry, as his ancestors used to think. He is now interested in a suitable match. He is not much concerned about family status but his stress is now on the qualities of the life partners. He does not believe in caste system, which he thinks is an indication of orthodoxy. In addition he feels that caste system has no scientific rationale. This was what was opposed by his ancestors. Today he does not hesitate to have inter-caste and inter-regional marriages. His approach is that caste is man-made and not a natural or religious phenomenon.

He is also opposed to both the child marriage and ban on widow remarriage. Both these things were dear to his ancestors.

He feels that every child should be married at an age when he is both mature and self-supporting. The widows should be remarried, particularly the young widows, because widowhood is not in the control of the widow herself.

In the social life his approach towards family is different. To the ancestors joint family system was dear but the youth of today favour single family system. He feels that joint family system stands on the way of growth of the family. He under estimates the advantages of joint family system and over-estimates those of the single family. His attitude towards the women too is different than what it used to be of his ancestors. Today he feels that the women should be given high respect. They are equal with men. There is no difference between the two. But his forefathers used to think that women are much inferior to men. The former have no thinking capacity and should thus be condemned. Approach towards marriage of both the generations has changed. Previously marriage used to be considered a religious bond, which was unbreakable. It was the duty of the wife to bring stability in marriage. But now in many sections of society many young boys and girls consider that marriage is a bond, which can be broken, if need be. That is the reason that in Indian society divorce rate has increased and is increasing day by day. It is now believed that it is not the duty of the wife alone to maintain stability in the family. It is equally the duty of the husband and that both must make efforts in this regard.

Inter-generational gap is visible in all the walks of Indian life. It is because India has made democracy as a way of life, which has made all equal participants in social, economic and political life. The state is enacting such laws which help removing many old barriers. Casteism has been legally abolished. Education has been made widespread. The people have been given Fundamental Rights which give them many protections. Means of communication and transportation have so developed that these have enabled the people to come closer and nearer to each other. Exchange of views has thus become very easy. Impact of West and modernisation has gone a long way in bringing inter-generational gap. This gap is likely to widen with the coming of every new generation to the front.

Status of Women

In the distant past Indian women enjoyed considerable social respect. In fact during Hindu age women enjoyed co-equal powers and position with men, if not more. They had equal opportunities with men for getting higher education and instances are not wanting when Hindu India produced many learned and socially advanced women. As the time passed Hindu society degenerated, with the result that the position of women also considerably went down. The women began to be considered lower than men both in social status and intelligence.

With the coming of the Muslims, the situation did not improve. Due to insecure political and social conditions evil of child marriage came to stay. The women began to be treated like servants in the family and men usually did not consult them on any important matter. It was around this time that *sati* system became deep-rooted and also a slur on the fair name of our society.

As the Britishers came to India, for quite some time they could not devote any attention and time to improve the lot of Indian women. They hesitated to disturb our social setup. But as these foreigners got political stability, with the cooperation of social reformers, like Raja Ram Mohan Roy, attention was paid to the pitiable conditions of women. It was during British regime that *sati* system was legally banned and girls below a particular age were not allowed to marry.

Women in Freedom Struggle: As time passed and political awakening came, the women also began to demand their rightful place in the society. Their cause was championed by

Brahmo Samaj, Arya Samaj and the Theosophical Society. They pleaded that the women should be provided educational facilities and high social status. Gradually women got political awakening. During our freedom movement we find them struggling with men against British imperialism. The name of Kasturba Gandhi, Vijaya Laxmi Pandit, Sarojini Naidu etc. deserve mention here. Along with men, women also picketed shops, institutions and participated in boycotts, strikes and *hartals.*

As the female education facilities expanded Indian women started movement for getting better social status and more political rights. In 1917 Women's India Association was founded. National Council of women was founded in 1925. It was due to the efforts of such like organisations, both in India and abroad, that in 1923 Indian women were given limited franchise.

In 1926 women were allowed entry to the legislatures and we find that when elections were held under the Government of India Act, 1935, quite a few women were returned to our legislatures. In promoting and championing the cause of women, Mahatma Gandhi, Jawahar Lal Nehru and many other national leaders significantly contributed.

Position of Women in Post Independence Era : After Independence it was realised that the nation could not progress without the active cooperation of women. Our Constitution accordingly clearly lays down that our women shall have equal opportunities with men both in the field of education, employment and in enjoying political opportunities. They shall be paid equal wages with men for equal work.

They have also been given the right to vote, which women, in other parts of the world, got after a persistent struggle. It is not in theory alone, but in actual practice as well that our womenfolk have held high positions in our states. They have held ministerial, executive and political posts. The late Prime Minister Smt. Indira Gandhi had created a name all over the world for guiding the nation and thus raised the status of womanhood.

In 1946 Hindu Married Women's Right to Separate Residence Act was passed. In 1955 Hindu Marriage Act and in 1956 Hindu Succession Act etc. were passed. In fact, as already mentioned, several Acts have been passed favouring Indian womanhood.

Purdah system is now a thing of the past and *sari* system is legally banned. Our women have now been given the right to have a share in the ancestral property. Women can now adopt a son and have a share in the property of their husband.

Today Indian woman is not satisfied with what she has already got. She is trying to become economically self-sufficient and quite a large number of high positions, both in the public and private sectors, are held by them. The women are demanding that education should be made compulsory for them and they should be made to follow the same syllabus of study as the boys.

Inspite of the fact that the conditions of women have considerably improved, as compared with the past, yet much remains to be done. However, a section of our population still gives second rate position to the women. They still feel that the women are less intelligent and have no brain to give serious thought to any serious problem. They are of the opinion that the women should not be given the right to vote or participation in politics. As compared with men, literacy rate among the women is still very low. In some cases the girls are sold by the parents and considered as their property. In some communities system of child marriage still exists and widow remarriage is looked down upon. But on the whole status of women is very much increasing and has considerably gone up.

Development of Industry

The interweaving of human relations results in society.

The human relations are determined by human attitudes. The pattern of human relations and the nature of civilisation and culture mutually determine each other. The pattern of human relations in an agricultural society is quite different from that of the industrial society. The measure of social relations in the primitive society is widely different. In short, the structure of society is determined by the trade and profession of the society and the attitudes of the members towards these. The social relations found in modern industrial society are very complex and intricate compared to the simple and straightforward social relations found in ancient societies.

The industrialisation has affected the society in every respect. The customs and traditions, the fashion and manners, the ways and modes of living all have been deeply influenced by industrialisation. The processes of industrialisation are intimately related with scientific processes. Therefore, the attitude of the members of industrial society becomes scientific. In an industrial society the superstitions and blind faiths have no place. People accept and demand rational explanation of every phenomenon. The reason and not faith is the touchstone of every action and belief in the industrial society. The freedom of thought and individualism are the cornerstones of the industrial society. The ancient institutions of marriage and family have also changed. The old values and rules pertaining to religion and morals are undergoing radical changes.

The new patterns of social stratification are being established. The caste system is being replaced by class system. Even the means of recreation and entertainment are undergoing change in industrial urban society. Thus it is apparent that industrialisation has influenced every aspect of society. It is not quite easy to judge if this impact is good or bad; but it is possible to study the consequences flowing from industrialisation. The following discussion is an attempt to make an in-depth study of the impact of industrialisation upon various aspects of society.

Marriage and Family Impacts

The institutions of marriage and family are to be found in every society. With the changes in the structure of society these institutions also undergo changes. Traditionally, the Indian society has recognised marriage to be a sacred and religious institution but in the modern industrial society it has been reduced to contract. In the past, marriage was considered to be a permanent and inalienable bond which could not be terminated at will. But now, under the impact of industrialisation, divorce and marriage go side by side. Now, it is not considered an evil to terminate the contentious and miserable marriages. The following discussion will make explicit the impact of industrialisation upon marriage.

Social Contract Aspect of Marriage : Prior to heavy industrialisation of India, marriage in this country was considered to be a religious and sacred institution. It was commonly believed by Hindus that marriage was necessary for emancipation or salvation and that anyone who did not marry could not find salvation in this life. Besides, marriage was regarded to be a permanent bond. But with the advance of industrialisation these beliefs are considered superstitious and anyone holding them is frowned upon. Today marriage is regarded to be only a social contract between a man and a woman. The aim of marriage in modern times has ceased to be spiritual and now its aims are economic, social and biological only.

Marriage in Higher Age : In Indian society only a few decades back parents used to get their children married at a very early age. Child-marriages were quite common. But with the industrialisation the age of marriage is advancing; it is getting higher and generally people are marrying at the ages of 25 to 35.

Non-marrying Practice : As we have referred to above, the aim of marriage in India is no longer spiritual: the marital consequence of rejection of the traditional beliefs and attitudes is that many young men and women in big towns prefer to live single. According to the thinking and beliefs of these young persons the major need fulfilled by marriage is biological and this can be easily satisfied out of wedlock.

Love Marriages in Practice : In industrial society men and women usually work together. In mills, factories, offices and other places men and women work together. Under these circumstances they get a chance of coming together, meeting and exchanging ideas and opinions. As a result of this human concourse individuals become intimate and this intimacy becomes love which ultimately blossoms in marriage.

Increasing Divorce : The industrial society is becoming more and more complex every day. The philosophy of individualism is flourishing in society. Even husband and wife have different outlook and attitude. Both of them, as a rule, work in separate social spheres. As a result of this, marital bonds are from time to time rent by discord. The mental conflict increases and the situation of divorce develops. In all industrial societies today there is legal sanction for divorce.

The foregoing discussion makes plain the influence of industrialisation upon marriage. Besides affecting the institution of marriage the industrialisation produces effects upon the institution of family. Following are some of the important effects of industrialisation upon family:

As a result of industrialisation the function of family has changed considerably. Compared to today the family had much more functions in the past. Now, a number of functions which used to be performed by families in the past have been taken over by other institutions. Traditionally, an Indian family used to be a centre of birth, rearing and education of children. The children used to get training in the ancestral profession. The function of socialisation of children, too, used to be performed by the family. But in the industrialised society of today the family is not required to fulfil these roles. Today children are born in hospitals. Even for the nurture of the children there are many a number of official and non-official institutions. In big towns we find today a number of Infant-Care Centres and Children Homes. The education of children, today is done in schools and not in homes. The professional training also is no longer the obligation of the family. What is even more, even feeding is no longer the exclusive obligation of the family. Many people in metropolises eat out of homes. In almost all big cities people rarely take lunch at home except on Sundays and holidays. In many families both husband and wife go out for work. In these circumstances the functions of a modern family are more formal than real.

Disintegration of Family

Traditionally, most of the Indian families were joint families. As a result of industrialisation most of these joint families are breaking up and are being replaced by nuclear families. There are a number of reasons for this. Firstly, in industrial towns there is acute shortage of residential accommodation. Most of the people have to content themselves with a single or two room accommodation. In these circumstances it is physically exceedingly difficult if not impossible to retain the joint family system. Secondly, as a sequel to industrialisation family trades and professions have been eliminated. The sons of the same parents differ widely in respect of economic and social conditions. Joint family is all but finished in industrial towns.

Nuclear Families : As a result of industrialisation the cost of living has gone up. At the same time the standard of living has also gone up considerably. Everybody wants good clothes, houses and other comforts of life. Obviously, it is not possible to maintain the standard in a big family. Therefore, people these days want to keep small families. The prevalence of contraceptives and abortion has made this goal easily attainable.

Thus we find that there is a strong trend towards small families in industrialised towns.

In past the status enjoyed by women in Indian society was rather low. Women were shut up in the fourwalls of the home. From economic and social points of view woman was subject to man. The woman enjoyed no independence. Without husband the condition of a woman was miserable. As a result of industrialisation there has been much improvement in the status of women. Alongwith men, women today work in all walks of life. They are therefore becoming independent economically. Their status and respect in society has therefore improved considerably. Nowadays women consider themselves equal, even superior, to men. As a result of this feeling many women today do not like to marry. They wish to assert their independence by defying the laws of the society.

Family Disintegration : As a result of industrialisation the outlook of intense individualism has grown. Everyone wants to have his own way; no one likes to be subject to anybody. Nobody these days appreciates the need for adjustment and give and take. Thus, we find in modern society families cracking up under least strain. There is continuous tension and conflict in the minds of family members. As a consequence of this situation it is small wonder that families are breaking up fast in urban society.

Family Goals Differences : The goals and ideals which nourished the traditional Indian family were spiritual and religious. The housewives used to regard their husband as a god or divine being. They willingly subjected themselves to each and every whim of their husband. Even children used to give unqualified respect to their parents. The father was regarded to be the head of the family and his command was rarely defied. In Indian homes Ram and Sita were ideals of paternal devotion and wife's dedication to husband respectively. In industrial society there is no room for such ideals. For a modern wife the husband can be at best an honourable colleague and, under no circumstances, a god. The status of father in a family is being lowered as a result of industrialisation. Compared to parents, children now have more say in the family affairs. In the past the functions which were regarded sacred duty and ideals are now considered acceptable only from utilitarian point of view. The father no longer holds sway over family members.

Effect of Industrial Development upon Caste and Class : From times immemorial human society has been riddled with inequalities and discriminations. From the very beginning of civilisation we find some or other form of hierarchy in society. The society has always been divided into various classes having different rights and privileges and each enjoying a unique distinction and status in society. The classification and stratification in society have always been governed by some definite principle. As a matter of fact neither all persons in a society are equal nor are the various functions in the society of equal value. Therefore, in order to maintain some system and order in society it is necessary to establish a hierarchy of functions in society.

In different societies the principle behind the hierarchical arrangement of functions is different. In some societies the distinction between classes is based on the relationship of master and slave while in others it is based upon the idea of high, low and middle classes. Still in some other societies the governing principle of this distinction is caste system. In the modern industrial society the classification and stratification of society is based upon the concept of economic classes. The society today is divided into the classes of capitalists and labour.

As referred to above the basis of distinctions between classes in society is different in different countries and at different times. This basis is sometimes biological, sometimes historic and sometimes religious. As a matter of fact in the stratification of any society are reflected its values and ideals. In a religious society the *gurus* and godmen enjoy a place of pride. In a marital society warriors and conquerors occupy top positions. On the other hand in a capitalist society the wealthy persons are on top. In some industrialised societies like Japanese the technocrats occupy privileged positions. Thus it is apparent that in different societies the basis of distinction among classes is different.

Impact on Social Stratification

In industrial societies there is a unique kind of social stratification. In industrial society the different strata of society are known as social classes. The basis of stratification in an industrial society is different from that of other societies. Generally social stratification in an industrial society occurs on the following fourfold bases:

(1) Occupation.

(2) Educational Standard.

(3) Level.

(4) Birth Rate.

Now we shall study these in a little detail:

Occupation : In industrial societies the main basis of social stratification is occupation. In these societies the status and prestige of an individual is determined by the position and rank he occupies, the nature of his profession and his rank and status in that profession. What is meant is that rank and status are of crucial importance in industrial society. Indeed in an industrial society rank and occupation are indicative of one's ability. The rank and status and occupation are not hereditary in industrial society; one has to strive and struggle for these. In a society where caste system is prevalent the occupations and professions are hereditary. The son of a Brahmin does the job of a Brahmin and enjoys the same status and respect in society as were being enjoyed by his father. The son of a

Brahmin becomes automatically entitled to respect and status of his father. On the contrary, in an industrial society the son of a manager cannot claim the post of a manager after the retirement of his father. He must possess all the necessary qualifications for it, that is, he must earn the managership. In order to gain status in an industrial society one has to strive hard. In an industrial society there is no value for heredity but one has to strive for status.

Educational Standard : In an industrial society education is an important determinant of the status of a person. The better educated are regarded more highly than the less educated. Of course in every society the poets, writers and learned have got top rank and status. However, in industrial society there is some difference in this regard from other societies. The industry has closer relation to science and technology than formal learning.

This is why a person who is highly learned is not regarded so well as a person who is proficient in science and technology. In an industrial society it is not literary learning but the scientific learning that commands respect. As a consequence of industrialisation the importance and value of subjects like philosophy and literature has gone down. The formal learning has been replaced by utilitarian subjects. The predominant outlook in education today is pragmatic. Naturally, training in science and technology is conducive of industrial advance. It is applied science that is responsible for industrialisation. On account of the utilitarian nature of science and technology, the scientists and technologists enjoy places of prestige in industrial society.

Level : Now-a-days in industrial societies the measuring rod of one's social status is one's income; the higher one's income, the higher one's social status. In materialistic societies one's material possessions are indeed the exclusive determiner of one's worth in the society. The rich are worshipped and poor are hated. According to the materialistic outlook the possession of material comforts and luxuries is the paramount aim of life and the more one's material possession the nearer is one to the *Summum bonum* of life. For acquisition of material comforts money is needed. Therefore a person's income or salary determines, his status in the society.

There is another reason also for regarding money and wealth as criterion of social status. In the industrial societies the various types of qualifications are needed for earning money. It is but natural to accord high status to men of ability. Thus, from both points of view money and income are the determinants of one's social status.

Birth Rate : In the determination of social status one's birth and pedigree have always been kept in view. In different societies the family into which one is born has been regarded important in various ways. In the caste-based societies the son of Brahmin was accorded the status of Brahmin without the slightest consideration of his actual merit.

In feudal societies the family had great importance in determining one's social status. In industrial society, too, the family has unique importance in determining the social status of a person. However, the reasons for the importance of family in social stratification in industrial society are not the same as in caste-based or feudal society. In an industrial society it is recognised that in order to develop, to flower one's talents the family plays an important role.

A successful manager and technocrat need special opportunities of training etc., only those families which can provide such facilities produce successful persons in industrial societies. A man born in a high class family naturally gets more opportunities of development than a person who is less fortunate in this respect. In socialisation the family plays an important role. Thus from the above discussion the role of family becomes apparent.

IMPACT ON CASTE STRUCTURE

In Indian society the caste system has had a unique role and importance. The social status of a person was determined by his caste. The industrialisation has diminished the role of caste. Following are the salient features of the impact of industrialisation upon Indian caste system:

Caste-System Disintegration : The industrialisation in India has led to breakdown of caste-system. Under the impact of industrialisation the traditional caste-based structure of society is collapsing. Traditionally, the social status of a person in Indian society was determined by the caste into which he was born. As a result of industrialisation the caste-based criterion of social classification has changed. In the industrial society it is the class and not the caste which fixes the social status of a person. Now the society is split into classes. Man gets status according to his class. Thus the caste system is now disintegrating.

Brahmin's Influence and Power Reduction : In the traditional social structure the Brahmins enjoyed the highest status in the society. But as a result of industrialisation the influence of Brahmins is on the wane; it is gradually losing its traditional hold on Indian society. Now there are other criteria of social stratification. It is no longer necessary that one should be a Brahmin in order to attain high social status. As a matter of fact the traditional role of Brahmins in society is all but finished. Those who are unable to adapt themselves according to the changed circumstances have only a parasitic existence in modern industrialised society. That is why a Brahmin today is looked down upon.

Arrival of Shudras

In the traditional Indian society a *Shudra* enjoyed the most inferior status in society. Indeed his plight was miserable and he was treated no better than a slave. The *Shudras* were subjected to all kinds of calumny and obloquy. They enjoyed little respect in society. As a result of industrialisation there is some improvement in the condition of Shudra. In the industrial society the criterion of social status is work and not birth. Anyone proficient in industrial know how is bound to get a place of pride in society irrespective of the fact that he is a Brahmin or a Shudra. Today, a number of persons born into Shudra family are occupying high ranking positions in society.

Elimination of Caste-based Functions : In the traditional caste-based society each caste had some functions. Generally, the entertainment was also caste-based. The Brahmin had the role of teacher, the Kshatriya that of warrior. Now all this has changed. It is no longer obligatory upon a Shudra to do menial jobs for upper caste. Due to these changes the traditional functions of the castes stand abolished.

Proficiency-Oriented Division of Labour : Under the caste system the division of labour was based upon caste and not upon the consideration of efficiency. A Brahmin was to perform the function of learned even if he was poor in learning. Under the influence of industrialisation the criterion of division of labour has changed. The industrialisation has encouraged specialisation. Now-a-days a person is not given a task unless he is specially trained for it. In every department of society a specialised training is needed for the successful performance of a job. The Shudras are today doing teaching jobs. On the other hand, Brahmins can be seen to be doing the menial jobs. A proficient Shudra can now easily attain the position of an industrial manager and a number of Brahmins may be working under him.

Control of Castes Vanished : In traditional society the caste system was an effective instrument of social control. Each caste had its own code of conduct which was strictly adhered to and any violation thereof attracted strong social reprobation. The violation of caste based code of conduct used to result in ex-communication. In modern industrial society the control of caste has become loose and lax. The industrial society is highly intricate and complex. Now -a-days persons of all castes work together and it is, therefore, well-nigh impossible, to observe the separate caste-based codes of conduct. In modern industrial societies the instruments of effective social controls are provided by law and law enforcing agencies.

Untouchability Loosening : Under the caste system there used to be no intercaste social mixing. The persons belonging to different castes did not get together and share a common board. As far as a shudra was concerned he could not even sit, stand or walk near the persons of upper castes. A shadow of a shudra was scrupulously avoided. On the other hand, there are cases where Shudras themselves did not welcome the opportunity of being in the company of Brahmin. They forbade Brahmins from entering their quarters.

As a result of industrialisation the spectre of untouchability is relaxing its grip upon the thought and imagination of people. Today members of all castes work together in mills and factories and eat foodstuff from the same canteens and tuck-shops. Many a waiter in restaurants are Shudra. Even Brahmins willingly partake of food prepared and served by these people. Besides in parks and public places there are no restrictions on the entry of Shudra. Thus industrialisation can be said to have come as a boon for the low-castes.

Inter-Caste Marriages Exist : Under the caste system inter-caste marriages were a strict taboo. Hardly anyone dared to defy this taboo and marry with a spouse of any other caste except one's own. The punishment for such marriages was nothing less than complete excommunication. In modern societies these taboos are giving way. Though inter-caste marriages are not very common, people do marry into other castes without much disapproval. In mills and factories persons belonging to different castes come together, develop common interests and form friendships. Some of these contacts bloom and flower into mutual love and attraction. The mutual attraction breaks the caste barriers and such persons marry. There is another reason for the prevalence of inter-caste marriages. Due to frequent encounters with members of other communities one comes to realize the fundamental oneness of all human beings. One begins to appreciate that stereotyped thinking with regard to other castes is not valid. Thus the factors like caste pride and hatred for other castes which help accentuate caste barriers become inoperative. Thus there emerges a rational outlook. The factor of mutual regard and love comes to be considered as the only relevant consideration in regard to marriage.

Impact of Religion

Industrialisation has deeply influenced the course of religion. Following are some of the important features in this respect :

Orthodoxy and Superstitions on Decline : Under the garb of religion, orthodoxy and superstitions flourish. As a matter of fact, that whole edifice of religion is built out of bricks of superstition and blind faith. Superstitions are due to ignorance. In practical life belief in superstitions and orthodoxy proves harmful. For material and industrial progress it is very essential that men should be free from the clutches of superstitions. They must have rational and scientific outlook.

The process of industrialisation helps the spread and dissemination of science and practical knowledge. As a result of industrialisation people learn the truth of physical reality. They begin to appreciate and value the practical results and are prepared to give up irrational beliefs. The knowledge disseminated and spread on account of industrialisation subverts religious orthodoxy.

Religious Patience and its Growth

As a result of industrialisation the outlook of general masses in respect of religion has become broad. Generally, orthodox, religious persons are of narrow and parochial outlook. On account of their parochial outlook they regard their own religion as supreme and infallible. Their attitude towards other religions is that of contempt. As a consequence of industrialisation the persons of different faiths come together and get an opportunity of knowing and understanding the truth about each other. This results in dispelling of wrong notions about other faiths and an appreciation of basic unity of all faiths. Therefore, as a result of industrialisation there is development of religious tolerance.

Secular States Foundation : Previously, the states used to be theocratic; each state subscribed to some or other faith. Each nation had a national religion. The citizens professing faiths different from that of the state did not enjoy full rights and privileges; they were treated as second-rate citizens. But as a result of industrialisation the concept of theocratic states has become obsolete. Due to industrialisation every state now has a sizeable number of minorities whose claims cannot be ignored. Therefore, now-a-days it is a practice for most of the states not to consider any religion as special or state religion. The states today subscribe to the ideology of secularism, according to which the state is neutral in matters of religion but accords equal status to all religions. This is secularism.

Social Concern of Impact

Religion and religious functions have dual aspect. The first is its spiritual aspect and the second is its social aspect. In an industrial society the spiritual aspect of religion is not very important. Its social aspect, however is quite important in industrial societies. Now-a-days, festivals are celebrated not so much as religious affairs but as social functions. Even going on pilgrimage today is more of a social necessity than a spiritual need. A visit to temple or mosque even has come to assume social overtones.

Ethical Impact

Following are the ways in which industrialisation has influenced morals:

Growth of Rational Outlook : The Indian society has been traditionally based upon morality and religion. In India there has been little critical thinking in regard to moral principles and beliefs. The moral principles were accepted as universal truths beyond the sphere of doubt and reason. As a result of industrialisation the outlook of common man has changed. Now people demand rational justification as to why a particular action is considered right or wrong. In industrial societies it is believed that the moral principles are man made and that morality is for the sake of human life and society and not *vice-versa*. The tendency to examine and evaluate every moral principle before acquiescing to it is gaining ground in modern society.

Growth of Materialist Outlook : On account of industrialisation the importance and value of physical progress and development is enhanced. An average citizen of today does not appear to be satisfied and contented. The maximum material acquisition seems to have become the aim of modern life. It is for this reason that a common man of today is averse to religion and spirituality. Today, there is a strong competition for acquiring as much wealth as possible.

Growth Individualism : The industrial societies are increasingly becoming complex and in all spheres of life there is reign of specialisation. Due to industrialisation large metropolises are coming up. In large communities there is drop in fellow feeling. In such societies therefore the community feeling or the feeling of mutual belongingness is rather missing.

The life has become rapid and mechanised and people have little opportunity to look after the welfare of others. The life in industrial societies becomes self-centred. As a result of this there is growth and development of individualism in these societies.

Tolerance of Sex Morals : As a result of industrialisation the sexual morals have become lax. There are numerous reasons for this laxity. Firstly, the opportunities for the mixing-up of sexes have increased. Now-a-days boys and girls can meet without much difficulty and social opposition. In mills, factories and offices men and women work together.

As a result of this frequent encounter of sexes there is laxity in sexual morals. Moreover, industrialisation has given rise to materialistic thinking and according taboos on sex are harmful and that free sex is consistent with health and sane life. This is why that today pre-marital sex is not considered to be criminal or immoral. Indeed sex without marriage is coming to be considered quite normal, healthy and moral. In Western society all taboos on sex have broken down. A new highly permissive sex morality is the order of the day.

Increasing Crime : As a result of industrialisation there is an all round rise in the incidence of crime. It is a common observation that the rate of crime is very high in industrial towns. In large metropolises family life is subject to many pressures. It is very difficult to have normal family life in those towns. On account of disintegration of family the control of family over individual is becoming lax. Due to absence of this control there is encouragement of crime. In every industrial town prostitution and liquor consumption are rampant. Besides, theft and dacoity also are common-place in industrial towns. The incidence of violence and murder is also high in industrial towns.

Harassing Social Control : In industrial towns, labourers and artisans from places far and wide come in search of jobs.

Having found jobs, they settle in these towns. In industrial towns like Delhi, Kanpur, Bombay, Calcutta etc., workers from all over India are settled. As most of these workers are outsiders they are not subject to usual social controls. Moreover caste and clan considerations are almost non-existent in big metropolises. On account of all these factors the social control becomes loose and lax. In industrial towns it is neither the family nor caste and clan nor society in general that exercise social control. It is exercised by law and law enforcing agencies like police, courts etc.

Impact of Entertainment

Entertainment and relaxation are essential to life. Relaxation is indispensable for the health of everyone. The means of relaxation and entertainment keep changing with time and circumstances. There is a big difference between the means of entertainment in pre-industrial and post-industrial societies. In India there has been significant change in means of entertainment as a result of industrialisation. Following are the important influences upon entertainment due to industrialisation:

Outside Family Entertainment : Traditionally, in India family was the centre of entertainment. All entertainment was focused upon family. Generally, all families used to be joint and therefore were very large. A single family used to have about a dozen adult members and a dozen children. On account of large families it was possible to find all kinds of entertainment within the family itself. The adult male members used to beguile themselves by playing cards or chess and females used to gossip, swing or sing.

As there were very many children in every family the entertainment of children was easy. In the modern industrial societies the situation is just the opposite of the old state of affairs. The families today are not joint. The size of families has shrunk. A family today consists of husband and wife and their two or three children. Besides, in many families both husband and wife are employed. Under these circumstances there is no scope of entertainment within the family. Today almost everyone goes out for entertainment. The entertainment today has become institutionalised.

Entertainment regarding Profession : In industrial societies entertainment has become a business and a profession. Today, there are a number of institutions of entertainment. The cinemas, dance clubs and gambling dens are all centres of entertainment. We buy entertainment today. Throw money and have fun is the situation today.

Entertainment in Artificial Manner : Due to industrialisation entertainment has become a business and a profession. A professional entertainment however lacks the true spirit of entertainment. It is artificial and usually debases the man instead of relaxing him.

Besides, entertainment in industrial societies is not only artificial but is base and low also. Today classical music and dance are little appreciated. Moreover, these days entertainment by liquor and drugs is becoming common. In bigger towns prostitution is also a big source of entertainment. From all this it is apparent that the standard of entertainment has fallen steeply as a result of industrialisation.

Effect of Urbanisation

Urbanisation concerns the movement of population from agricultural to industrial work and from rural to urban places of residence. People are attracted to the city by visions of a better life, or they feel compelled to leave rural places because they are disadvantaged there. For most urbanisation migration, the attractions and compulsions are intermingled. For most such immigrants, urbanisation means a transition from one way of life to another. They become urbanised by going to where the urban way of life is.

Urbanisation through migration to urban centres is a global phenomenon. It is also centuries old and has always been more or less necessary to keep cities alive since city populations are seldom able to reproduce themselves. They draw new inhabitants full-grown from their hinterlands. The modern city needs more than the migrant who is full grown and ready for work.

Before he can be put to work he needs the kind of experience and training that can be used. Urbanisation is not only cityward and towards industry migration, there is also the non-migration aspect of urbanisation. One can be urbanised by going to the city, but urbanisation can also come to him in a non-urban place. In this sense urbanism is outward reaching. People may be urbanised without migrating to cities and without changing from agricultural to non-agricultural work.

The impact of urbanisation on rural life is not unimportant to sociological studies. The rural population is necessarily dependent on agriculture and allied occupations. But as a result of increased contact with urban centres, this means of livelihood is forsaken by many in the lure of better prospect in industry. There is a general exodus from agriculture to industrial and Semi-industrial centres. Also, commercialisation of agriculture itself occurs. More and more cash crops are cultivated and the improved marketing facilities thrown to the rural folk afford an opportunity to market agricultural products into the city. The increased demand for these products necessitates the introduction of specialisation and sophisticated machinery, equipments etc. to face competitional cultivators. Economically, there is increased production with a market in view due to the effects of urbanisation, "optimum" being the rule of the agriculturists.

The influx of urban commodities into the rural market is purely an exchanged contract. The rural folk accept the new products, be they food commodities or labour saving devices. The leisure time resulting in the use of such sophisticated gadgets helps diverse activities, commercialised in most cases.

Urbanisation necessarily involves the movement of a major population to urban centres. These migrants bring back with them new way of life, culture, way of thinking etc. These introduced influences of urbanism affect the majority of the rural population. The entire social structure of the rural community suffers a change in being shaken. Economic relations, neighbourhoods, universality of human actions, brotherhood doctrines are all thrown open to the gullible rural folk. As such new classes and status functions are derived in social life. Hereditary leadership gives way to rational leadership based on legality and authority as well as on voting choice. Efficiency gives the people a rule of choice.

New forms of mass media like the radio, T.V., newspapers, magazines etc. are available to the rural folk who are influenced by these to a great extent. Individualism creeps in gradually replacing the age old collectivistic approach. Religion is less primitive, more rational. It is more a practical way of life than a threatening force.

The rural inhibition no longer threatens the development of personality. The urban culture placing as it does adequate emphasis on individual's action, shatters the inhibited pattern of life and affords a broader perspective.

Urbanisation Social Control : In almost all cities of the world there is progressive increase in the population consequent upon industrialisation. This is a simple and quite easily understandable phenomenon. Wherever some new industry is put up a large labour force and a sizeable managerial cadre are required. In order to meet this demand there is influx of population to the city where an industry is being set up. In flourishing cities of the world, every day some or the other new industrial unit is coming. Therefore, there is continuous influx of population to cities. This progressive increase in the population has resulted in the problems of overcrowding. The industrialisation and mechanization have given rise to a host of social problems. The main consequences of industrialisation for the social life in cities are the following:

Fall of Social Sympathy : The first consequence of overcrowding and increasing population is the decline in fellow feeling and sympathy. In villages we find a lot of sympathy and communal feeling. A villager knows almost every other man in his village; knows about his problems, joys and sorrows. He feels for them. On the other hand, the question of knowing others does not arise in cities. And obviously we can have little sympathy for those who are unknown to us. In cities everyone is concerned about himself or his friends and lacks sympathy for others.

Absence of Social Control : With the decline in fellow feeling, sympathy and concern for others, there is also decline in the social control in cities. As the population increases in cities there is decline in control of family and caste on the behaviour of an individual. The infection of no control and arbitrary behaviour in cities is catching even rural population. Now-a-days the control of caste and *panchayat* has declined considerably in villages.

Fall in Family Control : The rise in the urban population has led to decline in family control. The family ties have lost their orthodox value and have become rather lax. In cities there are a number of families, where there can be no control over children. Lakhs of labourers live in cities without their families. Obviously, there is no question of family control over their behaviour. After coming to cities they start indulging in licentious behaviour because there is no one there to check them. They start going to cinemas and also visit houses of ill-repute.

Fall in the Influence of Religion : In cities the philosophy of materialism is ascendant. Everybody has become self-centred and is madly pursuing his self-interest without any consideration for others. All this is a direct result of the decline in the influence of religion in the urban life.

Women Status on Change

There has been considerable change in the status of women in cities. There is a great awakening among women. They are on the way to achieving economic independence. They are no longer slaves to their husbands. Commenting on this great change in the status in cities, Earnest K. Mowrer writes "The husband is no longer the head of the household in many families, inspite of the fact that he still provides the family name.

The wife, on the other hand, finds herself quite equal of her husband in the family circle, if not superior". However, there is an evil side of this awakening among women. There is rise in the incidence of illicit sex contacts, divorce, premarital and extra-marital sex.

Changes in the Institution of Marriage : In India marriages used to be contracted by the parents of bride and bridegroom. But now a-days there is an increasing tendency to choose one's life partner freely and of one's own accord.

Family Organisation on Change

In cities the institution of joint family is disappearing. Everywhere there is an increasing tendency to have limited families confined to husband, wife and their offspring.

Male Ratio Superiority : The reasons for the greater number of males in the urban population are quite clear. In cities lakhs of labourers live: their families live in their villages. Hence in cities males outnumber females.

Entertainment Professionalization : In cities relaxation and entertainment are not natural. One does not participate in it but merely enjoys it passively. Of course one has to pay through his nose for this entertainment. One can go to a cinema, to a hotel to see a cabaret or even to a brothel to see dance or buy sexual pleasure. In short, entertainment in cities is commercial and one has to pay for the entertainment.

Lack of Living Accommodation : In cities there is acute shortage of accommodation. More industrialised a city is, the less is the living accommodation in it. In cities like Bombay, Calcutta and Delhi people are compelled to sleep on footpath. Even those who find a roof overhead, live like cattles. Even then ten to twenty persons may be staying in a single room. Naturally, this gives rise to all sorts of evils.

Slums : This really follows what has been said above. As a consequence of shortage of living space, there are sprawling slums in big Indian towns. In Kanpur these slums are called *Ahatas:* in Delhi *Basti;* in Bombay *Chaw* and in Madras *Cheri.* These slums are a blot on the fair name of India. What is rather distressing is that alongwith slums we find grand mansions of mill owners.

Moral Values Change : There is change in the moral attitudes of city dwellers. The industrialisation leads to mechanization and as a consequence of mechanization man becomes an automation and loses his independence and moral autonomy. The industrialisation has produced a man who functions in the manner of a component of a machine. He feels himself a victim of circumstances and is unwilling to assert his will. The attitude of working girls towards sexual relations has changed considerably. As industrialisation has created great demand for working hands, women get work along with men. Due to this they have achieved economic independence and are no longer prepared to play a second fiddle to their husbands. The old moral values have crashed. New gadgets have given household women a great deal of time to pursue their interests.

All this has brought about great change in moral thinking and moral values.

Disintegration of Joint Family

In cities the joint family system has broken down. In cities most families consist of husband, wife and their offsprings.

Increasing Evil Professions : In cities many evil professions flourish. Due to frustrating working conditions in the factory, workers drink, gamble and go to prostitutes.

Increasing Incidence of Crime : As R.K. Mookrjee has very aptly observed, in industrial centres manhood is unquestionably brutalized, women dishonoured and childhood poisoned at the very source.

Increasing Juvenile Delinquency : In cities there is a sharp increase in juvenile delinquency. Due to industrialisation unscrupulous employers engage child labour. This is an important factor in producing juvenile delinquency. Besides, the children those parents who go to work are not properly attended to by their parents. They are left to their own designs and tend to become juvenile delinquents.

Moral Deterioration Conflict and Competition : In cities we find cut-throat competition in economic field. Not only among businessmen but among mill-owners there is furious competition. When this competition becomes fierce, evil practices are resorted to. Black-market is a direct consequence of this fierce competition.

The above mentioned social impact of urbanization is to be found in all countries. Some effects are desirable, while others are undesirable. To control the undesirable effects there is town planning in advanced countries.

Changing Process : In social change a number of factors operate. Among these are cultural, technical, biological, economic, geographical, psychological and ideological. A survey of social change in India would reveal the presence of all these factors. Again, these factors are themselves inter-related and inter-connected. If we analyze any particular case of social change we find at bottom a web of numerous interlinked factors. These factors together produce a specific social change and it is not always easy to determine the relative strength and influence of these factors.

Culture is a field of values, styles, emotional attachments and intellectual trends. These values, styles and ideas affect social change. By value we understand the goal which any individual or institution tries to accomplish. For example, the goal of a Hindu marriage is performance of *Dharma* and sexual intercourse for procreation. In modern times the impact of *Dharma* has declined quite a bit and the necessity of limited family has tended to make pleasure the chief goal of marriage. Due to this change in values the institution of marriage has become rather unstable. This has encouraged disintegration of family. In past the father used to enjoy a privileged status; every member of the family considered it his sacred duty to follow his command. In contemporary Indian society a generation gap is visible. Among the important social processes of change operating in the Indian society the following are worth mentioning : Sanskritisation

The structure of Indian society is based upon caste system. There is a hierarchy of the castes and certain castes are considered upper and certain others the lower. According to *Varna* system *Brahmins* were on the top rung of the society because they were the preservers of the culture. After them Kshatriya, Vaishya and Shudra occupied the second, third and the fourth rungs. The *Varna* system was based upon the cultural values. The higher castes were considered to be culturally higher also. In the caste system the social hierarchy is not strictly based upon the *Varna* hierarchy.

At some places Brahmins were considered at the top but at other places, on account of political and economic factors,

Kshatriyas occupied better status. The higher castes control and govern the behaviour of the lower castes and the lower castes try to carry out the dictates of the higher castes. According to M.N. Srinivas, by Sanskritisation we do not mean only the adoption of new habits and traditions but also the expression of new ideas and values. In the phenomenon of sanskritisation, the dominant caste finds a place of pride in the social hierarchy but the lower castes follow it with great care and caution because blind following leads to harmful effects. According to Dr. D.N. Majumdar in India the processes of sanskritisation and non-sanskritisation are going on side by side.

Influence of Western Culture: In the modern times a widespread influence of the western culture has led to many important social changes. Therefore, westernisation is a vital factor in social change. Westernisation has produced profound changes in the structure of family and marriage, personal relations, female education, social mobility etc. It has also affected in important ways the ideological and value system; the means of social control has also undergone change. Alongwith Westernisation, the materialist and scientific outlook of the West has also produced profound changes in the thinking of Indians. The philosophies of utilitarianism, pragmatism and individualism have also affected the Indian society. Still the cultural fall out from the industrialisation and urbanisation due to West is less than what it could be.

Secularization : The ancient Indian civilization was dominated by religion; but under the influence of Westernisation it is becoming increasingly secular these days. Under the influence of secularization the influence of religion over social institutions, traditions, practices and usages is declining and in its place utilitarianism and personal predilections govern human behaviour. After Independence the Indian government has adopted the ideal of secularism. This has given impetus to the process of secularization.

Democratic Application : In modern times, democracy is generally regarded to be the best form of government in the West. The main reason for this is that the democratic values of freedom, equality and fraternity are in tune with modern consciousness and thinking. After Independence, a democratic government was established in our country. Though democracy in social relationships is a distant goal, there is sufficient progress in this regard in other fields. The decentralization of power and the recognition of democratic values is leading to a decline in the obscurantist forces and the differences based upon caste, sex and religion are becoming less marked. Untouchability has been declared illegal. All individuals are equal before law. Every individual has full freedom of undertaking any profession: he is also free to marry anywhere; receive education from any place and associate himself with any body, institution or organisation. Many important steps have been undertaken for the upliftment of women and backward classes.

Movement of Policy

After Independence the Indian Constitution conferred voting rights on every adult. This means that every worker, every peasant and whosoever is above 18, and not insane, is entitled to vote. This has indeed taken politics to every corner of India and all Indian villages are today agog with political activity. Almost the entire length and breadth of India is now covered by radio network and millions of people are now able to see the television. This has kindled deep interest in politics everywhere. Around the election time this interest is all the more intense.

In election every party and each candidate try their level best to wrest power. With the abolition of feudal lords the power is now concentrated in the hands of politicians. Therefore, the political factors have become dominant lovers of social change. Due to political factors mainly, people support and oppose untouchability. Due to political factors alone the disintegrating tendencies like casteism, parochialism, and communalism are raising their forehead. The linguistic chauvinism is encouraged on account of political factors. In many social communities there is new life and strength on account of politics. Today there is so much politicisation in India that the social changes in both rural and urban India are governed by politics.

Process of Sanskritisation

Feature of Varna System : The origin of caste system is traced to ancient Indian *Varna* system. Some of the characteristics of *Varna* system resemble those of caste. The important among these are:

(1) All over India without any regional exceptions same kind of classification is to be found.

(2) There are only four *Varnas*. But if we include Harijans these will be five.

(3) The social hierarchy in the *Varna* system is quite explicit.

(4) The social hierarchy of *Varnas* is not subject to change.

Being based upon *Varna* system, the caste system is to be found in the four corners of India. But, unlike Varna, there are some differences in caste system from one region to the other. For example, certain castes are to be found only in a particular region of the country such as *Bhadbhuja Kahar, Barot* and *Charan* etc. Besides, the social status of various castes varies from one region to the other. In fact, many castes operate upon regional basis. Harijans are the essential part of caste system.

As remarked earlier, in the *Varna* system the place and status of each *Varna* is fixed but in practice this is not the case with the castes. Before the British rule the dispute regarding the status of castes used to be presented before feudal lords for arbitration and they used to settle them and fix the status of the caste. Thus whereas in the *Varna* system the place of each *Varna* is fixed, it keeps changing in the case of caste. The ancient writers on *Varna* system fixed the rights and duties of the three upper castes, who, on account of *Upanayan* ceremony, used to be called Dviya (twice-born). Thus the duties of *Varnas* were fixed. The Brahmin occupied the place of supremacy. During the British rule the ideal of *Varna* system began to collapse and each caste tried to improve and reform itself by sanskritisation.

Definition : In his book *Social Change in Modem India,* M.N. Srinivas has defined the process of sanskritisation thus: "Sanskritisation is the process by which a 'Low' Hindu caste, or tribal or other group, changes its customs, rituals, ideology and way of life in the direction of a high, and frequently "twice, born caste" In this definition the following points have been stressed:

(1) By Sanskritisation a caste or a tribal community ventures to gain higher status in society.

(2) In Sanskritisation, a low caste takes to the conduct, customs and rituals of the higher caste.

(3) The process of Sanskritisation is found not only in castes but also in tribal communities.

(4) In Sanskritisation Brahmins alone are not the object of initiation. Kshatriyas and Vaishyas are also taken as models. But in all instances the lower caste moves towards the higher and therefore follows or imitates the higher caste.

(5) By Sanskritisation a caste or group adopts and follows customs and rituals which would qualify it for being treated as twice-born.

Ideals : In the process of Sanskritisation a claim is made for higher status in the social structure and it is therefore, a vertical movement. But in Sanskritisation only there is improvement of status, there are no structural changes. In India, besides castes, the process of Sanskritisation is to be found in tribal communities like Bhils of Rajasthan, Gonds of

Madhya Pradesh and other hilly tribes. By the process of Sanskritisation a tribal community tries to prove itself to be a part of Hindu Society. In his book on Coorgis, Srinivas had laid undue emphasis upon the ideal of Brahmanism. But in his book *Social Change in Modem India* , he admits that the ideal of Sanskritisation can also be Kshatriya, Vaishya and even Shudra.

Integration Vertical and Horizontal : In the *Varna* system the three upper castes, namely, Brahmin, Kshatriya and Vaishya are considered to be twice-born, because only members of these castes have the right of wearing the sacred thread during *Upanayan* ceremony. In Brahmins also there are a number of caste distinctions. As different castes are to be found in the same region, they speak the same language, celebrate the same festivals and take to worship of local deities.

M.N.Srinivas has called this process as vertical integration and this is quite different from horizontal integration. Horizontal integration occurs within a single *Varna.* On the whole, Brahmins have tried to keep aloof from the local influences and these are found mainly among Kshatriyas, Vaishyas and Shudras. The Kshatriyas and Vaishyas in different parts of the country are separated by deep differences. The maximum Sanskritisation has taken place in certain Shudra castes.

Dominant Caste

In the rural life of India, there is an agricultural caste which has the ownership of land. This is the dominant or *Prabhu* caste. For a dominant caste the following are the essential characteristics:

(1) The major portion of agricultural land is under its ownership.

(2) Adequate membership of the caste.

(3) In the local hierarchy it must occupy the highest status.

(4) In the presence of above features of lordship a caste will be called *Prabhu* or dominant.

In certain villages more than one caste enjoys the lordship of land and in the course of time the domination of one caste over the other gets reversed. In the last century various factors have influenced the lordship-Western education, government service, urban sources of income, etc.

After Independence, on account of universal adult franchise, Harijans now feel their importance, power and dignity. Now the reins of power are in the hands of rural rich and with the exception of those villages where Harijans outnumber others the seat of power is unlikely to change for some time in the rural India. A caste enjoying lordship in one village has to observe deference and respect to the caste which enjoys lordship in the whole region.

Thus a local dominant caste is less powerful than the regional dominant caste. In the establishment of lordship the ownership of land plays a crucial role. The ownership of land gives not only power but prestige also. The power and prestige of feudal lords affect their relationships with other castes—for example, in Punjab feudal lords treat Brahmins as their servants and the Thakurs of Madohpur in Eastern U.P. did not accept the food prepared by Brahmins except their preceptors and priests.

Though in secular matters, members of dominant caste are privileged, in matter of rituals the situation is very different. In India the sacred matter occupy more importance than the secular affairs. A millionaire Gujarati *Bania* dare not step into the kitchen of a Brahmin because this would pollute Brahmin food. If the dominant caste is Brahmin or Lingayat its ideal of Sanskritisation would be Brahminism and if it is Rajput or Bania its ideal would be Kshatriya or Vaishya.

Disposition of Caste System

Following two tendencies are to be clearly seen in India:

(1) Besides local religious and moral values, the existence of other cultures is recognized.

(2) The ways and manners of higher castes are followed. However it needs to be remembered that the local rural organisation is not entirely independent of the All-India organisation. The rules of moral conduct, sanctity of the places of pilgrimage, moral dramas and other sacred traditions are derived from various sources. In villages, the elders of dominant caste are the guardians of a pluralist value-system. The dominant caste maintains the structural distance between the castes under its influence. The lower castes also try to follow the customs and manners of dominant caste. The imitation of the life style of upper castes is done in a round-about manner because direct imitation of the upper castes will be frowned upon and may invite punishment.

Sanskritisation in Punjab : Dr. D.R. Chanana has mentioned about Sanskritisation in regions where prior to Independence in 1947 and consequent upon partition of the state the influence of Islam and West Asian countries was dominant. Sikh religion enjoyed subsidiary lordship. In the matter of religion Hindus were deeply impressed by Islam, particularly its Sufi Cult. In pre-partition Punjab and North Western Frontier Provinces, Muslims enjoyed the lordship and in certain areas Sikhs enjoyed the subsidiary lordship. Brahmins among Hindus had neither resources nor knowledge and the commercial classes were more important. Arya Samaj and its rival *Sanatan Dharma* did much to spread education. This encouraged Sanskritisation of Hindus.

Tribals Sanskritisation : The process of Sanskritisation is to be found among tribals. On the other hand, Shri S.L. Kalia has tried to show that a process of tribalisation is evident among the castes of Jaunsar Bawar of U.P. and Bastar of M.P. The elders of the dominant caste administer punishment to those who violate its rules. But at times, the twice-born upholders of great traditions yield to little traditions. It is of course not always true that maximum sanskritisation occurs in Brahmins.

Leading Caste Example : It is possible to draw a map of rural India in which the name of dominant caste in each and every village can be given, but this will be a very cumbersome task. Yet the names of dominant castes can be enumerated. In Northern India the rural folk nickname the dominant caste *Ajgar* which are indicative of dominant castes among the down-trodden castes. *Ajgar* is formed by the first letter of the names of *Ahir, Jat, Gujar* and *Rajput.* In some parts of West Bengal, *Sagdip, Patidar* and *Rajput* in Gujarat, *Maratha* in Maharashtra, *Kamma* and *Reddy* in Andhra, *Vokilagas* and *Lingayats* in Mysore, *Wellas, Gandar, Parchayi* and *Kallar* in Madras and *Nayar, Syrians, Ijwan* etc. in Kerala are the dominant castes. The dominant castes project ideals for the majority in the villages.

Kshatriyas and Brahmins maintained their lordship for long. The places of pilgrimage and religious monastries are the sources of sanskritisation. The spread of sanskritisation among the non-dominant castes living in the vicinity of places of pilgrimage and monastries used to be vertical and horizontal in other regions.

Varna Conflict : As we have mentioned earlier, there has been no single ideal of sanskritisation. There were three or four such models. There has been conflict among these ideals. For example, in Vedic scriptures we find references of conflict between Kshatriyas and Brahmins. Later on there was conflict between Buddhism and Jainism. In Buddhism and Jainism we find mostly trading communities who were resentful of the over-domination of Brahmins. Buddhism and Jainism pointed a way out to get rid of disqualifications imposed by caste system.

In the original *Varna* system, the place and status of each *Varna* was fixed. But during the Vedic period there were important changes in the life style of Brahmins. These changes are crucial because other *varnas* used to follow the ideals of Brahmins. In Vedic age the Brahmins began to be treated as *sannyasins*.

In post-vedic age Brahmins were influenced by Buddhism and Jainism. The spread of *Bhakti* movement gave an opportunity to the lower caste persons to become religious leaders. Many Harijans and women also attained the status of sainthood. *Bhakti* movement helped to spread the message of ancient scriptures which was in Sanskrit in the regional languages.

Sanskritisation's Political Elements : Before the British rule the instability of political system in India was a powerful source of social mobility. In the 18th century there were four stages of political organisation—Imperial, Intermediary, Regional and Local. At the imperial level there were Mughal emperors. At the intermediary level there used to be Nawabs. At the regional level the Jagirdars or feudal lords dominated. The Jagirdars used to rule through local 'Aamils'. Thus at the top there was a king under whom used to be Navabs and under Navabs there were Rajas who used to control the populace through local chieftains.

The officer at the lower rung was under obligation to provide soldiers to his immediate boss. The 18th century political conditions obtaining in Gujarat and Benaras were favourable for castes like *Bhoomiher, Brahmin, Rajput, Patidar* and *Koli*. In order to give instances of social mobility before the British, M.N. Srinivas has cited, examples from U.P., Gujarat and Kerala. In all these areas there was a lot of a political mobility. Due to political instability there was social mobility.

A Raja had the power to raise or lower the status of, caste residing in his region. This was so because in the pre-British India Rajas were considered to occupy the topmost position under the caste system. Rajas used to offer appointments to various posts in the castes. A person excommunicated from some caste for misdemeanour could approach the Raja who could grant him re-entry to the caste. The disputes regarding appointments in the castes were also adjudicated by the Rajas. The king had the authority to punish; he used to consult wise men before giving his judgement.

Sanskritisation's Economic Elements : During the pre-British period the so-called mobility of the caste was not only due to political factors; there were economic considerations too. There was no dignity of labour and higher the status, less the labour. The feudal lords were not supposed to do any work with their own hands. The manual labour was reserved for low castes. The ownership of land and the economic status were responsible for entitlement to high castes. During the middle ages the social mobility was linked with residential mobility. By change of residence new castes were born and they severed their links with their origins.

All the changes which have occurred in the castes are inter-caste changes and these have in no way affected the fundamentals of caste system. For this process of change, M.N. Srinivas has used the concept of sanskritisation. The rationality and validity of this concept has been critically examined by Dr. D.N. Majumdar and other contemporary sociologists. The discussion of this evaluation would show the significance and limitations of this concept.

Hiatus in the Concept of Sanskritisation : Sanskritisation is not a new concept in the sociological literature; but M.N. Srinivas has used this concept in a peculiar way. In his words, "Sanskritisation means not only the adoption of new customs and habits but also exposure of new ideas and values which have found frequent expression in the vast body of Sanskrit literature, sacred as well as secular *Karma, Dharma, Papa, Punya, Maya, Samsara and Moksha* are examples of some of the most common Sanskritic theological ideals, and when people become sanskritized these words occur frequently in their talks. These ideas reach the common people through sanskritic myths and stories". Thus Sanskritisation means the adoption of the values of a cultured society.

However, M.N. Srinivas considers this concept to be only useful but not very clear. According to him this concept helped him in analysing the religious life of Coorgis. He believes that the anthropologists would profit by the use of this concept, though he himself concedes that "Sanskritisation" is no doubt an awkward term, but it was preferred to Brahmanisation for several reasons".

Sanskritisation Process : In explaining the meaning of sanskritisation, M.N. Srinivas points out that sanskritisation was not always due to Brahmins. Generally sanskritisation qualifies a caste for a higher status. In the dynastic system, Sanskritisation emphasizes the status of dynasty. In sanskritisation sons were considered obligatory as a matter of religious duty and thus sons had a higher social status. Thus the status and value of daughters was downgraded. According to Srinivas sanskritisation spread during the British rule. With the spread of education and literacy it percolated to the lowest castes.

The Western technology radio, press, rail etc., greatly facilitated the process of sanskritisation. The Britishers introduced the system of parliamentary democracy in the country. This also helped Sanskritisation. According to M.N. Srinivas the economic status of the caste is not an essential factor in the process of sanskritisation though the better economic status did help. Besides, the attainment of political authority, spread of education and the desire for better status also helped the process of sanskritisation. Srinivas has recognized that mere sanskritisation does not 'help a caste to attain a higher status. According to Srinivas an untouchable caste, no matter how sanskritized it becomes, will not be able to cross the barrier of untouchability. But a thorough going sanskritisation taking place among the castes may ultimately overhaul the Hindu caste system. A question arises if sanskritisation is a one-way process. Srinivas believes it to be a two-way process.

Process not Universal : Thus, according to Srinivas sanskritisation is a process whereby a lower caste incorporates in itself the culture and values of the higher caste. This may not enable it to elevate itself to the higher caste but it does bring it nearer to it. But it must be borne in mind that under the caste system there is taboo on the lower castes against adopting the norms and values of the higher caste. According to M.N. Srinivas, "In short, it took over, as far as possible, the customs, rites and beliefs of the Brahmins, and the adoption of the Brahmanic way of life by a low caste seems to have been frequent, though theoretically forbidden". But here we encounter a difficulty. Srinivas accepts that in Hinduism the lower castes are taking to the norms and values of the higher castes.

This fact may be true with reference to a particular community or region but it is not universal. As Dr. D.N. Majumdar has shown in his study of Mohana village, in U.P., there is no tendency among the lower castes to adopt the customs and manners of the higher caste nor does it help in elevating the status of any caste. There are quite a few instances where the members of low caste seem to adopt the life style of the high caste but this does not qualify them to be considered the members of the high caste. If a "chamar" pastes a 'Tilak' on his forehead he would not be considered a Brahmin. Dr. D.N. Majumdar asks. "If it (Sanskritisation) is a process, where does the process stop and why"? In his study of the Mohana village Dr. D.N. Majumdar has shown that in the social stratification the movement among the castes is not vertical but horizontal.

That even the members of the same caste begin to regard some of them as low. For example all Brahmins are considered highest among the castes. But among Brahmins there are sub-castes like Gauri Kanyakubja, Saraswati etc. who consider themselves to be lower or higher than the others. This is horizontal expansion of Brahmins. Similarly, there are many sub-castes among Shudras. Not only among the Shudras, but even within the sub-castes of Shudras there are to be found further sub-castes. For a non-Chamar all *Chamars* are at the same level but for a *chamar,* another *chamar* may be lower or higher to him. From the above examples it should be clear that by the change in the life style in castes there come into being further sub-castes and this change is not a vertical progress but a horizontal expansion.

***Sanskritisation and De-sanskritisation* :** Dr. D.N. Majumdar is not only critical of the concept of Sanskritisation but doubts if it is really taking place. According to him there are more signs of the reverse process, namely, de-sanskritisation in evidence all over the country. In de-sanskritisation the members of the higher castes abandon their dress and rituals. For example, many among the Kashmiri Pandits have abandoned their traditional mode of life. Another symptom of de-sanskritisation is taking in professions traditionally reserved for the lower castes. According to D.N. Majumdar the shrinkage of distances between castes is not due to sanskritisation but its reverse. The lower castes are not' moving towards the higher but the higher castes are abandoning their life' style.

IMPACT OF WESTERNISATION

The Western culture has greatly facilitated the process of de-sanskritisation. Under the impart of Western culture the various castes are abandoning their traditions. The educated members of all castes are adopting the Western life style and hence coming together. D.N. Majumdar admits that the process of de-sanskritisation is slow in some places but it is going on everywhere. The social mobility among castes is horizontal rather than vertical. Therefore, D.N. Majumdar does not consider that the concept of Sanskritisation is scientific.

According to him, "Sanskritisation connotes a group of concepts and at best is a loose one, devoid of any special merit". He is against the use of the term sanskritisation in reference to cultural change. In particular it should not be used in reference to horizontal and vertical progress. But in the absence of a more refined concept it may be of a limited value. As long as a better concept is not formulated to explain the cultural change, the use of the terms sanskritisation and de-sanskritisation is indispensable. From the above examples it is evident that the changes in the life style result in the formation of new sub-castes which move horizontally. Dr. Majumdar is of the view that the process of de-sanskritisation is more evident than that of sanskritisation in Indian society.

Sum Up : As a matter of fact adequate study of the cultural changes in India have not been made to enable us to draw any safe and sure conclusions. But we will have to recognize that both the process of sanskritisation and de-sanskritisation can be seen to operate in our society, at some places the former can be more dominant and at other places the latter. But in the absence of sufficient scientific data, it is difficult to determine conclusively which of the two is more effective. But as far as probability goes the view of D.N. Majumdar seems more probable; though it cannot be strictly said to be true. In order to arrive at a more dependable conclusion more extensive research into this matter is called for.

In the modern times Westernisation has played a crucial role in bringing about social change in India. Westernisation means incorporation of the norms, values and culture of the West in one's own culture. India came under the influence of

Westernisation during the British rule. Therefore, M.N. Srinivas defines Westernisation thus: "I have used elsewhere the term 'Westernisation' to characterize the changes brought about in Indian society and culture as a result of over 150 years of British rule, and the term subsumes changes occurring at different levels—technology, institutions, ideology, value".

Impact of Western Culture in Urban Areas : The impact of westernisation is seen mostly in urban areas; but on account of this fact, it cannot be concluded that westernisation and urbanization are synonymous. In many parts of rural India more westernisation is in evidence than even in the urban areas. Though on the whole more urban areas have come under the impact of westernisation, nonetheless there are quite a few villages in India that are more westernized than urban areas. Therefore, it will be wrong to think that the westernisation is a result of urbanization. These are two independent entities or processes; that is why those have been treated separately in this book.

Comparison between Westernisation and Modernisation

Many people are under the wrong impression that westernisation is modernisation because the two are thought to be the same; but in fact the two must be differentiated. Westernisation is more a limited concept than the modernisation. All countries have not become modern due to the influence of west. For example some countries have become modern under the influence of Japan. In modernisation all those elements are included which come about by a revolution in the means of communication, more urbanisation, more literacy, increase in the per capita income, adult franchise etc.

Features of Westernisation : In as much as modernisation in India has come about due to westernisation, therefore the above mentioned changes of modernisation can be taken to be the result of westernisation. The following are the characteristics of westernisation :

Neutral Morality : Modernisation is generally considered to be good, but this is not always so with westernisation. Westernisation has been for good as well as evil. In fact westernisation is morally neutral.

Westernisation Limit : A distinction has to be drawn between westernisation and western culture. All the elements of the Western Culture did not originate in the West. For example, Christianity originated in Asia. The decimal system originated in India and via Arabia reached the West. Gunpowder, printing press and paper were invented in China. All these constitute the important elements of Western culture though these did not originate in the West. The manner in which westernisation operates in India is mainly the result of British influence. The culture of Germany, France and Russia etc., is quite different from the Indian Culture.

Meaning of Westernisation

The concept of westernisation is quite wide. It subsumes all changes which are consequent upon Western technology and modern science. Secondly, it has had varying impact upon the different aspects of the culture; hence it is a complex concept. Thirdly, westernisation has affected society on different levels. For example, in olden days people used to eat in *thalis* or *banana* leaves in squatting position but now they use dining table with all its accessories. While westernisation has had very wide impact, there has been resistance to it in some quarters. Thus westernisation has had variable impact on the Indian society.

Process of Westernisation : Westernisation has not been incorporated willingly everywhere in India. At places the copying of British manners and customs was deliberate; at other places it was a sub-conscious process.

Impact of Westernisation : The following are the consequences of westernisation.

Effect on Institutions : Westernisation has influenced caste system, joint family system etc. It gave birth to new institutions like press, electrical system, Christian missionaries, etc.

Transvaluation : Westernisation has encouraged modern values like humanism, egalitarianism and secularism. British Civil and Criminal law affected Hindu and Muslim laws. The system of slavery was ended and members of all castes were free to get education. Gradually, there was spread of education among women. Theoretically all were accorded equal economic opportunity. Many discriminative religious practices were ended. Among such practices, the practice of untouchability is foremost.

Reform's by Government : Under the impart of Westernisation, the states undertook a number of reforms. The steps were taken to prevent epidemics and famines. An effort to spread education was also made.

Hinduism Redefined : Under the impact of westernisation, many religious reform movements came into existence and they attempted to redefine the various aspects of Hinduism in the light of modern science and knowledge. In redefining Hinduism, Maharishi Dayananda, Ramakrishan Parmahansa, Vivekananda, Rabindranath Tagore, Sri Aurobindo, Raja Ram Mohan Roy did commendable job. They indicated to various aspects of Hinduism which required urgent reforms. By their laudable efforts *Sati* System where a wife was burnt alive on the funeral pyre of her *husband* was ended. The curse of child marriage was put to an end and widow-remarriage was sanctioned. An effort to eradicate the evil of untouchability was also made.

Activities in Politics and Culture

Besides religious reform movements which came into

existence under the impact of westernisation, many political and cultural movements were also started. Besides nationalist movements many parochial movements based upon caste, creed, language and religion came into existence.

The most significant impact of Westernisation is to be seen in the form of modern education taking root. During the British period, many schools, colleges and universities were opened to disseminate modern education. Press came into existence and many newspapers and periodicals were published which offered a number of viewpoints. An educated class came into existence which became the vanguard of freedom movement.

Factors of Westernisation : The British and Indians both helped to begin and accelerate the process of westernisation. Therefore both can be considered as carriers of Westernisation. Among Britishers three groups can be distinguished. Firstly there were soldiers and civilians occupying high ranks. Secondly, there were traders and the owners of orchards. Thirdly, there were missionaries. All of these three groups helped to spread westernisation. On the other hand many Indians also helped the process of Westernisation. Among them the following are included.

Persons who came in Direct Contact with Englishmen : The Indians who came in direct contact with Englishmen were influenced by their life style. Among them were the persons who were in the household employment of the Englishmen and also those Hindus who abandoned Hinduism and espoused Christianity.

Indirect Influence : The primary contribution towards Westernisation was made not by those who came directly in contact with the Englishmen but by those who were indirectly influenced. Among these are included the persons who received new education, entered into trades or served as petty bureau crates under the British. All were not middle-class persons. For example, Raja Ram Mohan Roy and Rabindra Nath Tagore belonged to aristocratic families.

These English educated gentlemen brought forth great change in society by launching various movements. Among the Muslims, Sir Saiyad Ahmed Khan belonged to this category. Among the backward class, Dr. B. R. Ambedkar, did a great job of modernisation. Besides the contribution made by the above mentioned luminaries certain castes among Hindus were especially westernized. These include *Vaids* of Bengal and *Parasi* and *Bania* of Western India.

The impact of westernisation was also felt through the patients who were treated in the British hospitals, the persons who had to go to law courts and through the medium of newspapers and books. The port cities near the sea coasts were particularly vulnerable to westernisation. For example, Calcutta, Bombay and Madras were the first cities to receive the impact of westernisation.

In India westernisation did not take place on a wholesale basis, rather it was selective. The westernisation in India was the result of the traditional tolerant, catholic and receptive attitude of the Indians. India always has had the tradition of catholicity, tolerance and self-criticism. The luminaries like Vivekanand, Ranade, Gokhale, Tilak, Tagore, Aurobindo, Gandhi, Patel, Nehru and Radhakrishnan who came under the influence of westernisation tried to re-evaluate and redefine the ancient Indian values in terms of modern enlightenment.

System of Modernisation

Definition : Before undertaking the discussion of modernisation in India, it is advisable to define the term modernisation first. According to S.N.Eisenstadt, "Historically, modernisation is the process of change towards those types of social, economic and political systems that have developed in

Western Europe and North America from the seventeenth century to the nineteenth and have spread to other European countries and in the nineteenth and twentieth centuries to the south American, Asian and African continents". Modernisation is the characteristic feature of modern society.

Features of Modernisation : The process of modernisation becomes evident from its characteristics. Following are its characteristics :

Social Mobility : The social mobilization is that process by which the old social, economic and psychological elements are transformed and new social values of human conduct are set up. The social mobilization is a peculiarity of modernisation.

Social Discrimination : Another feature of modernisation is social differentiation . In this process there is increase in the complexity in social, political and economic activities and there is progress in the activities of individuals in various fields. Industrialization is a result of modernisation. In politics the administrative complexity in the central and local bodies is a characteristic of modernisation. The political power gets dispersed among adults. Thus modernisation is a way to democratization. As a result of modernisation new trends ' in philosophy, religion, science and literature become visible. Briefly an increase in modernisation leads to a progress in social, economic, political and cultural fields, there is more differentiation in these.

Structural Discrimination and Change : Another characteristic of modernisation is structural differentiation and continuous change. In the social and economic fields old organisations break up yielding place to new. In politics new parties emerge. The cottage industries are replaced by big industries. The new means of production develop. Many new professions develop. The production becomes more complex.

Organisational and Status Change : A feature of modern society is the emergence of a number of specialised organisations. Secondly, there is greater division of labour. Thirdly, the organisation based on close kinship lost its importance. With the accelaration in the speed of change the status of individuals and families undergoes change. New classes emerge in society. From the cultural and economic viewpoint there come into being three classes, namely, upper, middle and lower.

PROCESS OF URBANISATION

The phenomenon of urbanization and modernisation are inter-linked, one leads to the other.

Socio-political Movements : An important feature of modernisation is the emergence of new social and political movements which aim at the transformation of society. This transformation becomes imperative in order to make man adjust to fast changing conditions. These movements also aim at casting off orthodoxy and paving the ground for change to modernity. In order to attain the new aims, a change of outlook becomes imperative.

Education Comprehensive and Multi-sided : An important aim of modernisation is the spread of education. In modern society it is tried that all should be educated. Besides academic education under modernisation, the need for technical and professional education becomes acute; therefore many technical and professional institutes spring up to meet this demand.

Growth of International Cooperation : Lastly, the development of international cooperation is the aim of modernisation. The national movements gave birth to many nations. For the development of mutual relations among nations, a League of Nations and later U.N.O. came into existence.

Modernisation Means : After discussing the characteristics of modernisation in India, the means of modernisation will now be discussed :

Growth of Industry

In modern India industrialization is going on at a fast pace. The Western model is being followed in this regard. The Western countries, in particular U.S.A., have helped India in industrialization. This has helped to bring India close to the Western style of industrialization. In order to meet the demands of fast growing population, every country must per force become industrialised. Therefore, India is fully resolved to bring about fast industrialization.

Urbanization : The fast growing of population of this country in the last 50 years has led to fast urbanization in India. The fast industrialization and consequent urbanization has led to many ticklish problems like slums, crimes etc. In order to solve these problems town planning is imperative.

Secularization : Secularization is a consequence of urbanization. The people of India have adopted the ideal of secularism according to which everybody is free to follow the religion of his choice. The modern society is pluralist. The compassion and tolerance are the chief characteristics of modernisation.

Evolution of New Social Classes : The traditional social classification in India is based upon caste system. The caste system is incompatible with the egalitarian social values. Under it the status of a person is determined by his birth. Whatever may have been the merit and use of caste system in the past, there is little doubt that in the modern society it is an obstructive force; it is retrograde; it is against the democratic values. Due to current politicization the importance of caste system is growing; but from all other viewpoints its value and importance is declining. Today, both in the towns and villages, the people are divided into classes which are based upon economic and political rather than caste considerations. The distinction between lower, middle and high classes is exclusively economic.

The classes based on economic considerations are non-hereditary. A low class person, by dint of his labour and application, may belong to upper class tomorrow. The importance of money and possessiones in modern society is paramount. With increasing politicization there is now clear-cut demarcation between those in power and those out of it. Mostly economically better off persons are politically also better off, but this is not essential. The political class in India is other than the economically rich but the economically rich support politicians with money and use them.

The industrialisation is giving rise to an organised labour class and the communist thinking is creeping into Indian society. With the organisation of labour class the capitalist class is also getting organised and they have formed many associations to protect their interest. While there are all India Labour organisations there are also all India associations of the capitalists.

Social Transformation

Modernisation accelerates the pace of change; it is quickened. The change is both the characteristic and goal of social change. Change is a cultural goal towards which every society advances. The change must be towards the achievement of greater human dignity and greater social equality. It is a progress towards democratic values.

The social change can be seen in diverse fields. On the one hand, social movements have greatly changed our ideas and concepts about various social matters and on the other youth movement has brought about revolutionary change in the thinking and aspirations of youth. The youth movement can be seen all over the world, this is an important characteristic of modernisation and the pace of modernisation gets accelerated by these movements.

The youth movement is a rebellion against the traditional

values and is a harbinger of new shape of things to come. Today, particular attention is being paid to encourage youth movements at the university level. From time to time youth functions and festivals are held in the universities in which young persons from all over the country participate. This encourages the national integration and also shows the basis for the building up of the future. In India the youth movements can be seen in the form of student movements.

The youth are demanding a right to participate in the administrative affairs of the universities. The modern youths are busy evaluating the educational curriculum and also the efficacy and utility of examinations. These matters become bone of contention among the students and university authorities.

Impact of Western Culture : The trend towards modernisation in India can be seen in the form of a movement towards westernisation of the society. The trend towards westernisation can be seen in all fields. In social, economic, political, cultural religious and educational spheres India is following the example of West. Even those who are in favour of retaining the traditional values also want to utilize the good traits of the western system.

They want a synthesis of western and Indian values. The westernisation leads to modernisation because the model of modern society is provided by the west. In the social sphere we are following west in matters like dress, life style and town-planning etc. The latest fashions of the West are quickly followed by the Indian elite. There is more of Westernisation in the technical and scientific spheres than in the social spheres. This has given rise to cultural lag. In the social fields we are still sticking to the obscurantist values of casteism, communalism and parochialism.

Democratization : In the field of politics the most characteristic feature of modernization is the process of democratization. India is becoming progressively democratized. There is in India universal adult franchise. Everybody above a certain age is entitled to elect his representative. Everybody is equal before law and enjoys equal rights and privileges. In the economic sphere an attempt is being made to reduce economic disparities. The compulsory primary education is aiming at universal literacy. All political parties are wedded to the value of equality, liberty, and freedom. There may be differing view points regarding the means to attain these values but there is no dispute about their validity and acceptance as the ultimate goals of political endeavour. Though it is understood that there was a tradition of democracy in ancient India, but modern democratic tradition in India is following the West. In the promotion of democracy, U.S.A. in particular, has helped a great deal.

Various Pressure Groups : Pressure groups, as the name indicates, are groups which exercise pressure in social change. Such pressure groups may be rural and urban. These types obviously differ according to the society in which they function. Indian society is primarily rural in nature. Even in cities a large number of people who have migrated from the rural areas maintain their rural customs and tradition.

Therefore in these sections of the cities, one may again find some pressure groups. Among the most important rural pressure groups are *Hokka* groups and social and political factions. Caste groups are the most dominant pressure groups in the villages and cities of India. Among caste pressure groups the dominant castes acts as a pressure group in the whole community. Many social elements are determined by the dominant castes. In every caste based social structure the caste *Panchayat* acts as a pressure group. This is particularly important in rural societies. Political parties act as pressure groups both in cities and villages. Political actions and dissident groups are important pressure groups within the political field. All these pressure groups are important determinants of social change. These will now be briefly described.

Hokka Pressure Groups : Smoking *hokka* is extremely common in Indian villages, young and old all are used to smoking *hokka.* It is a common sight in villages to find groups of persons taking puffs at *hokka.* Farmers, Ironsmiths, Goldsmiths, Potters, Barbers, in short, people from different walks of life find time between their working hours to smoke *hokka.* Smoking *hokka* apparently refreshes them and they re-engage in their respective works after short spells of *hokka* smoke.

Though smoking *hokka* is intoxicating and its use as narcotic cannot be condoned it serves an extremely useful social purpose. *Hokka* in villages provides an occasion for get-together and gossip. *Hokka* is symbolic of inter—caste and inter-group distinctions. If anyone smokes *hokka* is anyone's company he is considered to belong to his group. Smoking *hokka* in common is indicative of an expression or affirmation of friendship. This is why usually persons of high caste do not smoke *hokka* of low-caste persons.

This is because they wish to maintain and preserve their distinction and smoking *hokka* with low-caste is regarded degrading. If a group of persons sitting together belong to any single caste they can be seen to smoke from the same *hokka.* Whenever a guest arrives in any home in a village and if he is of the same caste as the host, he is entertained with milk or beverages and then in a relaxed atmosphere is offered *hokka* to smoke.

The guest and the host take turns at *hokka* and engage in slow relaxed conversation. At marriages *hokka* is freely used, and all persons belonging to one caste or group smoke from one *hokka* and this is considered to be an affirmation of fraternity and friendship. However persons from different castes do not smoke the same *hokka.* Among certain caste there is no barrier on smoking from a common *hokka.* For example, Brahmins can smoke the *hokka* of Jats and *vice-verse.* However, a Brahmin would never smoke a *hokka* of a *Chamar* and would not allow a *Chamar* to smoke from his hokka.

Though in general, there are no restrictions on *hokka* smoking in villages, there are some occasions on which smoking *hokka* is a taboo. For example, smoking *hokka* on Janamashtmi day is not considered proper, because on this day it is forbidden to take any foods, water or any thing which would involve introduction of any foreign thing into stomach. Naturally, therefore, smoking would involve breaking fast and this is considered bad.

On account of permissive attitude of villagers to *hokka* smoking, we find a number of *hokka* groups in villages. A *Hokka* group is that congregation of individuals who collect at certain places and smoke *hokka* and engage in gossip in a relaxed manner to while away their time pleasantly. Besides being a source of relaxation, *hokka* in villages serves as a symbol of acceptance or non-acceptance of someone into one's fold. Thus *hokka* group serves as an indication of one's social status. If someone accepts *hokka* of any person he expresses hereby his fraternity with the man. Therefore, if any one is to be punished with excommunication from any caste or group he is disallowed to smoke in that group or the *hokka* groups of a particular caste. To exclude someone from *hokka* smoking is a great punishment. It is a strong disapproval of the conduct of man excluded from a *hokka* group.

As exclusion from a hokka group is a special disapproval and punishment, it has great value in dispensation of social justice within a caste or group in a village. Therefore, whenever any person violates the code of his caste or does anything disgraceful to his community, a council is called to discuss his guilt. If it is proved, he is declared as an unacceptable person and is not to be allowed to smoke *hokka* of that community and no member will touch the *hokka* used by him. However, this excommunication from a group is not permanent. After doing the penitence prescribed by the community and making apology for her or his misconduct, the excommunicated person can be readmitted to the community and the ban on his *hokka* smoking repealed.

Even if a person unwittingly violates the restrictions placed on *hokka* smoking the person is punished. For example, if an upper caste person smokes the *hokka* served by a low caste and this fact becomes public he is liable to be duly punished and prevented from smoking *hokka* of his community till the time he makes suitable amends by tendering apology and performing penitence prescribed by the community. Thus in a *hokka* group, *hokka* is an effective means of exercising social control. Besides, *hokka* is a symbol of mutual relations and fraternity in villages. It keeps a person in a fold and provides an effective means of social disapproval and punishment. In modern progressive society, it would appear that mere *hokka* cannot be a thing of great social significance. Nonetheless it continues to be something of a great social significance in Indian villages.

Panchayats in Villages

In the matters concerning the whole village particularly in political and economic matters the village panchayat is the most important pressure group in the villages of India. The present system of village panchayat started in 1947 when after the Independence of the country, panchayats was reorganised in the villages. The *Gram Panchayat* cultivated in the village people the habit of working together, owing responsibility for the various activities of the village, understanding things of public interest and living in cooperation and charity. The panchayati court taught them to resolve misunderstanding through mutual negotiations.

The panchayats did much towards increasing the communal feeling by decreasing the effects of urbanisation which had been manifested in the village youths in the form of a lack of responsibility, selfishness and impetuosity. The tendency to look upon the entire village as a family was born in the village people as a result of the communal contribution of labour in the construction of roads, drains, tanks, schools and panchayat houses. In this way panchayat has a major role in removing the irresponsibility which had been the outcome of the disintegration of the joint family and the weakening of caste panchayats. By arranging for radio sets and lectures etc. the panchayats created awakening in the villages. Thousands of primary schools were opened in the villages to spread education among the village children. In order to educate the older members of the community, adult education centres and night schools were opened. Literacy weeks were organised and resolute efforts were made to remove illiteracy from the country.

Caste Pressure Groups : Indian society is divided into numerous castes. This is equally true about the Hindus, the Muslims and even about the Christians. The caste group sometimes has a caste panchayat constituted by the influential members of the caste which determines important matters concerning all the caste members.

It is this caste panchayat which exterminates those members of the caste who break its social norms. The caste panchayat rigidly imposes social control upon the members of the caste and observes endogamy and other rules. During the British rule the caste system suffered a severe shock in the village. Due to the British economic policy and new laws, different castes abandoned their traditional occupations and adopted other professions. Many Brahmins and Kshatriyas started farming.

The members of the untouchable castes became agricultural labourers. The control of caste panchayat weakened. It is seen in the villages now-a-days that the status of an individual in the villages is determined not only by his caste but also by his personality, financial condition and activities as well. Although the Brahmin is addressed respectfully, the wealthy untouchable is not the recipient of any the less respect even though he belongs to a lower caste.

And at some places it may even be that he may be respected even more than the poor Brahmin. Being assisted by government laws the lower castes no longer look upon themselves as inferior and in south India at some places the untouchables consider themselves defiled if they touch a Brahmin. If any Brahmin happens to come into their sector he is assaulted with brooms and in extreme cases strict measures are taken to purify the place which he has defiled by his touch.

In this way in the present age the members of each caste are engaged in strengthening their own organisation. Some castes have formed their own caste organisations by holding meetings, for the protection of their interests. But even then the power of the caste panchayat, exercised in the form of control over the individual's behaviour, food habits, ways of living etc. has gradually disappeared.

Even in such villages where the laws regarding untouchability in the caste are necessarily observed, freedom is given towards violating them in the towns. Although marriages are still contracted within the same castes even then there is no obstacle to eating, conversing etc., between different castes. But although in this way the caste system appears to be growing weak on the one hand it seems to be gaining in strength upon the other.

Casteism is increasing due to vested interests. In recent times it is seen that most of the people vote for the members of their own caste or one whose caste is in majority in that electorate. The same had been the case in the previous election and some elected persons, had even tried to gain advantage for their own caste. In this way due to political and other interests casteism is increasing. Most administrative authorities in government and non-government factories, offices, colleges and other works think it very necessary to employ only the members of their own caste.

Party System

Political parties help in the operation of checks and balances in a democracy. The existence of political parties checks abrupt revolutions as the parties provide a platform to express grievances and get them redressed in a constitutional way. Various political parties act as counterbalancing forces upon each other. They provide different sets of policies and programmes from which the people can choose as the ideal alternative according to their needs. Discussion between parties in parliament and in state legislatures brings to light these alternatives.

Rural Group : The main reasons for the formation of factions in villages are a sense of economic, social or political insecurity. Many a villager has no or a little land; they are therefore so poor that without external help they cannot maintain them. They need good organisation to be able to secure official or unofficial assistance. Similarly, for successful litigation and securing of justice a strong organisation is needed.

By belonging to some or other faction they can face the threat to their physical or economic welfare in a better way. Without belonging to any faction it is difficult to feel secure in villages. Each member of a faction feels a sense of political, social or economic security. In an event of difficulty or trouble the other members of the faction are ready to help him. In the event of his untimely demise, the group looks after his family and children.

In case of threat to his honour the members of his faction protect him and also help him in his bad times. Besides in times of need he can use the houses of others and seek financial help. For example, in time of marriage his guests can stay with his friends and his friends make their contributions towards marriage. A faction does not remove only a feeling of insecurity from the minds of its members but also fulfils many a social need of them. A member of a faction does not suffer from the sense of isolation and loneliness and feels a sense of gratitude as the powers and influence of an entire group are behind him.

Political Group **:** Political factions refer to groups within a single party with divergent interests and view points. Factions emerge when modern political society emerges in traditional societies like that of India. Factions with diverse interests are bound to emerge in loosely structured political organisations. In the larger society there are various caste, sectarian, regional and landed and industrial interests which often may converge and diverge depending on the fluctuating socio-economic situations. When a political party secures power either at the central or regional levels it will have to deal with these divergent interests, it has to sustain its control over the political administration. Consequently, factions representing these interests are bound to emerge in such parties.

Combined Family

An important pressure group in Indian society particuarly in the villages, is the joint family. In a joint family are included husband, wife, uncles, aunts, sons and nephews etc. In a joint family, the authority rests in the oldest male member in the family. The property is deemed to be the common possession of all members of the family. The head of the family uses it for the good of all members of the family. A joint family runs a common kitchen and every member shares common board and lodging.

Programme for Greater Change

As the social sciences have now progressed it is now considered desirable that the social change should be planned and well-directed. Though social changes are always taking place on account of various social factors, it is better if these changes are directed towards some particular goal which brings common-zeal to all. This work is known as planning. In India Five Year Plans have been taken up for economic planning. However, these plans are aimed at not only economic planning but also social planning.

The above account of social changes in India and an enquiry into the causes and factors responsible for the change clearly suggest that the pattern of social change in India is like that of the west. Though it must be admitted that the social change should suit the local conditions, unless the impediments like superstitions, beliefs, orthodoxy and blind adherence to traditions are removed no meaningful pattern of social change can emerge.

It is not possible to make rapid progress in social planning without abandoning the unscientific attitude towards life. The contemporary Indian society is passing through a period of transition. How the Indian society will shape itself in the future cannot be safely predicted but if the change has to occur in desirable directions, the goals that we wish to accomplish must be determined in advance and then an effort should be made to achieve them in a planned way. For this purpose cooperation between the government and people is essential: but above all the elite must realize its duty and must do the work of enlightenment. It must endeavour to inculcate the scientific outlook among people.

Without a powerful elite there can be little progress in the country and so far the elite is not a very effective class in India. Among the elite we find both rightist and leftist trends. Will these ultimately harmonize? Nothing can be predicted. Everything is in a melting pot at the moment.

Legislative and Executive Measures in Five Year Plan: Planning in India derives its objectives and social premises from the Directive Principles of State Policy set forth in the Constitution. The public „ and private sectors of the economy are viewed as complementary. The private sector covers not only organised industry but also small-scale industries, agriculture, trade and a great deal of activity in housing and construction and other fields. Individual efforts and private initiative are considered both necessary and desirable, the policy being to assist development on the basis of voluntary cooperation to the utmost extent. Economic planning also envisages a growing public sector with massive investments in basic and heavy industries.

The Government of India appointed a Planning Commission in 1950 to prepare a blueprint of development taking an overall view of the needs and resources of the country. The composition of the Commission as on 15 September 1982 was as fellows:

Smt. Indira Gandhi Prime Minister and Chairman, S.B. Chavan: Minister of Planning and Deputy Chairman, Pranab Kumar Mukherjee: Minister of Finance and Member, R. Venkataraman: Minister of Defence and Member.

Mohammad Fazal: Member

Prof. M.G.K. Menon: Member

Dr. C.H. Hanumantha Rao: Member

K.V. Ramanathan : Secretary

First Five Year Plan : (1951-52 to 1955-56) had a two-fold objective to correct the disequilibrium in the economy caused by the Second World War and partition of the country and to initiate simultaneously a process of all-round balanced development, which would ensure a rising national income and a steady improvement in the living standards over a period of time. Since the country had to import foodgrains on a large scale in 1951 and there were inflationary pressures in the economy, the Plan accorded the highest priority to agriculture, including irrigation and power projects.

About 44.6 per cent of the total outlay of Rs. 2069 crore in the public sector (later raised to Rs. 2,378 crore) was allotted for its development. The Plan also aimed at increasing the rate of investment from 5 per cent to about 7 per cent of the national income.

Second Five Year Plan **:** In 1954, Parliament declared that the broad objective of economic policy should be to achieve a 'socialistic pattern of society' under which the basic criteria for determining the lines of advance would be social gain and greater equality in income and wealth and not private profit. The Second Five Year Plan (1956-57 to 1960-61), therefore, sought to promote a pattern of development which would ultimately lead to the establishment of a socialistic pattern of society in India.

In particular, it stressed that the benefits of economic development should accrue more to the relatively less privileged sections of society and there should be a progressive reduction in the concentration of income, wealth and economic power.

The main aims of the Plan were :

(i) an increase of 25 per cent in the national income;

(ii) rapid industrialisation with particular emphasis on the development of basic and heavy industries;

(iii) large expansion of employment opportunities; and

(iv) reduction of inequalities in income and wealth and a more even distribution of economic power. The Plan also aimed at increasing the rate of investment from about 7 per cent of the national income to 11 per cent by 1960-61. The Plan laid special stress on industrialisation-increased production of iron and steel, heavy chemicals, including nitrogenous fertilizers and development of heavy engineering and machine building industry.

Third Five Year Plan **(1961-62 To 1965-66)** : The Third Five

Year plan aimed at securing a marked advance towards self-sustaining growth. Its immediate objectives were to :

(i) secure an increase in the national income of over 5 per cent per annum, and at the same time ensure a pattern of investment which could sustain this rate of growth during subsequent plan periods;

(ii) Achieve self-sufficiency in foodgrains and increase agricultural production to meet the requirements of industry and exports;

(iii) expand basic industries like steel, chemicals, fuel and power and to establish machine-building capacity, so that the requirements of further industrialisation could be met within a period of ten years or so mainly from the country's own resources

(iv) utilise fully the man-power resources of the country and ensure a substantial expansion in employment opportunities; and

(v) establish progressively greater equality of opportunity and bring about reduction in disparities of income and wealth and a more even distribution of economic power. The national income was to increase by about 30 per cent from Rs. 14,500 crore in 1960-61 to about Rs. 19,000 crore by 1965-66 (at 1960-61 prices) and per capita income by about 17 per cent from Rs.330 to Rs.385 during the same period.

Fourth Five Year Plan : The situation created by the Indo-Pakistan conflict, two successive years of severe drought,

2

Role of Social Stratification

As the families of a jati, in sufficient number, accrue a strong power base, and as their leading men become united enough to move together for higher status, they typically step up their efforts to improve their jati customs. They try to abandon demeaning practices and to adopt purer and more prestigious ways. They usually want to drop their old name for a better one.

A modern instance of this traditional process, that of the Yadavas, has been illuminatingly described by M. S. A. Rao (1964). This example illustrates a mobility effort which combines traditional and modern modes of disengaging from degrading customs and associating with respectable practices. The term Yadava has been taken by many different jatis, mainly of North India, whose traditional occupation was cattle keeping. They now maintain a national organisation which has published a well-edited and well-produced volume entitled *The Divine Heritage of the Yadavas* (1959). The book was originally written by V. K. Khedkar, a schoolteacher who rose to be private secretary to a Maharaja, and was later revised and enlarged by his son who was a surgeon. It argues that the jatis whose occupation was cattle keeping and milk selling are descended from the deity Krishna through a number of royal dynasties.

These jatis, among whom Ahirs are a widespread and numerous contingent, have usually been held in considerably less glorious repute by their neighbours. While an occasional warrior of a pastoral jati did establish his own state and dynasty, cattle keepers are ranked in many localities among the lower blocks of the Shudras. This was partly because they wandered about with their cattle and so their purity practices (so the explanation ran) could not be checked; partly because they performed castration operations on animals, and, perhaps mainly, because they were involved in the sale of milk (Baines 1912, pp. 56-58). The production of milk for one's family is entirely proper, but economic transactions in the sacrosanct product are thought to be unseemly. A cow's milk, like mother's milk, should be for one's children, not for customers and cash.

As some herdsman families became prosperous in the late nineteenth century, the campaign to take the Yadava name and Kshatriya style was begun, backed largely by a new business elite. Some men from these jatis, long accustomed to trading at cattle markets, became successful city tradesmen; others, who had traditionally contracted for the care of animals, became wealthy as contractors to government for the same purposes.

The book by Khedkar combines a traditional origin myth and a highly modernised improvement campaign. It postulates divine and noble ancestry for a good many jatis in several language regions covering hundreds of thousands of people who share little more than a traditional occupation and a conviction about their rightful prerogatives. The editor's introduction begins by giving the credentials of the authors, including the eight British diplomas, degrees, and certificates garnered by Dr. Khedkar. The editor also tells that the authors' manuscript was corrected, revised, and brought up to date by one Professor and two Assistant Professors of Indian History from the University of Allahabad. (It must be said that a very modern apparatus of historical scholarship is shown in the footnotes and references of the text.) B.N.S. Yadav concludes that "In this way we find that in the hoary past the Yadavas were associated with a political ideology which is considered to be progressive" (1959, p. 200).

This contemporary mobility drive was preceded by many earlier struggles carried on separately in various localities. At one stage Ahirs in the Punjab and U.P. joined forces to improve Ahir status (Marten 1924, pp. 231-232). Parallel but independent efforts were being made at about the same time in other linguistic regions. Representatives of the separate organisations met at Allahabad in 1924 to found the All-India Yadav Maha Sabha (the "great league" or "great assembly" of Yadavas). This association has published a journal ever since, and its resolutions urge that all adherents conduct themselves in a life style befitting the name Yadava.

Certain components of this improved life style are quite like those traditionally prescribed by the jati panchayat of almost any ambitious group. Jati fellows are told to discard demeaning practices, particularly the eating of meat and drinking of liquor. They are urged to take on prestigious customs and symbols, one of which is the wearing of the sacred thread. When a good many Ahirs in Bihar actually began to wear the sacred thread there was intense, sometimes bloody, opposition from the dominant Bhumihars and Rajputs (Marten 1924, pp. 231-232; Lacey 1933, pp. 267-268; Rao 1964, p. 1440).

Other reforms urged by the Yadava Sabha are more rooted in modern social and political conditions than in the traditional ideals. Thus the delegates to Yadava Sabha conventions have frequently resolved that dowry payments among their members should be lowered, the age of marriage of their children raised, the duration and cost of weddings lessened, and marriage alliances between families of different Yadava jatis increased. The wealthier brethren are encouraged to contribute to Yadava welfare causes and, as M. S. A. Rao reports, "They gave liberal donations to build schools, colleges, hostels, hospitals, and temples, to scholarship funds and toward the expenses of running caste journals and of holding conferences and meetings" (Rao 1964, pp. 1441-1442). With popular elections, opportunities opened to put fellow Yadavas in office in constituencies where Yadavas are numerically strong. By 1964 there was a "sizable group" *of Yadava legislators* in both the Bihar and the Uttar Pradesh assemblies, and some twelve members of the central legislature were Yadavas. At the top, "there is an Ahir Minister in the Union" (Rao 1964, p. 1443).

A new proposal for Yadava improvement came as a result of the fighting of 1962 in the Himalayas. One company that fought gallantly was the 13th Kumaon composed entirely of Ahirs. One hundred fourteen of this company were killed; their brave stand received wide sympathy and admiration in the Indian press. It stimulated the Yadava Sabha to press for the formation of a Yadava or Ahir regiment in the Indian Army (Rao 1964, p. 1440).

The modern Yadava campaign includes many more people, uses more rationalised techniques, and seeks broader achievement than a more traditional effort waged by a single jati to improve its local lot. But in essence the modern campaigners follow similar patterns of action for similar purposes. On the one front they must disengage themselves from low jatis and their demeaning customs. Hence there is still the plea to give up meat and liquor. On the other front, they seek to associate themselves with the more prestigious customs and groups. Putting on the sacred thread is a gesture of self-association with the category of the twice-born, although this symbol no longer is as important to young men as it was to their fathers and grandfathers. Refining the jati's origin story is another traditional move. Other reform proposals associate the rising group with the educated and modern elite.

CUSTOMARY CHANGE

In both the older and the newer means of cultural adaptation for jati mobility, a characteristic step is to change the name of the group. Either a respectable term is added to the old name, or an entirely new name is proposed.

A case in point is that of a sheepherding jati of the Poona district in Maharashtra. A number of families in this jati have become landowners and have given up their rather lowly former occupation, claiming the occupation of landowner, soldier, and village headman, and assuming the sacred thread. Known formerly as Sagar Dhangar, the latter being the term for shepherd, they now call themselves Sagar Rajputs. Orenstein reports a speech given by an official of their caste organisation, who cited the "historical" reasons that they are not Dhangars and should not be so called. He demonstrated, to the loudly voiced satisfaction of his fellows, that they are really Rajputs (which links them to the mythology of the martial nobbles) and also Marathas (which links them to the dominant jatis of Maharashtra). The historical contradiction involved in their claim to be both was as irrelevant to his appeal as the fact that historically they were neither. His peroration was, "Then tell everyone that you are Marathas!" (Orenstein 1963, pp. 6-7).

Similarly, in parts of Bengal the dominant cultivators are called Mahisyas, a name that has come to be the standard term for them only in the past fifty years. "Previously in Midnapore and still in parts of Bengal where they are not dominant, they are known by the despised name Kaibartta or Hali Kaibartta (ploughing Kaibartta) in order to distinguish them from the lower-ranking Jati or fishing Kaibartta, with whom they now admit no connection" (Nicholas and Mukhopadhyay 1962,

p. 19). Such name changes are an old story in India. In eighteenth-century Gujarat, members of the Kunbi group who became landlords and revenue collectors were called Patidar, the title for revenue officials. This title carried such great prestige that in time Patidar became the name of the jati-cluster (A. M. Shah 1964b, p. 90; Srinivas 1966, pp. 35-381 Pocock 1955, p. 71).

When a decennial census was established, it provided a new arena for mobility efforts, especially in the matter of name changes. At the time of the first nationwide census, taken during 1867-1871, some groups formally registered their claims to a grander name than that commonly given them. Two jatis of cultivators in Madras, for example, asked to have varna terms affixed to their jati name. Vaishya in the case of one, Kshatriya in the case of the other.

In the 1901 Census, information was collected and published on the relative ranking and varna affiliations of each jati. This had the effect of certifying that the Census was indeed an arena for mobility struggles and precipitated a new phase of the competition. Many aspirant jatis thereupon concentrated their mobility efforts on the census operations. By 1911, census officials were inundated with petitions for name changes and other status certifications; one officer reported receiving about 120 pounds of petitions from the districts he covered (O'Malley 1913, p. 440).

A count of the claims for higher rank in four census regions of the 1931 Census (United Provinces, Bengal and Sikkim, Bihar and Orissa, Central Provinces and Berar) shows 175 such claims, of which 80 are to Kshatriya status, 33 to Brahmin (including two untouchable jatis claiming Brahminhood), 15 to Vaishya. There were 37 requests for new names without specific varna reference; 9 Muslim groups asked for new labels. Twenty-three groups entered more than one claim; a few claimed two or three prestigious names, perhaps in the hope that one would stick (Srinivas 1966, p. 99). In the 1941 Census and thereafter, the listing of jati and varna names was largely eliminated, terminating the use of the census as a tool for jati mobility.

Only certain elements of group custom are deliberately altered for mobility purposes. A great part of the jati's life style is kept quite the same, partly because of economic necessity and habitual response, partly because the members of an aspiring group see no need to make completely sweeping changes. If they are farmers seeking to be known as Kshatriyas rather than as Shudras, they commonly take pride in their work on the land, perhaps seeking to add a bit of martial luster to their yeoman status or to be known as overseers as well as tillers. Their aspirations do not require that they abandon farming. Many of the artisan jatis too, are not necessarily eager to give up their respective crafts, but rather to have traditional carpenters (or masons or whatever) recognised as practitioners of a high-ranking calling. Rising families do not try to change those domestic practices that have no deleterious implications (cf. Marriott 1959a, pp. 67-68).

All agree that certain practices degrade the practitioners. Hindus who seek a social status above the lower echelons avoid the eating of beef or of any carrion meat, the disposal of corpses or carcasses, the handling of products of dead animals (particularly cows), and the disposal of excreta. Muslims have different but parallel standards. Although there is solid agreement about what should be avoided, there is less consensus as to what should be emulated. Alternate models of prestigious conduct are available; different strategies for social rise are possible, and a combination of models may be feasible.

In sorting out the processes of mobility, it is useful to distinguish reference categories, that is, general principles for proper conduct, from reference groups, actual exemplars of conduct. A main reference category is that of the "twice-born" varnas in the three classic variants. Another is that of modern, educated, elite conduct. Each category is invoked in certain contexts and has particular appeal at certain stages of mobility. Commonly the two are combined, as when a jati organisation exhorts its members to become strict vegetarians and also to be zealous proponents of college education for the children. The reference principles are usually interpreted according to the living example of a prestigious reference group. These are people whose life style can be seen and copied by those who seek similar rank, privileges, and respect.

Importance of Reference Category

"Twice-born" is a generalised category. Ambitious families of Shudra or Harijan category select one of the three varna models to emulate, but all three models share common elements. The general label for the three is from the scriptural sacrament of the second "birth," the *Upanayanam* rite, at which a boy is formally separated from his preinitiation status and takes a last meal as a child, with his mother. He undergoes a token transition status, acting for a few moments or hours as an ascetic student bound for the great religious center, Banaras. He is incorporated into his new status when he receives a sacred verse from his spiritual mentor and is invested with the sacred thread worn across the left shoulder (cf. Kane 1941, pp. 268-316; Stevenson 1920, pp. 27-45). All birth rites proclaim a child's legitimate membership in society; this rite of second birth endows a boy with an important aspect of his full status and identity.

In religion, the "twice-born" are expected to show greater concern for the transcendental complex than do other folk and to have less to do with the pragmatic complex. Rites conducted by any of the "twice-born" should not, and rarely do, include blood sacrifice. If they want to propitiate local deities by such sacrifices they should contribute indirectly or vicariously. They are expected to follow the main tenets of Sanskrit scripture more closely than do others; their customary diet is supposed to be more pure than that of the lower orders in their locality. Those of Kshatriya status need not be vegetarians and teetotallers, but they still do not eat the lower forms of flesh, especially beef, nor do they offer alcoholic liquor in religious ceremonies. They usually have closer Jajmani relations with local Brahmin priests than the lower jatis can have.

Closer adherence to scriptural teachings entails more stringency in family relations, especially for women. A girl should become a wife as early as feasible and a mother as soon as possible. Her fate depends on her husband; as a wife no divorce is open to her, as a widow no remarriage is possible. "Among Hindus generally, there is a preference for virginity in brides, chastity in wives, and continence in widows, and this is especially marked among the highest castes" (Srinivas 1956a, p. 484). This last phrase is important. It is not that people of the upper varnas can claim exclusive rights to these family practices, as traditionally they did to the sacred thread, to the initiation sacrament, and to Sanskrit learning; it is rather that they should carry out these practices in purer fashion than do others.

The division between "twice-born" and all other Hindus was reflected and probably reinforced by the way in which British courts interpreted Hindu family law. For the purposes of British-Indian law there were only two kinds of Hindus, the "twice-born" and the Shudras. Any Hindu whose jati did not qualify as being of the three upper varnas had to belong in the fourth. The converts to Hinduism and untouchables were classed as Shudras. One kind of law was enforced for Shudras in matters of marriage, succession, and adoption and another kind for the "twice-born." The chief legal tests for the higher category were whether the sacred thread was customarily worn and whether marriage ceremonies followed Sanskritic patterns. If there was evidence that widow remarriage, inheritance by illegitimate sons, and divorce were allowed this was taken as an almost decisive index of Shudra status. In various legal decisions, other criteria were mentioned as indicating membership in the higher rank. These pronouncements tended to focus the reform efforts of mobile groups on these criteria (Derrett 1963, pp. 28-29; McCormack 1963, pp. 68-69; Galanter 1963, p. 545).

The process of cultural adaptation to these higher standards has been called "Sanskritisation" by M. N. Srinivas. He defines the term as "a process by which a 'low' Hindu caste, or tribal or other group, changes its customs, ritual, ideology, and way of life in the direction of a high, and frequently, 'twice-born' caste" (1966, pp. 1-45; 1952a, pp. 30-31; 1956a). The concept has been a fruitful one, which has stimulated a number of further explorations (*e.g.*, Chanana 1961b, Gould 1961b, Barnabas 1961, Singer 1964, van Buitenen 1966), but the earlier formulation of it has drawn criticism, notably that there has been great regional and historic variation in the content of "Sanskritic Hinduism" (Staal 1963).

That is quite so. Sanskrit scripture is vast; different sources lay down differing standards for conduct; the same source has been held by different interpreters to sanction different action. The Bhagavad Gita testifies to this (Edgerton 1952, vol. 2, p. 103). In Sir Edwin Arnold's translation of the relevant passage it is rendered as follows:

> Look! Like as when a tank pours water forth To suit all needs, so these Brahmins draw Texts for all wants from the tank of Holy Writ. But then, want not! Ask not! Find full reward of doing right in right.

Doing right, as we have seen, is taken by many to mean trying to raise one's jati rank; their superiors in rank usually view such striving as being quite wrong.

Yet most villagers agree that certain canons of conduct should be followed by those who legitimately count themselves among the "twice-born." These standards have long been upheld by the higher jatis and they do underlie the many varieties of Sanskritisation. These themes of conduct are repeatedly brought home to villagers, as has been noted, through religionists of many kinds, visiting entertainers, itinerant preachers, revered mentors. Some of the most effective agents of Sanskritisation, paradoxically, have been devotees of anti-Brahmanical sects. In their missionary zeal, these sectarians reached into groups which were not already imbued with the scriptural standards for the "twice-born" and were sometimes as successful in implanting these ideas as in making converts to their opposing sect. This was true for Lingayats of Mysore in earlier centuries and for the Arya Samaj in North India in the twentieth century (Srinivas 1966, pp. 21, 101).

Mrs. Karve has commented that among the illiterate people of Maharashtra, there is far greater knowledge about the literary tradition of the last seven centuries of this land than among the people who have received their education in schools and colleges. Through village channels there has been effective communication of the "fundamental theoretical framework underlying the social structure" (1961, pp. 117-119). This is true in other parts of India as well; religion remains a propitious code for communication (Gum-perz 1964).

People of the "twice-born" varnas are thus differentiated from the rest of society by standards that are based on scripture and accepted by most villagers. When a group becomes resentful enough about being classed as Shudras or Harijans, powerful enough to do something about it, and united enough to launch effective action, its members change their personal habits and jati manner to conform to a particular varna model. The model is also a marker. If such a group can succeed in being accepted by their neighbours as a jati of the higher varnas, they have arrived. Untouchables do not usually try to become Shudras; they aim for one of the higher categories, most frequently Kshatriya. Those classed as Shudras do not often use that term for themselves, though other villagers do (Karve 1961, p. 47); when they gather strength for a mobility leap, they generally aim for one of the "twice-born" categories, rather than for higher place among Shudras.

Which category is selected by those of an aspirant group depends on such factors as their origin myth, the attraction of a locally dominant group, and on calculation of the most feasible strategy for status gain. Whatever model is chosen, the general requirements for each are well known throughout village India. In simplest terms, jatis classed as Brahmins are expected to stress purity, piety, learning, and priesthood more than do others in their locality. Kshatriyas, for their part, emphasise honour, virtue, force, and masculinity. Vaishyas pride themselves on steadiness, thrift, intelligence, as well as on purity and piety.

These various features are known in the remotest corners of the land because, together with the basic "twice-born" standards, they are presented, assumed, and repeated through all the media of the civilisation—in sacred stories and plays, in local tales and anecdotes, in the information picked up by pilgrims, in the talk of genealogists and other professional visitors to the village, in daily interchange. A villager knows from his everyday experience that there are considerable variations of occupation and custom in every varna category. Yet certain directives for behaviour are postulated for each varna category and they do regulate the conduct of those classed in it or of those who aspire to be so classed.

Kshatriya Pattern

The warrior-ruler model of the Kshatriya has been the most popular for ambitious men of lower jatis. It best accommodated those who cut their way up with their swords in earlier centuries (Karve 1965, p. 116). Under the Pax Britannica, it remained a popular and feasible model. In the sample from the 1931 Census, there were 80 claims to Kshatriya status made by lower groups, as against 33 claims to Brahmin and 15 to Vaishya standing (Srinivas 1966, p. 99).

Those who proclaim themselves as Kshatriyas are expected to be ready to use force to gain their honourable purposes and to be zealous in defence of their honour. It does not much matter, for purposes of the Kshatriya ideal, if they be slow in learning, lacking in wealth, deficient in ascetic piety. In those jatis whose men pride themselves on their warrior tradition, the beau ideal of the Kshatriya is absorbed from childhood; a youngster learns it from his elders' frequent reference to the glories of their own kind and to the craven conduct of others. It is lovingly and lengthily depicted in stories and dramas from the Epics. A man of true Kshatriya breed should be easy to anger, hard in combat, magnanimous in victory, freehanded with his possessions, closefisted with his honour.

Rajput jatis have particularly upheld and cherished their Kshatriya character. A sketch of the martial Rajput as seen in Khalapur village ninety miles north of Delhi, is given by John Hitchcock. He writes that a Rajput who faithfully follows the warrior tradition looks a bit old-fashioned now to the educated young men of his jati, but even they share some of his attributes. The older Rajput still dresses the warrior part, with a long mustache and a high turban; he goes always armed with a heavy, wire-bound staff, which he stands ready to wield with skull-cracking skill. He considers himself to be one of the rulers of society by birthright and natural endowment, and "regards it as his duty to see that the proper relationships between all castes are maintained, and that the hierarchical order of society is preserved."

He takes great pride in his warrior ancestry and has fine scorn for all who do not share his heritage and tradition. If he acts rashly, he explains it as a sign of his valour; if he grasps for power, it is evidence of his destiny to be a ruler. As for ritual piety, he "regards it as a kind of warrior's dispensation that he is permitted to hunt, eat meat (except of course for beef), drink liquor and eat opium" (Hitchcock 1958, pp. 216-221).

Other Rajputs across northern India take a like Kshatriya posture. In a Gujarat village the Rajput overlords are described as being dedicated to the achievement and maintenance of power; they proudly say that a Rajput who bears an insult commits a thousand sins (Steed 1955, pp. 114-115). In a Madhya Pradesh village the local Rajputs run village affairs and are considered to be "the prime Kshatriya caste" (Mayer, 1960, p. 63). According to a description of the Rajputs in a Rajasthan town, "their traditional duties are to rule, and to fight" and although they did not have much good to say for their hereditary ruler "every Rajput insisted on his loyalty to him: if it came to fighting, even those families which were out of favour would claim the privilege of carrying arms in his support" (Carstairs 1957, pp. 106-107).

A Bengali version of the martial style is the Ugra-Kshatriya jati, Ugra meaning "hot-tempered." They are characterised in Lal Behari Day's novel of 1872 about his village in Burdwan district as "a bold and somewhat fierce race, and less patient of any injustice or oppression than the ordinary Bengal raiyat." An account of the same village as of 1962 quotes this passage and comments that the Ugra-Kshatriyas ("a strong, courageous community") still show the same characteristics. Their origin myth (from *Manu* X.9.) told of their descent from a Kshatriya man and a Sudra girl, and so they were not given unequivocal Kshatriya standing, but "they are now claiming themselves to be Kshatriyas and are trying to acquire the status of the twice-born themselves" (Basu 1962, pp. 24, 36).

Bold, ambitious, pugnacious men have found little difficulty in taking on Kshatriya attributes. No great revisions of diet or of routine are required in doing so. People of the Kshatriya category are not expected to be as stringent about food, drink, and ritual niceties as are Brahmins, nor as skilled in trade or crafts as are Vaishyas. What is required is a display of force and fortitude, useful qualities in any event in a struggle for higher rank. Ambitious cultivators frequently own to these qualities, and the Kshatriya ideal is based on control of land.

Moreover, it is not difficult to construct a mythical or even historical association with warrior ancestors. During millennia of battles many warrior bands rose to power and many also were toppled and dispersed. A genealogist can usually manage to find one such forgotten ancestor for an ascendant group (Srivastava 1963, pp. 264-265). K. M. Panikkar indeed concluded that practically all Indian rulers had been successful fighters who were then elevated to Kshatriya rank. "Every known royal family from the time at least of Mahapadma Nanda in the fourth century B.C. belonged to non-Kshatriya castes" (1956, p. 8): So sweeping a statement may be doubted by other historians and challenged by proud scions of the former princely houses, but there is no doubt that once a group fought its way to power, it was likely to be re-classified from Shudra to Kshatriya status.

Such rectification has occurred in many a village scene. In the village of Gaon of Poona district, for example, two jatis assert that they are Kshatriyas. One is Maratha, of the jati-cluster dominant in the region. The other is known as Sagar Rajputs, whose change of name was mentioned above. They are dominant in Gaon village and its vicinity. Other villagers of Gaon tell that not so long ago (as the older people well recollect) the present Sagar Rajputs were Dhangars, shepherds by traditional occupation and Shudras by traditional classification. They grew in strength and ambition to the point where they were able to change their name, declare their Kshatriya status and wear the sacred thread. One of them hired a genealogist who proceeded to trace their ancestry to a chief officer in the armies of the great Maratha leader, Shivaji.

Those of the Maratha jati in Gaon, much longer and more securely established in their warrior repute, are apt to sneer at these claims. And the Sagar Rajputs have not fully adopted certain Kshatriya practices, particularly the ban on widow remarriage. They counter Maratha aspersions about this by accusing Marathas of covertly allowing a widow to be unofficial wife to her dead husband's brothers. Most of the other villagers take the Marathas' view about Sagar Rajputs' claims, but they do so more in private than openly because the Sagar Rajputs are quick to take offence and ready to beat up the offender (Orenstein 1965a, pp. 145, 159).

Yet Marathas themselves have not always been universally accepted as Kshatriyas. In the nineteenth century they were labelled as Shudras by some Brahmins *(ibid.,* p. 145). Mrs. Karve cites an account, dated 1697, of the elevation of Shivaji to the category of Kshatriyas. A Brahmin found a suitable genealogy for him and counselled that the sacrament of the sacred thread be performed as was the custom of the northern Kshatriyas. "So in a sacred place Shivaji had the thread ceremony performed on him and was made a pure Kshatriya and then crowned King in the year 1674" (Karve 1961, pp. 43-44; 1958a, p. 88).

In the Dravidian-speaking regions, there were not many jatis that had long-standing claims to Kshatriya or even Vaishya standing (cf. Dubois 1928, p. 15). The Nayars of Kerala, warriors by preference and profession, were classed as Shudras by the Brahmins of the region, and only the ruling lineages among them were known by the term Kshatriya (Mayer 1952, pp. 26-27). During the nineteenth century, several Tamil groups began to declare Kshatriya affinities. One of them, the Padayachis, petitioned for the title of Kshatriya at the time of the first census in 1871, and by the 1891 census, they had produced a book on their rights to the name and rank. To judge by their ranking in Tanjore district, their efforts have not been wholly successful; there they still are placed below the jatis they were trying to surpass (Beteille 1965, pp. 87,97).

The Coorgs are an example of a people who have effectively secured their reputation as Kshatriyas, as was noted earlier, despite certain lapses from the usual Kshatriya standards. They were a compact body of warriors and landholders and as they became more closely incorporated into the mainstream of the civilisation they retained these characteristics, fitting well into the category of Kshatriya (Srinivas 1952a, p. 33).

Brahmin Pattern

Some ascendant groups take to the Brahmin rather than the Kshatriya style. They stress ritual purity and purifying ritual, they become more meticulous about avoiding pollution. They do not have to perform priestly services or acquire scriptural learning because many Brahmin jatis do not provide such services and a great many Brahmins have little learning. A Brahmin jati needs mainly to be more ritual-directed and purity-focused than are the other local jatis. Their degree of purity is always relative to the practices of the others. Many Brahmin jatis are strictly vegetarian, especially those of the South and those of Vaishnavite seas. There are also-many Brahmin jatis of North India whose members do eat meat and fish (Sharma 1961a), but they do not eat the more defiling kinds of meat and although their diet is not vegetarian it is still at least as pure as the customary diet of jatis in their locality, and usually more so (cf. Carstairs 1957, pp. 115-116).

As for learning, the ideal of the scholar was wholly fulfilled by relatively few Brahmins. Yet the ideal was and is revered by Brahmins more than among other village jatis. Kshatriyas may consider a very learned Brahmin, one who has a whole Veda in his memory or who is accomplished in scriptural exegesis, as worthy of respect but scarcely of emulation. Brahmins and would-be Brahmins see the scholar's pursuits as an exalted version of their own; Kshatriyas do not. In the traditional Brahmin view the earth belonged to Brahmins, but Kshatriyas were allowed to rule it so that Brahmins could avoid the necessity of taking life and could devote themselves to ritual (Ingalls 1958, p. 212).

Those who aim their mobility efforts in a Brahmin direction need not stress power over others but rather control over their own group so that its members are uniformly disciplined to Brahmanical standards. This discipline is a standard theme in the pages of caste journals. N. K. Bose gives a characteristic example from a Bengali caste journal of 1908, the journal of the Namashudra, cultivators and boatmen, who despite their name have waged a long struggle to win recognition as Brahmins. In translation this passage reads, "prompted by envy or anger, people may dislike us; but if one observes our clean Brahminical way of life as practised generation after generation, they will have to admit unanimously that the Namashudra caste is descended from the ancient sages and *Rishis, i.e.*, from pure Brahmins."

Another Brahmin-oriented group in Bengal are the Yogis, weavers by traditional occupation. Their caste journal began advocating Brahminhood from about 1911; by 1921 the priestly section among them claimed Brahmin status and in the Census of 1931, the leaders of the jati claimed that all Yogis were properly of Brahmin status. Discrepancies between Brahmin standards and Yogi practices were thrashed out in their publications. The question whether Yogis who had taken the sacred thread could still be farmers was answered with a clear "yes," but on the former Yogi custom of allowing widows to remarry there was some disagreement. Those who took the stricter Brahmanical line wanted to forbid it, but other members of the jati were not so sure, perhaps because they saw new respectability for the old practice under modern Western influence (Bose 1958b, pp. 86-88).

Some jatis emulate the Brahmin model without campaigning actively for Brahmin rating; others take the warrior-ruler model without trying to be known as Kshatriyas.

In two of the jati blocs of Ramkheri village in Madhya Pradesh, for example, the several jatis of each bloc are accepted as being about equal in ritual rank; both blocs are ranked just below the local Brahmins. The people of one are vegetarians and teetotallers, those of the other eat -certain kinds of meat and drink liquor.

The leading jati among the vegetarians is that of the farmers (to use the author's terms), the other vegetarian jatis are gardeners, carpenters, smiths, tailors, and Bairagi. All these are most confident of the superiority of their style of life. Mayer notes that "They are supported in their contentions by the emergence of popular Governments since 1948 which are dominated by vegetarian castes, and they look forward to national policies which will eventually ban all animal slaughter and so bear out their superiority" (1960, p. 45). Whether the government has actually been so dominated or whether such influence may long continue does not affect the confidence that these jati-groups have derived from the Gandhian movement and its political consequences. They are oriented to the Brahmin mode yet do not claim membership in the Brahmin category.

Rajputs are most numerous in the other bloc and set the tone for the seven jati-groups who are their firm allies in the village. These allies consider the vegetarians to be "weak and effeminate" and take pride that theirs is the style of the former Rajas and, as they believe, of the meat-eating rulers of Western countries. They scoff at the farmers' prudence and exclusiveness. Rajputs are more generous, civic minded, and outgoing; they present a model that men of lower jatis feel they can readily emulate. The origin story held by these jatis lets them circumvent the question of old Kshatriya status. It is the story of the god Parasurama who scoured the country, looking for Kshatriyas to kill. In their flight from this supernatural scourge, Kshatriyas took to different occupations as a disguise.

Hence when Parasurama came upon a Kshatriya working

as a gardener, he spared him and that man's descendants became the gardener jati. Rajputs alone carried on their martial occupation; the others can then claim to be ex-Kshatriyas if they wish, or avoid the question as many do (Mayer 1960, pp. 44-45, 60-62, 88).

A similar example from South India is from Sripuram village, Tanjore district. There, also, two blocs of jatis display different life styles, one prizing force and rule without raising the Kshatriya banner, the other following a more ritualised pattern without claiming to be Brahmins. Each set is known by the name of its leading jati, Kalla and Vellala respectively. Kallas are described as being physically larger and as having a distinctive "domineering" appearance. "They can be distinguished particularly from the Vellala group by their close-knit organisation (their 'tribal' character, as some call it), the comparative unimportance of Sanskritic elements in their culture, and their tradition of lawlessness and violent life which still makes them feared by the generality of people" (Beteille 1965, p. 84). Vellalas follow a more ritualistic, "Sanskritic" style of life and proclaim themselves as Vaishyas. While the Kallas are the more important politically, the Vellalas are the more influential ritually (Beteille 1965, pp. 82-85; Gough 1956, p. 827).

Artisans, in many villages of the South, show a special kind of mobility striving. The five allied jatis of artisans have made long and insistent claims to being Brahmins. They say that they are Brahmins of a special and most superior kind, descended from the god *Visvakarman,* builder and architect of the heavenly realm. Included under the collective title of *Panchala* are jatis of goldsmiths, copper and brass workers, carpenters, stonemasons, and blacksmiths. Through much of the Tamil-, Kannada-, and Telugu-speaking areas, these artisans are allies. They tend to spurn the proper Brahmins, those so recognised by the rest of the local society, and they do not seek priestly services from them, relying instead on priests of their own jatis. They disdain Brahmins as a reference group, but identify thoroughly with Brahminhood as a reference category.

Men of these jatis wear the sacred thread; they are so ritually meticulous that they will accept food and water from few if any other jatis; they use Sanskrit gotra names for their clans; they observe scriptural sacraments; some of them have even studied the Vedas. Yet despite all their scriptural ways, they are not taken as equal to proper Brahmins by their neighbours. In some places even untouchables will not take food and water from blacksmiths, though they are vegetarians. Perhaps the very audacity of their claims has led to special discrimination against them (Epstein 1962, pp. 162,294; Srinivas 1955a, pp. 22-24).

Their claims are not new. Accounts of the seventeenth century hint at them (Jackson 1907, p. 243; Ghurye 1961, p. 6). Dubois noted at the beginning of the nineteenth century that the five classes of artisans "refuse, in some districts to acknowledge Brahmin predominance." They were also principal partisans of the Left-Hand faction, arrayed against the Right-Hand faction of the higher Shudra jatis and their allies (Dubois 1928, pp. 23-25). Reports from the beginning of the twentieth century note their continued assertions that they are Brahmins of the purest water and highest degree and the continued response of their neighbours that they are no such thing (Baines 1912, pp. 58-60; Thurston 1909, Vol. III, pp. 106-125).

These artisan jatis of the South adapted culturally to the Brahmin category but failed socially. Perhaps they were able to keep themselves ritually isolated and relatively pure because they had a grip on the economy. Without the services of carpenter and blacksmith, other villagers would have difficulties in farming and without the services of goldsmith, coppersmith, and stonemason, other parts of village life would be impaired. Hence when blacksmiths took on the sacred thread, other villagers could not maul and harass them lest the next harvest suffer for lack of tools and repairs. Yet the artisans did not have enough power to compel others to respect their claims. For several centuries there was a standoff. The local systems worked quite well, these artisans and cultivators maintained Jajmani relations with other jatis for economic purposes only. The unresolved controversy apparently was not a great impediment to the functioning of the local caste systems.

Vaishya and Shudra Pattern

The Vaishya model, like the Brahmin, is ritualised, stringent, and ascetic, but it includes, as the Brahmin does not, a mandate to engage in a mundane occupation, commerce. (cf. Srinivas 1966, pp. 31-32; Carstairs 1957, pp. 119-120). Those who seek Vaishya status can keep any clean occupation and still show their Vaishya affinity whenever they market their produce or open a shop.

The Telis of Orissa, traditionally oil-pressers and ranked as Shudras, have insisted that they are really Vaishyas whose trade was halted by external circumstance; they had to fall back temporarily on the less respectable occupation of extracting vegetable oils. In the resolutions passed by the Teli caste organisation there is regular mention of this origin story.

The resolutions also include rules about the kind of trade proper for Telis. For example, they may sell betel leaves but may not sell betel prepared for chewing. The former is a respectable wholesale trade carried on by growers, the latter smacks of the petty peddler's traffic. "Those of our caste who earn their living by cultivation of betel leaves, may sell leaves at the plantation. On no account should they carry baskets of betel leaves to distant markets either on their heads or in bullock carts." A resolution taken at another meeting allows for selling betel leaves in a shop but not "by wandering from place to place." Several resolutions indicate that some Telis continue to carry on inferior kinds of trade, and they are urged to transact only the more honourable kinds of trade, those suitable for people of Vaishya status (Patnaik and Ray 1960, pp. 31-32, 34, 42).

Farming as well as trade is permitted for Vaishyas. The Vellalas, farmers who lay claim to being Vaishyas, stress the purity of their practices rather than the pursuit of commercial profits (Beteille 1965, p. 97; Gough 1956, p. 829; Thurston 1909, p. 366). But other jatis take to the Vaishya category just because of its mercantile feature. The numerous and influential Patidars of Gujarat are shifting from Kshatriya to Vaishya affiliation, as we noted above, mainly because of their increasing involvement in trade and because of the high prestige that businessmen have come to have in Gujarat.

The term Patidar, meaning landowners who had a particular kind of tenure, became the name of the jati-cluster. For several generations Patidars proclaimed themselves as Kshatriyas; they argued that they, like the local Rajputs, wielded political power. Like Rajputs, they supported genealogists to create and keep ancestral records and they became fond of the blood-and-thunder recitations of the bards. But in recent generations, a good many Patidars have been giving up the genealogists and their tall tales. They now prefer to have the same status as the local Baniyas, the trading jatis who are indubitably Vaishyas.

When the kingly model was dominant in their region they adhered to it, but it seems a bit obsolete to them now that many Patidars have been successful in trade. Both Baniyas and Patidars took to English education at an early date; both have prospered and, in general, have adapted to modern conditions more successfully than have people of the traditional Kshatriya jatis of Gujarat. Hence a number of Patidars see little to gain by clinging to the old kingly model and have shifted their adherence to the model which is now more suitable, realistic, and profitable (Shah and Shroff 1958, pp. 268-270).

The fourth varna, the Shudra, is rarely taken as a goal for

mobility, though presumably an untouchable jati could try to rise by claiming Shudra status. In the sample taken from the 1931 Census, twenty-six untouchable groups gave themselves Kshatriya status, five claimed Vaishya, and two even claimed Brahmin titles. Thirteen untouchable groups demanded to change their jati names without giving a particular varna. None in this sample of 148 claims argued for Shudra status (Srinivas 1966, p. 99).

Not all rising Shudra jatis lay claim to a higher varna. One such group, the Mahanayaka Shudra of Puri district in Orissa, convened caste assemblies in 1935 and again in 1959. In the published reports of these meetings there is no mention of superior varna. There are, however, many resolutions for improvement and reform, as for more meticulous birth ritual and stricter endogamy, against pre-puberty marriage, for the education of poor boys of the jati, and against demands for exorbitant dowry gifts, like a gold ring or a bicycle (Patnaik 1960a, pp. 81-118).

Both traditional and modern elements are typically included in such resolutions; recommended ritual improvements are from the "twice-born" repertoire, educational uplift is from the modern sector. There are other reference categories used by particular groups. Rising Muslim families attempt reforms in special Muslim terms while also calling for secular improvements and purer practices much as do ambitious Hindu families.

Reference Combination

When jati brethren change their ways to raise their status, they not only adopt a reference category but also follow the specific example of a reference group, a life model. They insist, however, on keeping their own group identity. They do not want to merge with those whose rank they esteem and whose ways they emulate. They feel no need, therefore, to copy all features of their reference groups, but only those they need for better rank. The standards of behaviour for the reference *categories* are learned, indirectly as it were, from books, rituals, tales, schooling, dramas, and latterly from movies, newspapers, magazines, and radio. The standards of the reference *groups* are vividly seen as enacted in life.

The life style of a strongly dominant group generally influences others in its area. We have mentioned the example of Gujars in a Maharashtrian village who were changing their marriage patterns to conform with the ways of the locally dominant Marathas. Some of the Brahmins of Maharasthra also follow the Maratha practice of cross-cousin marriage, even though it is against scriptural prescriptions and is contrary to the common practice of Brahmins. Excommunication for this offense was decreed in the eighteenth century under the Peshwa government but such marriage arrangements among Brahmins are still known (Karve 1953, pp. 9, 17, 162; Raghuvanshi 1966, p. 149).

In Gujarat, Rajputs are taken as a prime reference group by the jatis known as Koli. The term Koli, as A. M. Shah and R. G. Shroff explain, once covered about a quarter of all Gujarati Hindus and refers to an assortment of people who owned little land and who were presumably of tribal origin. In recent years, prosperous Kolis have employed genealogists who provided ancestral records linking them with Rajput history and prehistory, and ultimately showing divine provenience. They have taken clan names and some of the marriage customs of Rajputs, and now have Brahmin priests to guide them in the sacramental rituals performed by Rajputs proper.

These Kolis, Shah and Shroff observe, are "fast Sanskritising as well as Rajputising themselves." One of their genealogists commented that they still pay less than do Rajputs and do not know the niceties of Rajput hospitality, "but they have great reverence for us." This reverence has declined or vanished among many of their former clients, notably Patidars. As is true elsewhere, the Kolis are adopting practices from a group whose members are discarding the same practices for others that they deem more estimable (Shah and Shroff 1958, pp. 264-268).

An example of these tendencies comes from two villages in central Gujarat, which are only a few miles apart. In both places Patidars are dominant and set the cultural style for other jatis, particularly for the Baria (formerly Kolis). The Patidars of one village have become wealthier than those in the other, they belong to a much higher hypergamous section of their jati, and they have departed more widely from the former Patidar devotion to Kshatriya symbols. The Barias of each village take their cues from their own Patidar neighbours, modelling themselves in the one after the more traditional Kshatriya pattern and in the other after the ways of the newer elite (Pocock 1957b, pp. 25-27).

The cultural influence of socially dominant groups was strikingly demonstrated among Hindus in what was the North-West Frontier Province. Hindus were a small minority among Muslims there; the tradition of Muslim rule and prestige remained strong even under the British. Brahmin priests were not much used among Hindus; they commanded little reverence and less learning. A Hindu of "twice-born" varna would eat meat and eggs "even in the bazar, generally put on the sacred thread only at the time of marriage, recited no *mantra* (save Rama-Nama), knew no Sanskrit and sent his children to the local madrasa run by a Maulvi." Hindu children taught by a Muslim teacher in an Islamic school grew up to be deeply influenced by Islam. But with a shift in political tides these Hindus turned to greater interest in Hindu scripture and acquired it chiefly through the non-Brahmanical Arya Samaj movement (Chanana 1961b, pp.409-411).

Though the attraction to the life style of the dominant group is strong, it is far from total. The Hindus of the northwest frontier remained Hindus, observing some scriptural ritual even if in attenuated form and maintaining jati differentiation.

Where the Rajputs were the overlords, not all the lower jatis emulated them. As we have seen in Ramkheri, some chose the ascetic rather than the warrior model.

The Kshatriya model in all regions includes the broad characteristics of devotion to honour, rule, and martial valour. The Rajput version of that model adds certain traits, such as hypergamous clan organisation. That version itself is observed in different regional varieties; Rajputs of Gujarat differ in certain ways from those of Rajasthan or Uttar Pradesh (Baines 1912, pp. 29-33; cf. Steed 1955; Carstairs 1957; Minturn and Hitchcock 1966).

So the men of a rising group who chose the ruler-warrior road of mobility adopted Kshatriya principles for conduct, oriented themselves to, say, Rajput standards, and actually guided their conduct according to the example of those Rajputs whose behaviour they could see. The example of the visible reference group is usually much more influential than are abstract principles of scripture or indirect examples in legend and literature.

Attempt of Modernisation

Such cultural adaptations were part of recurrent changes. The overall system of society remained relatively constant even though (and partly because) there was continuous struggle for higher rank. The pervasiveness of these struggles within local systems and across the land, helped to reinforce a villager's conviction that higher rank was attainable and was eminently worth the struggle for it.

In the nineteenth century, European influences began to reach strongly into village society. Villagers were confronted with new conditions, of police and government, for example, with which they had to cope and which had somehow to be fitted into their social organisation. There was some adjustment of the system. When the new temporal rulers would not intervene in caste ranking as indigenous rulers might, the ritual criteria came to be more rigidly applied and litigation became a main instrument of caste manipulation. Yet the structure of the villagers' social order was not drastically altered, the mobility efforts observed in the mid-twentieth century are similar in process and phases to those reported in the eighteenth century (cf. Raghuvanshi 1966, pp. 167-169).

Modern influences, however, especially those that came with political independence, are cumulatively bringing about long-range changes, which we will discuss later. Village society was not static under the colonial regime; there were some systemic adjustments, but generally villagers tended to assimilate the main innovations in government, technology, and communications into the established pattern of jati relations. British culture was too alien from the village world to provide a new reference category and British society in India was far too isolated and aloof from village life to yield a new reference group for mobility.

A few quite exceptional Indian groups did adapt their ways to an English model, as some Coorg landowners did to the example of the English planters, but this was far from common and even the Coorg adaptation was limited to selected outer traits, as the club, plantation management, and men's recreational pursuits; it did not pervade religion or family relations (Srinivas 1966, p. 57).

Villagers of middle or low jati who gained assets in modern ways typically used them to acquire the accoutrements of high status in the traditional ways. As they did so, those of the higher jatis who had also benefited from modern accretions began to revise their status symbols and standards. Hence ambitious people of lower jatis, as has been noted above, tend to take on traditional symbols of high status that are being relinquished by the higher jatis. The latter are adopting new symbols that are not only indicative of their modern sophistication but also serve as new indicators of their superiority.

This is illustrated in Sherurpur village of Faizabad district of U.P. where one man of low jati has become wealthy as a contractor. "He has symbolised his new-found opulence not by becoming a 'modern man' but by building a residence in the village which outdoes the high castes in its traditional architectural style." He has also built a grand rest house for pilgrims, a gift traditionally made by benefactors of high jati rank. The local Brahmins and Rajputs "have little choice left to them than to turn to westernisation as a means of maintaining the social distance between themselves and the lower castes which is no longer possible within the old order in the face of the latter's current ability to Sanskritise themselves" (Gould 1961b, p. 947).

The Brahmins and Rajputs here and people of traditionally high rank in other villages do not relinquish their respective varna standards, but add modern standards of education and occupation to them. They are no less eager for substantive privileges of high status; they have taken a new view of the proper symbols and content of that status. Nor do prospering people of low jati ignore the new standards. Many have taken to whatever modern ways they could assume (cf. Srinivas 1966, pp. 66-67). Some of the lowest jatis have struck directly for better status through modern political processes. Most aspiring groups now combine the older and the newer means of raising themselves in the social order.

The Yadava example with which we began this chapter shows the eclectic approach. Those who call themselves Yadavas are urged toward such traditional ways as the wearing of the sacred thread and abstinence from liquor and meat. Yadavas are also advised to abolish child marriage and high dowry payments, practices formerly honoured but countered by modern influences. Intermarriage among all jatis now known as Yadavas is endorsed, even though such vast expansion of endogamy is quite contrary to former rules for marriage. The older preference is overridden by the prospect of united political strength which broader marriage ties may bring (Rao 1964, p. 1440).

To take one other example, the Telis of Orissa were notified through the 1959 constitution of their association that all the separate jatis calling themselves Telis should allow complete freedom of intermarriage among them, that high dowries and child marriages should be stopped, and that the children should be given more education (Patnaik and Ray 1960, pp. 73-76).

Some of these resolutions are more readily put into practice than others. Determination to wear the sacred thread in the face of opposition from higher jatis is usually much more appealing (especially when there is a good chance of overcoming the opposition) than is the advice to arrange marriages more broadly. While resolutions against lavish dowries and expensive weddings get resounding votes as tokens of devotion to social progress, it is quite another thing when a member, even a leader of the organisation, has to marry off his own daughter and must then demonstrate his own family's status in the jati.

Such contradictions between ideal and real practice, between scriptural standards and modern notions, are generally glossed over without much difficulty. The goal is clear. The purpose is to get more respect and esteem from others in the society. A rising group uses all its resources from both the traditional and modern repertoire in order to accomplish that purpose, and combines them in whatever way seems best suited to reach the goal.

The term "Westernisation" has been used to refer to the modern repertoire, to those adopted practices and ideas that originated outside Indian civilisation (cf. Srinivas 1966, pp. 50-56). But though these traits were originally introduced from European sources, this is not often relevant to villagers. Most of the patterns of government, technology, and communication that were first brought in by Europeans are now firmly part of the village world. Some of them have been so for generations. As far as the villager is concerned they are indigenous and long established. He certainly recognises the difference between scriptural edict and modern law, between traditional ritual and national ceremonies, but no opposition among them is necessarily assumed.

Secular education, railway and bus lines, newspapers and postal service, introduced food and cash crops, are no longer seen as alien by villagers. Moreover, most innovations are soon adapted to the Indian milieu and take on characteristics notably different from those of the prototypes. Perhaps the term "modernisation" avoids the unwarranted implications of "Westernisation" provided it is not taken as a slogan of invariably good and desirable progress.

Villagers, in sum, are altering modern patterns, such as those proffered by government agencies or presented through the mass media, to suit village conditions. They are also rephrasing the still powerful reference models of tradition to accord with modern conditions.

Change in System

The people who together engage in a social system must share certain critical psychological characteristics if the system is to work. The following summary of our social analysis therefore begins with a discussion of two psychological factors that are particularly important in this system. One is a cognitive assumption, the other is a personal motivation. The two are used as generative principles in the grammar of social action. Both are applied in much of a person's social interaction. These themes of personal behaviour underlie the social competition that is carried on at all levels. The very acts of waging competitive conflict help to confirm the contestants' conviction that status is worth the struggle.

Contests for status are part of the adaptive capacity of the whole social system. Groups that came to be materially successful (whether through their abilities, or fortunate opportunities, or both) could rise in their local social orders and did not feel impelled to disrupt the general system. Also, a local order could be adapted to accommodate new groups and institutions. The people of a locality could set up relations with alien groups without feeling that their own social integrity and status were necessarily endangered by such relations. The groups that were absorbed socially generally became assimilated culturally to the precepts of caste society.

These processes resulted in recurrent change in local social orders and in the long-term stability of the fundamental system. The parameters of that system are now being altered and with them some of the systemic principles appear to be changing. The shifts may possibly affect the psychological modes of perception and motivation that have supported the traditional social concepts and structure.

Personal Behaviour

The cognitive assumption is that most interaction occurs between a superior and a subordinate, or between representatives of a dominant and of a dependent group. One's society is therefore seen as a hierarchical order; that order defines the relative positions of the actors in a social situation in advance of their interaction. Dominance and subordination are fundamental dimensions in all societies, not only in India, and advance definition of social position is a requisite condition in all social systems.

In Indian village society the hierarchical assumption is applied particularly widely, stringently, and intensively. It is constantly reinforced by being linked to a person's bodily experience as well as to his religious beliefs. Each person's biological functions, especially his acts of ingestion, are in some measure the concern of all in his jati. If he falls below the jati's standards of ritual purity and pollution, then all may be in peril of sinking to a lower social position. His body thus becomes an arena in which weighty issues of group status are at stake. Each child learns that he himself becomes more defiled or more pure according to his daily acts and experiences. The criteria of ritual purity and pollution that mark off these different states of an individual's being are also used to demarcate the social strata of his society.

Some important exemptions from the hierarchical perspective have been noted above. Within the family, relations between brother and sister and between mother and child are construed with a different emphasis. A self-dedicated holy man, a sadhu, has presumably removed himself from the social frame. There are situations in which hierarchy is not a primary assumption, as among those who are struggling together against a common opponent, whether they are persecuted sectarians or college classmates. These and other exceptions are not few, but they are nonetheless exceptions to the prevailing assumption of hierarchy.

In relations among people of different jatis, the hierarchical assumption has been linked with postulated differences in ritual pollution and purity. One outcome of holding these linked assumptions is that the ritual superiority of Brahmins has been acknowledged by most of those who held secular power. Brahmins could legitimate power and sometimes made skilful use of this prerogative. Another reason Brahmins possessed such durable influence was that the dominant jatis (and the Rajas in earlier times), in acknowledging the ritual superiority of Brahmins, were also affirming the validity of the hierarchical principles central to their own conduct.

For this reason also there has been considerable inertia

about untouchables rising and Brahmins falling in a local order. In maintaining clear extremes of their social order, the people of a locality were also maintaining clear exemplars of the assumptions by which they regulated their lives.

Those assumptions are translated into a social map by the varna categories, to which have lately been added the overlapping categories involving modern conduct. Muslims, Christians, and Jews set upanalogous divisions of their own. Ambitious villagers model their conduct according to the reference category of a high varna and, more particularly, after the living examples of the reference groups whose behaviour they can see. In their emulations and mobility struggles, villagers demonstrate to themselves and to all their society, in the characteristic circular way, that their hierarchical assumption is indeed true.

Coupled with this image of hierarchical society is a characteristic image of one's self as worthy of being a superior within a close bracket of rank. A man does not typically feel impelled to challenge the superiority of those high above him in any hierarchy; dependency on such superiors is not deprecated, whether the superior is a revered guru or a powerful official. Subordination to someone in a proximal rank, however, is often felt to be uncomfortable and something to be changed as soon as possible. This personal motivation is the other source of the perennial press toward recurrent change.

How this motivation and confident self-image have been inculcated are matters about which we can only speculate, since detailed studies are not yet available. Certainly these ideas are absorbed early in childhood from family experience. Perhaps one factor is the great importance to a mother, at almost all social levels, of the birth of her child. The child, particularly the first son, becomes a kind of social saviour for her; each of her other children, in turn, can be the subject of her open emotional expression in a milieu that provides few other approved emotional outlets for a young woman. It may be that this focusing of maternal attention and affection gives a child an especially strong sense of his own worth. Whatever the causal factors in Indian family life may turn out to be, it is clear that these motifs of personality have been widely shared by men and women of the various regions and social strata on the subcontinent. This same personal motivation bestirs untouchables at the bottom of a local order (provided that they are not utterly crushed by poverty) as well as the elite of the upper ranks.

The response to acts rising from this motivation is defensive. The same man who gathers his strength to challenge a superior knows that some of those subordinate to him are probably preparing to challenge him. This makes him very sensitive about the prerogatives and symbols of any superior status he may hold. It leads to a style of personal relations that I have elsewhere termed "aggressive defence" (Mandelbaum 1955, pp. 235-239).

As against the instability of proximal relations there is the relative stability of distal relations. Villagers not only agree that there is a hierarchical frame to society but also that certain parts and figures are outside the arena of open competition.

Within a family a man's father has the more distal role, his brother the more proximal role. Solidarity among brothers is apt to weaken once the authority of the father is gone. One brother challenges another, eventually the family separates, with added bitterness because each tends to blame the other for rupturing the ideal. Both also blame the women, partly to gloss, over fraternal hostility, partly because the women of the family are also competitors among themselves. The young bride must be subservient to her mother-in-law, but as she becomes a mother and a matron she can begin to challenge her mother-in-law and to contend with any other of the sons' wives in the family. Although certain aspects of family relations do indeed differ by social level and by region, these family processes are shared across regions and jatis. When a low-ranking family begins to rise, its members tend to take on the family patterns of the higher jatis.

Beyond the family, one lineage of a jati may challenge another; the people of one village, under some circumstances, try to outstrip another village. The principal group for challenge and confrontation, however, has been the jati. It is, as we have seen, a main unit of a man's identification, a principal agency for individual and group power, the chief vessel of status. A villager's aggressive defence of his honour—the term izzat, as previously noted, expresses the concept for many in North India—combines defence of personal and family status with defence of the integrity, standards, and prestige of his jati.

Complieation in Systemic Processes

Competition among jatis is common and is better understood as an outcome of the basic motivation than as the root cause of village conflict. The importance of this motivation is shown when a jati or a jati-group is so firmly entrenched that its members fear no challenge from others. Challenge and conflict are then likely to come up within that group. Some of its members will feel subordinate to other members and will sooner or later dispute their superiority. The personal motivation toward challenge of immediate superiors is constant, and so is social competition.

It is a competition without end, not only because every superior feels that some of his subordinates will eventually defy him, but also because a man who is a superior in certain contexts generally feels himself to be a subordinate in others. He may be impelled to try to improve his position in those contexts while being warily defensive in others. The competition can yield enlivening rewards as well as nagging anxieties. A man may get considerable personal satisfaction from the results of his status strivings, as he does when he brings off an advantageous marriage in his family, or gains a precious ritual symbol for his jati, or helps put a kinsman into a position of power and prestige.

Competition is pervasive in many life situations, but there is also much in a villager's life that it does not pervade. As we have noted, there are exempt relations and situations. Relations between fully acknowledged superiors and reciprocally valued subordinates tend to be secure and assured (cf. Carstairs 1957, p. 106).

The subordinate then prizes rather than resents his dependency. For some people religion is a secure resource against the abrasions of competition. In the scriptural ideal a man who has fulfilled his family duties opts out of the social competition and into religious devotion. There are also some individuals and groups who prefer to be neutral and who try to remain on the sidelines of any competitive arena. Often they succeed in doing so for a time, but they are apt to be nudged periodically into competition by forces of the social system.

Failure in mobility efforts is allayed by the very assumption of social hierarchy. A defeated group is not obliterated or condemned to complete helplessness. Some of its members may be beaten, a few even killed, a number of its wealthier families may lose much of their wealth, but the group is generally not much worse off than it was before. The victors are usually satisfied to have the defeated resume their subordinate positions. The superiors need their goods and services, and they also need inferiors below them to shore up their position as superiors.

The ideology of non-competitive varnas is firmly believed while competitive social action among jatis is zealously waged. At any given time and place, some groups may be rising and others may be losing ground in their local order. This fluctuation is one reason for differing opinions about just where a particular group is to be placed.

Conflict within families is also disapproved in the villagers' ideology yet is inherent in their actual relations. In a family the stress point at which conflict is likely to erupt occurs when grown brothers, bereft of parental regulation, must reach some important decision about their domestic economy.

Among jatis, village ceremonies have often been occasions for outbreaks of conflict when each jati at the feast must be seated in order of relative rank. Such conflicts may consolidate each contesting group and reinforce the idea that higher rank is highly important. So quarrels about rank result from and also buttress the psychological themes.

Adjusting Capacities

The traditional social system was putatively closed and immutable but actually provided openings, if difficult and limited ones, for the rise of ambitious groups. The *Manu* version of fixed varnas was rarely denied, but the real possibility of status rise promised success to those who could best adapt. Adaptive success for a group within the society could be initiated by skilful development of economic resources, by military conquests, by settling new lands, by adroit trading or political acumen, or through any other fortunate exploitation of the environment.

Military prowess has not been a means for jati rise for some time, but the other avenues to status gain are still in use. Few can achieve much ritual advance in their own lifetime, but they may raise their material base enough to glimpse the self-promised niche that may be occupied by their descendants.

A main adaptive feature of jati society as a whole is the capacity to absorb alien groups who then become contestants for rank and thus supporters of the whole system. Such groups could readily be absorbed because jati villagers did not feel threatened by cultural differences among their neighbours. They could carry on restricted relations with those of different customs without loss to their own standards or status. Tribesmen have been continually absorbed socially and then assimilated culturally; jati folk could accept them as low-ranking dependents or, if circumstances so dictated, as dominant landowners, without impairing their own caste society.

Immigrants from another region of India or from outside the subcontinent were similarly accommodated. The early Christian, Jewish, and Muslim traders were absorbed into jati society and retained their religious identity. Foreign raiders who settled down to found dynastic kingdoms made their peace with the jati system. The British tried to keep aloof from the system of caste relations, but as wielders of paramount political power they did affect the system. Yet for all their influence on it they did not change the fundamentals or the pervasiveness of caste relations.

Jati people could cope with introduced institutions as well as with introduced groups. The British brought in new kinds of bureaucracy, law, learning, and technology, all were promptly utilised for jati as well as personal purposes. When the colonial bureaucracy was established, for example, there was not much question as to whether taking part in it was good for one's family and jati. Those who understood that they could get a respectable place in that hierarchy were usually far more concerned about how to get the highest possible place than whether it was good to participate at all. They took to the new institutions as providing auxiliary criteria of high status, new opportunities for attaining higher rank and additional channels for mobility.

Long before the impact of European influences, villagers dealt with strong outside influences—economic, governmental, and religious—without changing the bases of their social structure. The economic effects of irrigation, for example, were anciently felt in villages of the Tanjore area and the jati structure was fully maintained. It was maintained in Totegadde in Mysore where a cash crop has been grown for centuries. Such economic forces have had important consequences. They have affected the order of the jatis in a locality but they have not disrupted the jati order.

In governmental matters, villagers had ways of giving a Raja his minimal due while actually managing their local affairs through their own devices. British institutions of government were potentially inimical to the traditional system, but as we have seen, villagers quite successfully subsumed British law and police order within their own political code and jati order.

The introduced religions of temporal rulers, Islam and Christianity, attracted millions of converts and influenced the whole civilisation. Their influence did not undermine the traditional social system. Moreover, the internal tendency toward religious revolt against the system created social groups that were regularly incorporated back into that system.

Transformation of Society and System Maintenance

The system was used so adaptively because people applied the thematic principles both steadfastly and flexibly. They applied the hierarchical perspective steadfastly to new as well as to habitual situations; they applied it flexibly, not insisting on any single or completely calibrated hierarchy for all occasions. There is a certain flexibility even at the extremes of a local jati order. Most in a locality agree that certain jatis are lowest, but members of each of these low jatis typically insist that at least one of the others should be ranked below their own group. In this sense there is usually no absolute bottom to a local ladder of rank and in a parallel sense there is no absolute top.

Those who occupy the topmost rung are apt to compete among themselves for the best place along that rung, or they may look to a grander struggle in a wider arena. During the British regime, for example, a Maharaja might be the unchallenged suzerain within his state, with only a very few and broad constraints imposed on his conduct by the paramount British authority. Yet many such princes constantly tried to improve on the honours officially allotted to them at ceremonial occasions from, say, a ceremonial salute of nine guns to the eleven-gun class.

The drives toward social advance are quite constant, but the tactics for advance are varied. Different routes are possible; the traditional alternatives are in the three "twice-born" varnas. Though these reference categories are very different in certain respects, all three stipulate certain broadly similar kinds of behaviour, as in the relations between men and women and in the discipline of conduct. Those who attempt to move up into any one of these higher echelons must conform to the broad standards required of all leading groups in Indian civilisation. A convert to Islam or Christianity from a low jati is urged to discipline himself in ways that are similar in general, though different in details, from those he would follow in seeking high varna status as a Hindu.

Whatever route may be chosen, effective rise begins with the prospering of individual families. Hopes for higher rank are futile unless steeled with secular strength. Individual families can achieve real advance only as part of a larger group and so prospering families deploy their secular resources to achieve ritual gains for their group. To succeed, their leaders must simultaneously cope with external opposition and maintain internal strength.

Success against opposing jatis is usually achieved gradually, in a series of steps beginning with changes to which others cannot well object. As the aspiring villagers build a base of wealth and purity, they begin to make more open assertions that are more objectionable to those who rank above them. In Senapur village, the Earth-workers decided to wear the sacred thread. It is at such points that escalating aspirations and growing hostility to them come to a head and there is a confrontation, commonly a whole series of physical, legal, and societal encounters. The confrontation may be delayed if the higher groups have taken to modern standards and therefore set less store by the traditional symbols that the aspirants are trying to attain. The confrontation may be postponed but it is not annulled.

To overcome in such confrontations, an aspiring group must mobilise united effort. Unity is usually a difficult problem. All sections of a jati do not improve their resources and local standing at the same rate. The most advanced sections may have reformed their practices so greatly that they can scarcely admit to being jati partners with those who have not reformed. Moreover the success of some tends to arouse challenges from others within the jati.

If the more successful members find that they cannot muster enough cultural and social unity for their purpose, they may redefine the boundaries of the group. In the traditional process the more advanced or dissatisfied families split off and declared themselves to be a separate jati. Occasionally such sections joined with similarly mobile sections of other jatis in an action that entailed fusion as well as fission. With fresh unity, they then proceeded to battle for higher rank.

Individuals identify with different kinds of groups as different situations require and may compete for higher rank in each context. A vigorous villager strives mightily to advance and defend his family's rank among the families of his jati, but when he participates in a village panchayat on an issue affecting his jati, he is apt to be a firm proponent of the jati more than of his family. Should the repute of his village be at stake on some occasion, he is likely to identify with the village and to challenge those of other villages.

In some contexts he may fight to advance the status of his religion, or his region, or his language group. To be sure, he may not always know where to put the greater effort. He does not always switch identification smoothly; a village leader may sometimes be torn between advancing the interests of his village or that of his jati.

Moreover, an ambitious leader must be task-oriented as well as rank-oriented. He must focus on what is to be done for the village as well as on who gains rank advantage by what is done. The two interests are usually not completely separate; the one impinges on the other, but neither should be scanted if the leader is to be successful in an enterprise. Balancing off each consideration is a constant problem for leaders at all levels. This is indeed true in all complex societies; it is a particularly potent problem for village leaders in India.

Those who strive for social mobility do not challenge the hierarchical frame but believe rather that they are only trying to restore their proper place within it. Those who oppose them believe that the climbers are trying to alter the ordained order of society.

From the wider view of our analysis, the challengers are right, though not for the reasons they give. They are right because their efforts are part of the grand counterchange within the general social system through which secular power and ritual rank are kept in a broad parity. That parity, however, is not without exceptions. There are poor and ineffectual Brahmins, even whole jatis of them. Conversely, an occasional village Harijan may be rich and influential.

Yet by and large, the higher jatis of a locality are the wealthier and more powerful, the poorest are also lowest in ritual rank. So, as we have noted, acts that are intended to disturb an existing, static local order of rank, simultaneously serve to maintain the dynamic, adaptive general system of jati relations.

Abrupt and Chronic Change

The system of society in India was changed in the ancient past; the earliest Vedic scriptures reflect a social order of relatively open classes rather than of bounded jatis. After the classic system of caste became established, perhaps a millennium ago, temporal rulers sometimes intervened in the ranking but did not alter the systemic principles. A freebooter who seized state power could enhance the rank of his own jati and could manipulate the village ranking of other jatis through grants of land and of privilege.

During the period of British rule, ranking seems to have become more rigid. Greater emphasis was apparently given to the ritual criteria for rank, and greater power apparently accrued to jatis whose men were already high and dominant. These were not really systemic changes. The major social units remained the same; the assumptions about high and low status were unchanged; relations among jatis were carried on in the same way; and mobility campaigns continued, though with some shift in mobility tactics.

Political independence has set in train a series of social and economic changes that are still very much in the making. In some ways the trend seems to be a return to the precolonial condition when state power could directly impinge on jati ranking. Modern political power is based, not on military conquest, patents of nobility, and grants of land, but on voting influence, official positions, and such boons as tube wells, roads, and import licenses. Changes in the avenues to wealth and power have brought about changes in mobility procedures. Some low-ranking groups, obstructed in their villages, have appealed to higher political authorities, have organised for voting purposes, and have acquired offices, grants, and local influence. They have detoured the traditional step-by-step procedure and have struck directly for respectable status through political action.

With the increasing success of such actions, there has come a consequent decline in the attractions of the traditional symbols of high rank. Thus those Noniyas who succeeded after long and bitter struggle in wearing the sacred thread now find that their sons are quite uninterested in doing so. Men of the higher jatis are no longer so concerned as they were about who wears this ritual badge because many of them, like the younger Noniya, are more concerned with badges of higher modern education than with badges of higher varna status.

Ambitious men now find the fusion of jatis for political strength more effective than the fission of jatis for ritual purity. Hence many jati leaders urge the enlargement of their endogamous group by encouraging marriages among previously separate, though similar, jatis. The trend is toward fewer, wider, better organised jatis.

Villagers continue to assume that endogamy is a central factor for social solidarity, that social groups are ranked, and that one's own group must constantly try to advance or to defend its social position. The systemic changes that are in view do not point directly toward an unstratified society but toward fewer and more homogeneous social groups. These changes will not necessarily be rapid; much hinges on the rate of economic improvement.

The major changes in Indian society are in the same direction as that taken by broad changes in other contemporary societies. The general trend is toward the narrowing in cultural disparities and in social distances between groups in a society, though scarcely toward any total elimination of stratification. There is a general shift

3

Role of Development

Strategy and ideology of planning; poverty; indebtedness and bonded labour, strategies of rural development—poverty alleviation programmes; environment, housing, slum and unemployment; programmes for urban development.

Atmospheric Conditions

It was during the fourth-five year plan that our government gave direct attention to the issues related to environment. Consequently the National Council of Environmental Planning and Coordination was established in 1972 in department of Science and Technology. Another department on environment was set up in 1980 which late emerged in the form of Ministry of Environment and Forest in 1985. At present, the ministry of Environment and Forest has been entrusted for planning, promotion and coordination of environmental and forestry programmes for the country.

The State Departments of Environment, Central and State Pollution Control Boards, the Botanical and Zoological Survey of India, the Forest Survey of India, the National River

Conservation Authority (formerly Central Ganga Authority), the National Afforestation and Eco-development Board, the Indian Council for Forest Research and Education, the Wildlife Institute of India, the National Museum for Natural History, etc., are, the Ministry's partners in carrying out activities related to environmental protection. A Social Audit Panel has been set up to review the activities of the Ministry and to make recommendations whenever needed to mobilise people's support and participation.

Various institutions related to environment were set up. The Zoological Survey of India (ZSI) was established in 1961. Its headquarter is at Calcutta with other 16 regional stations located at different places. Its main function is to survey the faunal resources. The Forest Survey of India (FSI) was also established in this direction. Its headquarter is at Dehradun with regional offices at Bangalore, Calcutta, Nagpur and Shimla. It prepares thematic maps on 1:50, 000 scale and forest vegetation maps on 1:2,50,000 scale of the country. Since the beginning of the thematic cycle in 1986, 2,139 topographic sheets corresponding to an area of 13,13,325 sq km have been covered so far.

The vegetation maps are prepared on a two-year cycle for the entire country by the management of zoological parks in the country. It coordinates the activities of over 200 existing zoos and also supervises the exchange of animals on a scientific basis. Project Tiger, one of the premier conservation efforts of the country has completed 20 years in April 1993. Under this scheme, 23 Tiger Reserves have been set up all over the country. A Global Tiger Forum has been set for Tiger Range countries and an interim secretariat has been set up at New Delhi. A Tiger Crisis Cell has been set up to obtain all the information essential for conservation of the Tiger. Under the Project Elephant, states having free-ranging population of wild elephants are being given financial as well as technical and scientific assistance to ensure long-term survival of identified viable populations of elephants in their natural habitats.

Board for Welfare

Its main function is to conserve the forest resources. The Animal Welfare Board of India, established in 1962 under the provisions of the Prevention of Cruelty to Animal Act 1960 is an autonomous organisation of the Ministry of Environment and Forests working for the cause of animal welfare. Various camps for training the members of SPSAs and animal welfare organisations takes place all over the country, in collaboration with the Royal Society for Prevention of Cruelty to Animals, London. The Board has undertaken a scheme of Animal Birth Control in six metropolitan cities and about 13,500 sterilization were carried out on stray dogs under this scheme. The Board also celebrates Animal Welfare Fortnight from 14th January every year. The board works under the provision of the prevention of Cruelty to Animal Act.

Assessment of Environmental Impact : Impact assessment tool was introduced in 1978 to assess the environmental compatibility of the projects relating to the suitability, location and technology efficiency in resource utilisation and recycling. This assessment further covers the following projects.

It was started in 1975 and now covers following types of projects (a) (i) river valley; (ii) thermal power (iii) mining; (iv) industries; (v) atomic power; (vi) rail, road, highways, bridges (vii) port and harbour (viii) airport; (ix) new towns and (x) communication projects; (b) projects requiring approval of the public investment board, central electricity planning commission authority (c) projects referred to the Ministry of Environment and Forest by other ministries (d) projects which are sensitive and located in environmentally degraded areas—public sector undertakings of the Centre where the project cost is more than 50 crore.

The notification issued in January 1994 makes Environmental Impact Assessment statutory for categories of developmental projects under various sectors such as industrial, mining, irrigation, power, transport, tourism, communication etc. An amendment to this notification stipulates that all applications complete in every material aspect have to be examined and decision conveyed to the applicants within 30 days in the case of site clearance and 120 days in the case of environmental clearance of projects.

Once an application has been submitted by project authority the preliminary scrutiny of the project is done by the respective technical divisions and the overall appraisal of the projects is undertaken by specially constituted environmental appraisal committees of experts. In addition special groups, committees and task forces are constituted as and when needed of expert, inputs on major projects. After detailed scrutiny and assessment, the appraisal committee makes its recommendations for approval or rejection of the projects. Depending on the nature of the project, certain safeguards are recommended. For monitoring and timely implementation of safeguards suggested, six regional centres have been set up by the Ministry at Bhopal, Bhubaneshwar Chandigarh, Bangalore, Lucknow and Shillong.

The Ministry of Environment and Forests takes the management and control of hazardous substances including responsible hazardous chemicals, wastes and micro-organisms. In pursuance of these activities, the following rules have been notified under the Environment (Protection) Act, 1986: (i) Manufacture, Storage and Import of Hazardous chemicals, 1989; (ii) Hazardous Wastes (Management and Handling) Rules, 1989; and (iii) Manufacture, Use, Import, Export and Storage of Hazardous Microorganisms/ Genetically Engineered Organisms of Cell, 1989.

Crisis management plans are being set upto meet chemical emergencies in units handling hazardous chemicals, a control room to deal with emergencies caused due to hazardous chemicals has been set up, guidelines for preparation of crisis management plans have been issued to the state governments and financial support is being provided to them to strengthen infrastructure for the purpose. Emergency Response Centres have been set up at Bhopal, Baroda, Manali and Khapali. A Red book entitled 'Central Crisis Alert System' which includes names, addresses and telephone numbers of the Central and State authorities and experts to be contacted in case of emergency has been prepared and circulated to all concerned. A public Liability Insurance Act was enacted to provide immediate relief to the victims of accidents by hazardous chemical industries.

India is a signatory to the UNEP sponsored Convention on Control of Transboundary Movement of Hazardous Wastes which has been adopted at Basel, Switzerland by 126 governments of the world in 1989. The Convention aims at checking the reported illegal traffic in hazardous wastes from one country to another. A scheme on National Register of Potentially Toxic Chemicals (NRPTC) has been started with a view to set up the basic infrastructure for implementing the London guidelines for the exchange of informations on chemicals. Under this scheme the requisite hardware and software are obtained and the electronic network of state, central and boards are established through MICNET and SIRNET.

Implementing the London guidelines for the exchange of information on chemicals in international trade including the procedure for prior information. Under this scheme the requisite, hardware and software have been obtained and electronic networking of carious central and state government and boards has been established through NIOM and SIRNET. Eight Regional Registers PRPTC have been set up in UP, MP, AP, Gujarat, Orissa, Kerala, HP and Punjab. An approach paper for establishing a National Inventory of Chemicals has been prepared. National Foreign Information Centre has been set up at the Department of Pharmacology at All India Institute of Medical Science, New Delhi. The Ministry has constituted a National Waste Management Council to suggest ways and means for effective utilisation of wastes generated in the country.

Three subgroups have been set up by the Council to deal with the major categories of wastes *viz.*, industrial, urban and rural. The sub-groups have been entrusted with the task of identifying wastes, suggesting technological action points including legislation, taxes and incentives. A Pilot Project on Municipal Solid Waste Management has been sanctioned to Hyderabad Municipal Corporation. Special emphasis is being laid on promoting the use of flash in various fields and the state governments have been asked to prepare a perspective action plan for 50 per cent utilisation of flash by the turn of the century. For the disposal of hazardous wastes, 15 sites have been identified in the country for preparation of secured land fills. The Hazardous Wastes (Management and Handling) Rules, 1989, have been amended. The Manufacture, Storage and Import of Hazardous Chemical Rules, 1989 are being amended. Draft Rules on Biomedical Wastes also have been notified.

Facility of the House

It has become one of the major concerns for governmental policies and planning for which the National housing policy was instituted.

Eradication of houselessness, improvement in housing condition, provision of a minimum level of basic services and amenities, facilitation of housing activity of the lower and middle income groups, upgrading shelter are the main tasks of the housing policy and the policy related to these has been incorporated in the eight five year plan.

Monetary Concern of Housing

Public Sector outlay for Housing in Central and State sector during Eighth Plan is Rs. 6,377 crore. The following initiatives have been taken during the last five years for augmenting the flow of funds in the housing sector :

(a) The National Housing Bank (NBH) set up in 1988 is a subsidiary of Reserve Bank of India (RBI) launched the following schemes :

  (i) Home Loan Account Scheme--a contractual deposit scheme linked to guaranteed loan. Under the scheme, above seven lakh accounts have been opened in various commercial banks and housing finance institutions and an amount of Rs. 373.14 crore mobilized as deposits at the end of June 1995;

  (ii) The cumulative refinance assistance provided by NBH upto 31 March, 1995 is Rs. 2,254.04 crore;

  (iii) Land development and shelter programmes of public/private agencies to be operated through Housing and Urban Development Corporation (HUDCO) and commercial banks to increase the supply of serviced land and houses-Rs. 218.28 crore advanced till March 1995;

(b) During 1994-95, Rs. 723.78 crore have been allocated as banking finance, as 1.5 percent of incremental deposits with the commercial banks for housing loans, out of which 30 per cent will be channelised to individual/ household sector. Compared to total allocation of Rs. 567.27 crore for 1993-94, the total disbursement, made by scheduled commercial banks was about Rs. 425.25 crore. The amount of Rs. 114.77 crore was invested by the banks in the guaranteed bonds and debentures of NHB, HUDCO, state housing boards and other state agencies. For 1995-96, loan allocated to states by LIC and GIC are Rs. 274.54 crore and Rs. 15 crore respectively;

(c) About 21 housing finance institutions both in the public and private sector have been recognised by the National Housing Bank and now operating,

(d) During 1995-96, HUDCO sanctioned loans worth Rs. 1,967 crore and the actual loans released were Rs. 1,229.50 crore. About 90 per cent dwelling units financed by HUDCO are for economically weaker sections and low income groups. In 1996 over 60.02 lakh units have been sanctioned under various housing schemes of the HUDCO of which about 34.48 lakh units are in rural areas. In addition, over 4.12 lakh developed plots and 38.48 lakh basic sanitation units have been sanctioned till 31st March 1996;

(e) Under the Nehru Rozgar Yojana (NRY) scheme for upgradation of the housing stock of the poor, a subsidy of Rs. 1,000 per household is provided by Central and State governments along with Rs. 9,950 loan from HUDCO. This is implemented in collaboration with municipal bodies and

(f) As an Action Plan item, Footpath Dwellers Night Shelter Scheme is being implemented as a Centrally sponsored scheme in the metropolitan and other major urban centres. Since April 1991 and as on 31st March 1996, 60 schemes benefiting over 23,000 footpath dwellers have been sanctioned by HUDCO in various parts of the country.

As part of the Eighth Plan exercise, the demand and likely shortage of some of the major building materials have been estimated along with the potential for production of alternative building materials. Some more fiscal concessions for innovative and cost-effective building materials have been granted in the 1995-96 budget. The Building Materials and Technology Promotion Council under the ministry of urban Affairs and employment has taken up initiatives to effectively utilise Wastes and flash and above 15 flash based units were set up. In order to create awareness even among the ordinary and common people regarding the issues related to environment, the ministry has taken special steps which could be implemented through education such as the promotion of environmental education, creation of environmental awareness.

Education, Consciousness and Information : Priority is accorded by the Ministry of Environment and Forests to promote environmental education, create environmental awareness among various age groups and do disseminate information through Environmental Information System (ENVIS) network to all concerned. Special emphasis is given to non-formal environmental education through seminars/ symposis/ workshops, training programmes, eco-camps, audio-visual shows etc. The National Environment Awareness Campaign (NEAC) has been instituted since July 1986. As part of this campaign, 19th November to 18th December every year is observed as the National Environment Month. The main theme for the 1995-96 Campaign was "Women and Environment". The Ministry also provides financial support for setting up eco-clubs at schools and for production of films on environment and other activities related to environmental protection.

"Paryavaran Vahini" was launched during 1992-93 to create environmental awareness and to ensure active public participation by involving the local people. Paryavaran Vahinis are proposed to be constituted in 134 selected districts all over the country which have high incidence of pollution and density of tribal and forest population. The Vahinis also play a watch dog role by reporting instances of environmental pollution, deforestation, poaching etc. They function under the charge of District Collectors with active cooperation of the state/union territory governments. This scheme is entirely financed by the Ministry of Environment and Forest.

The ministry has also established centres for conferring research and training in environmental science and management. For the effective utilisation of land, steps are being proposed for increased supply of service land through land acquisition, negotiated purchase and land readjustment, suitable amendments to LA Act; modification of development plans and regulations for cheaper legal shelter and intensive land use; and HUDCO and NHB have been financing land development schemes.

The Non resident Indians have been encouraged to invest by the central government by announcing a scheme such as under the first scheme, existing or new companies, both private and public limited, engaged or proposing to engage in the urban development and housing sector including roads and bridges, manufacturing of building materials and application, to issue equity shares/convertible debentures to non-residents of Indian nationality/origin upto hundred per cent of the new issue with repatriation benefits.

The repatriation of original investment will be allowed after a lock-in period of three years from the date of issue of equity shares/ convertible debentures with prior permission of the Reserve Bank of India; The second scheme relates to the acquisition of immovable properties by individual NRIs. This foreign citizens of Indian origin and non-residents holding Indian passports are to be allowed, against application to repatriate the original investment in equivalent foreign exchange in residential properties upto a maximum of two houses. General permission has been granted to foreign citizens of Indian origin, whether resident in India or not, and to non-residents holding Indian passports to acquire by way of purchase or inheritance and transfer or dispose of by sale, commercial immovable properties situated in India. Repatriation of original investment in equivalent foreign exchange will be allowed by the Reserve Bank of India on receipt of an application. General permission has been granted to foreign citizens of Indian origin, whether resident in India or not, to acquire, transfer or dispose of residential properties upto two houses situated in India by way of gift from or to a relative who may be an Indian citizen or a person of Indian origin, whether resident in India or not, subject to the condition that gift tax, if any, shall be paid.

The last part relates to overseas corporate bodies owned by NRIs including investment in the development of serviced plots, construction of built up premises, residential and complex construction etc.

Besides these, the ministry of urban development established material building organisation in 1954 to take up research in low cost building designs, improvement of the building and housing conditions along with the socio-economic aspects. Its other functions are housing for ESCAP. Regarding the current requirements under the National Housing Policy, NBO has been restructured during 1992 to take up mainly the socio-economic, management information system and creation of date bank functions.

The Urban Land (Ceiling and Regulation) which came into force on 17 February 1976 was instituted to prevent concentration of urban land in the hands of few and to curb speculation and profiteering with an aim to facilitate equitable distribution of urban land to sub-serve the common good. It applies to all the state governments and union territories except Jammu and Kashmir, Kerala, Nagaland and Sikkim which have not adopted the Act and it excludes Tamil Nadu which had enacted its own law in 1978. The Act is mainly implemented by the state governments. As per the information furnished by various state governments/union territories, 2,20,675 hectares of land have been estimated as excess vacant land. Out of this 43,944 hectares have been vested in he state government/ union territories.

Slums : Slums can be described as an area in a city or a metropolis characterised by sub-standard housing, dilapidated houses under destruction, poverty, poor hygienic conditions, multi family dwellings, conflicts, fights, gambling, alcoholism, etc. Slums lack the basic needs of life such as food, shelter and clothing and corresponding with these, there are many socially created and perpetuated ills. Juvenile delinquency and mal-socialization of more or less orphan juveniles of the slum society whose parents have not enough in their hands is a curse of the slum upon the city. Thus a slum is a highly destructed area of worn out buildings which provides housing facilities to the city's poor and needy. Slums provide as a breeding ground for many ills of the society.

Slum can be original one abounding the industrial or factory or mining site. They are aged old slum which can not be removed. Transitional zone slum is created by the departure of middle class families to other areas. Or when an industry or construction starts, such slums prevail. The worst and the most pathetic slum is the one characterised by complete physical deterioration and its corresponding social ills such as characterised by flap houses, overnight accommodation for the destitutes, prostitute's home, tramps, vagrants, chronic alcoholics, beggars, homeless, criminals etc.

Thus slums differ in both the physical and social conditions and hence administering them demands slightly different approaches.

The Unemployment

Unemployment has been one crucial area of all the problems facing this country. When a large section of a population is rendered unemployed, one can well imagine of the possible problems including high incidence of poverty, ill-health, death, demoralisation, unrest. This is a phenomena of complete failure to realise the social investment in human capital.

According to Fair child, "Unemployment is forced and involuntary separation from remunerative work on the part of the normal working force during normal working time, at normal wages and under normal conditions." Generally speaking, unemployment means the non-availability of work even though there is desire to do it.

The various forms and the nature of unemployment differs for example two types of unemployment are found in India which could be different from that of America in varying degrees. India has been facing seasonal unemployment as well as open form of unemployment.

The Second Five Year Plan recorded the first official estimate of the quantum of unemployment in India. Estimates of the backlog of the unemployed were obtained by comparing the additions to the labour force during the plan period of Third Plan and Fourth Plan. By examination of these estimates it was concluded by Dantwala Commission that the estimates of Planning Commission were inaccurate. It was pointed out that the unemployment situated in rural areas was not properly estimated. The Committee of Experts on unemployment estimates recommended attempts to measure the number of the unemployed by different segments of the labour force. It asked Planning Commission to give up such efforts. Therefore, Committee on unemployment known as Bhagwati Committee was appointed to assess the number of unemployed and underemployed and to suggest remedies.

The eleventh and twelfth National Sample survey disclosed that the incident of unemployment in rural areas among male agricultural labour was four times than of the other rural males. Among the female agricultural workers it was as much as seven times of that of the other females. Thus, agricultural labourers are the worst victims of unemployment and underemployment in India. Similar is the position of landless labourers. They have to be protected against economic crisis. Again; in rural areas the incidence of unemployment of the educated is higher as compared to the urban areas. The rural residence has also been a handicap since urban residence and long period is required for searching a job. Besides unemployment, underemployment is very much visible among the above mentioned class in rural areas. In fact agricultural sector in India suffers from surplus labour. In the urban areas the trend of increasing educated unemployment and underemployment is on the increase.

Plans for Urban Development

Today's urban growth can be attributed to the industrial revolution of the West. While industrialisation has stimulated city growth, trade and commerce have played an important part in urban expansion. This expanding urban community calls for certain developmental programmes in all its dimensions to make the living of urban people comfortable and livable. Planned urban development is a social problem. In India, the undesirable developments in urban areas show serious attention for adequate urban planning and programmes. In various parts of India, there are municipalities and municipal corporations in which the function of maintaining public cleanliness, health care, town planning, registration of births and deaths, provision of services offered at the time of natural calamities have been corporated.

Separate Town Planning Acts were enacted and these Acts empower the local authority for planning and development functions. Thus, MMDA was set up in 1975 to carry out major development policies, and approve regional plans. Urban Housing is a complex one which involves Housing Schemes for various types of groups.

(1) Housing for labourers;
(2) LIG and MIG;
(3) Housing by Government and local authorities for public and displaced persons;
(4) Housing for private enterprises;

(5) Slum clearance schemes. National Building Organisations, House Boards (centre and state) and the cooperative house building societies are constituted to look into this problem of urban housing. Other urban development projects are slum clearance schemes, accelerated slum improvement, sites and service schemes, shelter for shelterless, pavement dwellers housing schemes, cash loan scheme, Nehru Rozgar Yojana, self financing schemes, land bank scheme, community development wing, Housing cooperatives, shelter upgradation in urban areas, Environment and improvement scheme.

Water Supply and Drainage Boards : The board has developed expertise in the fields of geology, drilling water quantity and surveillance. Underground sewerage facilities have been provided either fully or partially in the towns. The Board is implementing a project with World Bank assistance also. Chennai Metropolitan water supply and sewerage Board is implementing two major projects. Provision of supplying adequate drinking water to urban population is undertaken by this board.

Domestic and commercial electric power are under the control of Electricity Board. Central Electricity Board is responsible to control and coordinate the generation of electricity. The problem of traffic or transportation presents specific position for transport and terminal improvement. The location and planning of Airports, Railways, major roads, and Highway systems, Terminals, arterial, cycle tracks etc. within the urban areas is very essential. The transport plan has been based on the proposed land use pattern for the urban areas. In Indian cities, the prevailing condition of the transport service are not upto the desired standard. So a planned policy for the same is essential. Various schemes for improving traffic flows are in progress in Indian cities.

Transport and communication network is another major problem in the urban area. The law and order problem, security problem, criminality are other areas to be looked into.

The urban environment has to be kept pollution free. So the Pollution Control Board has been established to check the pollution. The Board promotes environmental awareness among public. Recreational facilities are also taken care of by providing licence to run cinema halls, stage theatres etc. Press, Radio, T.V. play constructive role besides providing entertainment. Tourism Development authority is responsible for conducting short and long tours, identifying sight seeing places, developing pilgrimage centres, arranging Trade fairs, water sports, etc. Social security services are on the increase as a result of increasing urbanisation and industrialisation. Labour legislations, social assistance, social insurance, family welfare, child welfare, youth welfare are looked after by Centre and Social Welfare Boards. Many NGOs have come into existence. Economic development services like Banking, Business and Commerce, Industries, Market and Shopping Centres, Employment Exchange, Employment Information Bureau, Vocational Guidance Bureau, self-help programmes, Animal Husbandry, Cooperative societies, Consumer Protection Acts and Forums are also taken care of by both Government and private agencies. These services require considerable planning especially in an urban milieu, where ample economic opportunities are available.

Education, medical and health services are other social and cultural developmental activities. The role of religious organisation is vital in the present context, as the urban society is heading towards without any sense of direction.

Urban community welfare services like, library, restaurant, guidance and counselling, Destitute and Delinquent centres, reformative and rehabilitative services, old age homes are part and parcel of planning. But waiting for response simply from the government will not serve the purpose of developing the urban areas in its overall aspects.

4

ROLE OF ECONOMY

SYSTEM OF JAJMANIS

Jajmani system is the backbone of rural economy and social order. Oscar Lewis has defined it thus: "Under this system each caste group within a village is expected to give certain standardised services to the families of other castes." Thus barber dresses the hair of villagers; carpenter meets the wood work requirements and iron smith makes agricultural implements and other household effects like tongs, hammers, buckets etc. which are made of iron. The class of shopkeepers, *Banias,* makes the provisions and numerous articles of daily use available by collecting them from a wide variety of sources and Brahmins help in carrying on various religious rites and ceremonies.

Everyone works for a certain family or a group of families with whom he is linked hereditary, that is, his forefathers and father were rendering same type of services to same group of families for whom he is working presently. Even his sons will perform same kind of duties for the specified families in future as well. Thus professions and services in villages are determined by the caste and have become fixed by long traditions. Under *Jajmani* system the family or families entitled tot certain services from certain persons are called *Jajmans* and the persons rendering those services are called *Kameen* of the *Jajman*. The term *Kameen* means one works for somebody or serves him. The terms *Jajman* and *Kameen*, patron and auxiliary are popular in Northern Indian villages. Though *Jajmani* system is found all over India, the terms used for *Jajman* and *Kameen* are different. The first detailed study of *Jajmani* tradition in India was made by William H. Wister in his book, *The Indian Jajmani system*. He for the first time drew attention to *Jajmani* as a tradition and system.

However, Wiser did not know that *Jajmani* system is nearly universal in Indian villages. In fact Wiser had no idea about the extent to which *Jajmani* system was prevalent in India. Oscar Lewis had made more elaborate study of this system. The sociological studies of Eastern Uttar Pradesh, Malabar, Cochin, Mysore district, Tanjore, Hyderabad, Gujarat and Punjab regions have revealed that *Jajmani* system prevails in all regions though there are minor local differences. Therefore we are fully justified in saying that *Jajmani* system is universal in rural India, some minor regional variations notwithstanding.

Indian Society is structured on caste patterns and the economic and professional relationships between various castes in this set-up is called *Jajmani* system. It is a pre-established division of labour among the castes sanctioned by religious and social traditions.

Jajmani is a peculiarity of Indian villages. In India professions are generally hereditary and there is a long tradition of families carrying on same professions over generations. Normally there is no deviation from the hereditary professions. Thus the son of a carpenter will become carpenter and the son of an iron smith will become an iron smith. Every Indian villager considers it natural and right to engage in professions peculiar to his caste and, on account of long tradition, feels at home in it and easily acquires proficiency.

According to Webster's Dictionary a *Jajman* is "a person by whom a Brahmin is hired to perform religious services hence a patron a client."

Etymologically the word *Jajman* is derived from the Sanskrit word *Yajman* which means a person who performs a *Yajna;* and for the purpose of performance of *Yajna* one has to hire the services of a Brahmin. Gradually, this word came to be applied to everyone who hired services or to whom some service was given. As N.S. Reddy observes, the fanner who engages carpenter or iron smith for manufacture repair of his tools is *Jajman* and the carpenter and the iron smith are *Kameen* or *Parjan*. Between *Jajman* and *Parjan* the relationship is hereditary and is based on tradition. *Jajmans* get a variety of jobs done by *Parjans* as for example, the barber dresses the hair and shaves the beard; *Kahar* brings water from the well or river as the case may be; sweeper does sanitary jobs. For these services *Parjans* are paid something. In majority of cases farmers in Indian villages give wheat for the services of the *Parjans*. In modern times currency notes are fast replacing all other media of exchange even in villages. In *Jajmani* system, *Jajman* enjoys so much respect that he is often referred to as *Rajah* (King) and *Parjans* as subject.

Jajmani System: A Study: Various studies *of Jajmani* system in India have been made. As referred to earlier, Oscar Lewis studied *Jajmani* in North Indian Villages. *Jajmani* in Eastern U.P. was studied in 1948 by Oplera and Singh in 1955, N.S. Reddy studied this system in North India. Miller studied *Jajmani* system in Cochin in 1952, and 1955, Sri Niwas and Bir Singh studied the same system in Mysore District. S.C. Dubey's *Indian Village* is based on his classic study of *Jajmani* in Hyderabad.

Jajmani in Tanjore was studied by Gough in 1955. In Gujarat *Jajmani* was studied by Steel in 1953. An earlier study, in 1934, of *Jajmani* in Punjab was made by Darling. All these studies revealed and confirmed the universality of this system in rural India but they also revealed that there were minor variations in the system from region to region.

Traits of Jajmani System

Jajmani vs Permanent System : As is obvious from the various definitions given above the most striking and essential feature of the *Jajmani* system is that it ensures the availability of certain essential services to farmers. Thus on account of this system certain individuals or groups of them needed for assistance in agriculture or to meet the essential requirements of the agriculturists stay permanently in villages. Thus a village is able to function as a relatively self-sufficient unit. It is on account of this system that if any *Kameen* leaves a village he provides for his substitute. We also come across examples where *Jajmani* rights are sold.

According to Shri Inderdatta Singh a sweeper can sell his *Jajmani* rights for about Rupees 200. However, generally *Jajmani* rights are not sold. These are not even exchanged or transferred, because a *Kameen* does not like to leave a particular village to go to some other village. Thus the system of *Jajmani* ensures that no one moves away from the village in which he was born so that there may be no disruption of services available in a village. Thus a permanent structure of economic order and relationship among various classes in the villages is provided for and its continuance ensured by *Jajmani* system. Infact, abdication *of Jajmani* rights amounts to abandonment of natural birthrights. The abdication of these rights is not only economically hurtful but hurts also the prestige. Sometimes in order to prevent migration of *Kameen* from a village, great pressure is brought to bear upon his caste members. S.S. Nehru has cited an instance of a village in which a law was framed by its Panchayat according to which no iron smith could leave the village. According Dr. S.C. Dubey while a *Kameen* had no right to desert his *Jajman,* the *Jajman* also has no right to replace his *Kameen.* That is, the spirit behind *Jajmani* system was to ensure life long fixed and permanent relations so that the rural economy was undisturbed.

According to S.C. Dubey, "It is not easy for an agriculturist to remove a family attached to his household and secure the services of another. For example, A, a barber is attached to the family of B, an agriculturist. If for any reason B is greatly dissatisfied with the services of A and wants those of another he cannot abruptly dismiss A. His difficulty will not be in dismissing A, but finding a substitute. Each of these castes has its own inter-village council. Occupational castes have a developed trade unionism. No one else would be willing to act as a substitute for fear of being penalised by the caste panchayat.

Hereditary Concern : Second major feature *of Jajmani* system is its being hereditary. According to Shri N.S. Reddy, the rights of *Jajmani* jobs are considered to be proprietary. These are passed on to sons from his father and in case of separation of brothers these rights are also split among them. If someone has no son but only a daughter *Jajmani* rights pass on to the husband of the daughter. However, *Jajmani* rights are equally distributed among families.

For example an iron smith may be giving services to 30 families, whereas another may have only 10 or less clients. Moreover with the increase in the number of male members in a family *Jajmani* rights are split among them and this leads to reduction in the number of clients. On the other hand, if there is rapid increase in the members of *Jajman* families the number of clients may grow.

Course of Payment

Another important characteristic of *Jajmani* system is that instead of receiving cash payment against his services, the *Kameen* is paid in kind, that is, he receives goods like wheat, rice etc. Thus under *Jajmani* system the relation between *Jajman* and *Kameen* is not that of employer and employee, as is the case under the capitalist system. In fact in return for the services of *Kameen, Jajman* is anxious about the needs and welfare of *Kameen* and *Kameen* serves *Jajman* with devotion and dedication. *Jajman* not only provides *Kameen* with food but also gives him clothing and residential accommodation. The amount of foodgrain given to *Kameen* depends upon the nature of services rendered. In his study of *Jajmani* system in Rampur, Oscar Lewis collected following data regarding the amount of food given for each kind of work:

S.No.	*Caste*	*Nature of Service*	*Compensatory Rights*
I	Carpenter	Repair of Agricultural Implements	One mand food-grain in a year. 2½ *seers* of foodgrain at time of harvesting.
II	Ironsmith	do	do
III	Potter	Provision of earthen vessels and odd jobs during marriages	Foodgrain according to the value of pots and grains according to situation and capacity at time of marriage.
IV	Sweeper	Removal of filth Making gobar cakes Stringing beads	Two meals per day. As much foodgrain as he can carry at the time of harvest. More foodgrain at marriages.
V	Shoemaker	Assistance in agriculture Removal of Carcasses.	1/20th of produce and skins of dead animals.

As can be gauged from the above mentioned list, *Kameens* get enough food to meet their personal requirements. That is why they prefer payment in kind rather than in cash. However, these days there is a tendency to substitute by cash payment the payment in kind.

Peace and Contentment : According to W.H. Wiser, a significant feature of *Jajmani* system is the peace and contentment which it provides to villagers. The *Kameens* of a *Jajmani* feel a sense of security. They are free from the worry of finding employment to make both ends meet. As the nature of the tasks they have to perform is well-known to them in advance, they feel great mental peace and are well prepared for these tasks; and this saves them the botheration of adjustment. However, the picture is not altogether rosy. There are quite a few instances in which *Kameens* are exploited and given too little for their services.

Scope of Work Differences : Under *Jajmani* system the range of activity of different *Kameens* is not uniform. It is not necessary that certain *Kameen* should work only for a single family or even a single village. If the nature of his work or activity is such that he can effectively cater to the needs of two or three villages, there is no provision in *Jajmani* system against such an arrangement. For example, a family needs the services of a barber once or twice a week and that too, for an hour or so. Naturally, therefore, a barber can easily cater to the needs of a dozen or so families. He can even work in more than one village. In certain instances, a shopkeeper is able to carry on his activities of making general provisions available in range of 10 to 20 miles from a village. Thus in many villages we do not find one shopkeeper carrying on his duties exclusively in one village; he may be covering one or two villages in the vicinity of the village in which he has his headquarters. The range, scope or spread of activities of any *Kameen* is determined by the nature of his activity. For example, while it is not possible for a sweeper to cater to the needs of more than a handful of families a barber or a shopkeeper may be able to operate in more than one village. Another factor which restricts or widens the spread of one's activity is the nature of demand and supply. If a village is prosperous it may have one or more shopkeepers but if the village is small and demand of goods is low, there may not be one exclusive shopkeeper in that village. We do not find shoemakers in every village. S.S. Nehru studied 54 North Indian villages and found that only in 18 of them there were shoemakers.

Potters were in 30% of the villages and shopkeepers only in 16%. *Ahirs* were found in 60% and Brahmin, barber and ironsmith and *teli* were found each in 40% of the villages. From the above survey it is plain that not every type of *Kameen* is to be found in every village. In the absence of a particular *Kameen* people perform that task by themselves or go to other village for it. For example, residents of a village may get their hair dressed from a neighbouring village.

Critical Evaluation Jajmani System : The foregoing account brings into clear light the advantages and disadvantages of *Jajmani* system. Chief advantages are:

Service Security : As has been mentioned earlier, the professions in *Jajmani* system are hereditary; and are, therefore, fixed and permanent. The sons of a *Kameen* do not have to look for jobs; they get jobs as a matter of birthright.

Financial Security

In *Jajmani* system *Jajmans* look after each and every need of their *Kameens*. Thus a *Kameen* enjoys economic security.

Relations very Close : In as much as *Jajmans* and *Kameens* are related with each other by heredity and long tradition their relationship is intimate and personal. They know each other very well and are, therefore, sympathetic to the needs of each other. Their relationship is not purely economic or professional. As a matter of fact their lives are interlinked.

However, *Jajmani* system is not free from faults. Like caste system it was of great value in past but has now degenerated into an instrument of exploitation and discrimination. As Oscar Levis has pointed out in his study of *Jajmani* system in Rampur village, whereas in past it was based on personal relationship it has now become an instrument of exploitation of *Kameen* by *Jajman.* In *Jajmani* system, the *Kameens* are treated as inferior and low-bred. In fact the word *Kameen* itself means lowly or inferior.

Thus *Jajmani* system tends to perpetuate distinctions among men. Thus the upper castes exploit and abuse the low castes. Dr. Majumdar and colleagues found in their survey of the villages that the conditions of *Kameens* are miserable and the upper castes subject them to great harassment and trouble. These days there is a gradual change in *the Jajmani* system. This system is disappearing because old caste-system is giving way to groupism and class struggle.

Another important factor contributing to the disintegration of *Jajmani* system is the gradual weakening of faith in religion and performance of rituals. This has resulted in decline of Brahmin's prestige. They are no longer in much demand. The rapid expansion of the fast means of communication and transport has made it easy for workers to seek work outside their town and for *Jajman* to receive improved services somewhere else. However, professions are no longer heredity based.

It is possible, indeed is quite the case, for a village Brahmin to take to shopping. The agricultural profession is no longer an exclusive prerogative of any particular caste. People of different castes are engaged these days in agriculture. Finally, the greatest set-back to *Jajmani* system has come from reform movements like Arya Samaj. In brief, it can be said that all the factors which are responsible for decline and disintegration of the caste-system are also responsible for the decline and disintegration of the *Jajmani* system.

Changing Rural Life

But the element of village life which have been delineated above can be found to exist only in those villages which have remained unaffected by the influence of the towns. Otherwise, as a general rule, these elements are vanishing from the village life. The community consciousness in village life is steadily decreasing. The control of the caste panchayats is almost non-existent. The villagers who work in the towns as labourers acquire such habits as drinking, prostitution, telling lies, unnecessary show and needless boasting etc., and when these villagers return to their native village they spread extreme immortality. The village youths studying in the towns also become addicted to irresponsibility and pedantic habits, and when they exhibit the same habits in their villages the other simple minded adolescents are also corrupted. The village belle living in the town is even more adept at the use of cheap cosmetics.

Effect of Market Mechanism

Markets are a place of social action. Markets can be held on specific days, in specific places and on specific economic like festivals. These markets are, however, temporary markets. Permanent markets are places where goods are exposed for sale. Permanent markets are of two types: wholesalers and retailers. Here goods which are locally available are sold in bulk for further distribution.

Markets can be of a specific type: a fruit market, vegetable or cloth market. Then we have the super bazaar system which are meant for the convenience of consumers who want a number of commodities at a specific place.

Trade in Market

Market exchange involves competition between buyers and sellers. This exchange is regulated by business ethics which is dependent on demand and supply, quality and price relations. The market equilibrium gets disturbed if any change is made in any one of the variables.

The law of supply does not, however, apply to the 'professional market'. In the case of the 'professional market', the efficiency of the person is taken into consideration. To secure the services of a lawyer, a doctor, an engineer or a chartered accountant, the client, patient or customer will look for satisfaction of services rendered.

Method of Market Control

Business and professional ethics have always been in force in regulating the market conditions. In ancient India, *srenies* or guilds were functioning in India and medieval Europe. These agencies fixed the prices of commodities, regulated the relations between the supplier and the purchaser and enforced professional ethics.

Perfect and Imperfect Market : In a market where price is determined by the laws of supply and demand, the market is perfect. In such a market the rate of profit and interest is charged according to the business ethics, customs or market regulation. There is no monopoly system. However, a perfect market ceases to be perfect market when it is influenced by political authority. In those cases when the domestic supply of goods becomes erratic and are not of the required quality, the government, due to competition forbids the import of similar goods and instead raises the tariff or supports it with subsidies, such a market is called an imperfect market.

Market Economy till Now : Brahmanism had given full emphasis to *Artha* but it was bound to ritualism which was a limiting factor. However, by the 6th century B.C. the limitation of ritualism got released because of the origin of new religions like Buddhism and Jainism. Both these movements were anti-ritualistic which appealed to the urban classes who were affluent, educated and emancipated. The guilds were thus, free of priestly domination; they encouraged individual's right to property. The combination of business expertise and ethical systems rooted in the society, gave the Buddhist and Jain traders a basis for free action in trade and commerce with greater efficiency.

The commercial development cut across, caste and regional barriers. Large family business empires were developed, banking houses and commercial towns like Ahmedabad.

Occupational Variation : In India under caste system, it was almost an accepted fact that occupation of the father will be followed by the son. There was therefore, no occupational diversification. The social structure was based on immobility of occupations. The Brahmins were to impart education, Kshatriyas to fight, Vaishyas to trade and the Shudras to do other jobs. All this served its purpose for a long time and as long as the economy was simple, the people, tradition ridden and outlook, narrow.

But as the time passed outlook of the people changed. Their outlook widened and they thought of adopting new occupations. Those who got higher education and technical and other qualifications joined the occupations which suited their qualifications, no matter whether these were of their parents or not. Similarly those who could amass wealth began to trade both inside and outside the country irrespective of the fact whether their parents were traders or not. The high caste Brahmins in many cases found that they should work in factories and other establishments at even low jobs to make both ends meet. In some cases they even became cooks of the rich people. The low caste people also gave up, as and when they found an opportunity, their dirty work and instead adopted good professions.

There was, therefore, wide occupational diversity. For the

spread of education, contacts with the people, quick means of transportation and communication etc. were responsible.

Occupational diversification very much affected traditional social structure. The low castes who could start healthy and good occupations began to be socially respected. Those who could manage to get high jobs, were invited by their subordinates to their own residences, by the so called high caste people. The people belonging to all castes began to freely mix with each other and thus caste rigidity became less. Some of the high caste people did not mind marrying their sons and daughters with the low caste but highly placed people. In this way inter-caste marriages started. Not only this, but one effect was that new sub-castes came into existence. These were the result of the marriage of high caste with low caste and inter-caste marriages.

Diversification of occupations implied occupational mobility. It could be possible only when there were chances of entering into other fields. Obviously those chances could be only where the people who diversified left their families and places. They came to their native places after a very long time. They lived away from their kith and kin. Thus their love for their near and dear ones much reduced. They developed new relationships with the people near them. They were close to them rather than their dear ones who were away from them. Being away from their homes, their approach and outlook to the whole social system changed. In fact whole social structure came under heavy strains. Caste marriage, religion, family and traditions all came under strains.

Those who could manage to enter the new occupations and that too successfully, found that their life partners were not helping them in new efforts. They therefore, thought of dissolving marriage partnership, if that was possible. If that was not found feasible, they began to under-estimate the value of marriage. Family relations got worsened. The women then began to lead a miserable life. No less was the problem with religion. The hold of religion over the people very much reduced. Religion began to be characterised as blind faith full of irrational superstitions and so on. The traditions which had bound the society for a very long time were broken. The very fact that the people decided to join a profession which was not of their ancestors was in itself a proof of the fact that the traditions were being under-estimated. Thus occupational mobility and diversification of occupations in India very much affected social structure and continues to affect that even now.

Various Professions

Professions can broadly be categorised as rewarding and unrewarding. Some of the important professions in the villages are priest, barber, carpenter, iron smith, potter, washerman and shepherd etc. Money lending is another important occupation of the villagers, which has proved a great source of exploitation and drawn the attention of the government.

Zamindari system is one of the characteristics of the villages. The system was quite common at the time of independence and considered as a profession. The system has however, been abolished now.

As already said the profession can be both rewarding and non-rewarding. Under the former fall such professions which are paying and labour put in those occupations and professions either adequately or more than adequately rewards the person concerned. Such a profession can be adopted either by the person individually or group of persons collectively. In India trade, commerce and in many cases even shopping is considered as rewarding profession. The people engaged in these professions fall under the category of upper class or elite, upper middle class. The people who are engaged in these professions usually try to guard themselves from outside interference. They do not allow or encourage others to enter their business circle or to adopt a profession which they are following. It is because, these people feel that their monopoly will be challenged and profits shared. It is also just possible that some of the new entrants might excel them as well. Accordingly there is keen competition in India for entering into rewarding business and professions.

But each rewarding profession is not always prestigious. Only such professions and occupations enjoy social prestige which are socially acceptable. Moreover, prestige to an occupation which is highly rewarding comes when the goods produced are socially useful and accepted as such by the society. If in service there is security of service and the one engaged in a profession or occupation enjoys and commands power and prestige in the organisation and outside, that is prestigious.

Then there are unrewarding professions. These professions are usually dirty. In these more of manual than mental labour is involved. The people engaged in these professions are supposed to possess good physique. The people usually are illiterate and work hard. The wages are low. In many cases the people even do not know of the ultimate end of the work to which they are contributing. Sometimes the whole family gets engaged to make their both ends meet. Such professions are working in offices at low jobs, in industries as unskilled or semi-skilled labourers and workers, working on hired labour, labourers engaged in construction, road building and similar other activities or petty shop-keeping.

In India in the past the people belonging to scheduled castes and scheduled tribes were engaged in unrewarding professions. They used to work from day till night, but were paid very little. The people engaged in unrewarding business and profession can never economically come up because they can hardly save any money for doing any business.

The people whether engaged in rewarding or unrewarding business, all try to maximise their wealth. They wish to raise their profits and bargain with the employers for more and better wages. There is a movement from down to upward. Those engaged in unrewarding or less rewarding professions try to come up and join the ranks of those who are engaged in rewarding professions. But the movement is slow because the people are economically poor and their economic resources meagre. The rate of capital formation is slow. In addition, purchasing power of the people is low and they are more interested in purchasing traditional rather than new and traditional goods.

Agriculture still continues to be the main occupation of the people. Of the total population of India, only 32.92 per cent is working population, whereas remaining is just non-working. Broad division of the people by work and occupation in India is as under:

Agricultural Labourers	14.28%
Livestock, Fishing etc.	0.78%
Mining and Quarrying etc.	0.17%
Household Industry	1.16%
Other than Household Industry	1.95%
Construction	0.4%
Trade and Commerce	1.83%
Transport and Communication	0.80%
Other Services	2.88%
Non-working Population	67.08%

Trade Unionism

In India, those who are engaged in some sort of profession try to organise themselves in the form of trade union. They feel that only collective bargaining can help them in getting more concessions and facilities.

After Industrial Revolution large and big factories were set up which employed thousands of persons on different jobs. These factories were owned by individuals who exploited the workers to the maximum. They wanted to get maximum work by paying minimum wages. Working conditions of workers were miserable and many a time workers were found patients of T.B. and other fatal disease due to unhygienic conditions which prevailed in the factories. These conditions continued for a long time in Europe.

Prelude of Trade Union System : But all the labourers continued to work under those conditions. Raising voice meant loss of job and also starvation. Since the governments were under influence and control of the factory owners no laws could be passed which favoured the workers. But slowly there was consciousness and awakening among the workers and they felt and thought of uniting. But even these attempts were opposed by the Government.

British Act of 1799 is an Example to Quote : As time passed and the workers found factory working conditions intolerable they thought of coming together and forming their unions. The main object was not to bargain but to request the owner to give some concessions and facilities so that the workers could live and work in a good atmosphere.

It was with the philosophy of Karl Marx that the workers realised their value and worth. They began to feel that profit of factory owner was closely linked with their labour and that the both were inseparable. They also realised that if organised they could also bargain with the employer. It is this which gave birth to trade unionism.

TYPES OF TRADE UNIONS

Trade Unions today are found in each and every industry and also in each good establishment. It is therefore; difficult to name or count the number of trade unions in a country.

Generally speaking however, trade unions can consist of members who believe in the use of force and those who do not at all believe in the use of force, as a means and method for getting the demands redressed. There are other unions which usually believe in non-violent means, but if violence is a must, they will not hesitate to use that as well.

Working Method : In our set up trade union system has come to stay. Today we cannot think of an establishment which has no trade union. To begin with the leaders in the organisation enrol members from among the workers. These members usually indicate their strength and following. Usually membership is paid. Since it is considered that trade unions are essential for the industry, therefore, these are recognised by the management as well.

After the trade union has been recognised it is expected to use only legal and constitutional means for getting their demands met. The trade unions, in the first instance, put all the demands including their grievances before the management. First step is then that of opening negotiations. In this system both the representatives of the managements and workers sit round the table and on equal footing they discuss the problem. Efforts are made to settle the dispute amicably and in a friendly atmosphere.

After negotiations, comes the arbitration. If the negotiations fail, then both the parties refer their points to a mutually accepted arbitrator whose jurisdictions are decided beforehand. Such an arbitrator tries to settle the dispute.

Next comes the most effective and commonly used method of strike. Under this method, in order to get their demands met and grievances redressed, the workers stop working altogether. This is done with a view to reducing the profit of the employer or dislocating his work and organisation. This method is now very much in vogue. In almost all the advanced countries of the world right to strike is recognised. Syndicalists believe that strike is so powerful a weapon that it can dislodge the most powerful government from authority and supremacy. It is hoped that the strike, if successful, will force the management to come to terms with the workers.

These are some of the constitutional means for getting the grievances redressed, but in some cases trade unions have adopted other means as well. Some of the organisations have adopted the method of sabotage and destruction of property and machinery and that of creating anarchy but so far methods of these organisations have not been much appreciated.

Historical Review of Trade Unionism : Though in times past India had an agricultural economy yet the country knew of trade union system in the past, though in a crude form. But in its present form it has short history. It started by the middle of 19th century. It was during this period that the industrialists of the country organised themselves to protect their interests. But even at this stage the workers did not organise themselves. Credit of organising the workers and labourers goes to our social reformers who took initiative in this direction as well. In 1857 first Indian Chamber of Commerce, known as Bengal National Chamber of Commerce was set-up.

In 1875 MSS Bengali took the responsibility of reforming the conditions of the workers by drawing government's attention towards miserable conditions in which workers worked, but he was not a success in that in 1881 Mr. N.M. Lokhande organised a conference of Bombay mills workers and demanded that workers be given a weekly holiday, paid some compensation when they met with an accident while on work and also half an hour rest during their work. These demands were accepted by some of the mill owners. Lokhande thereafter founded an association of mill workers and helped in the publication of a labour magazine named Deenbandhu. The movement continued to progress during his life but slowed down considerably after his death.

In the year 1900 Marwari Chamber of Commerce, Calcutta was founded.

In the wake of partition of Bengal in 1905 the workers organised themselves in several parts of the country and organised strikes etc. The result of the awakening was that in 1905 in Calcutta workers of the printing press formed a union. In 1907 postal workers in Bombay formed a union. In the same year the Indian Merchants' Chamber, Bombay was founded. In 1909 South Indian Chamber of Commerce, Madras was founded. In 1910 a Labour Welfare Association was founded in Bombay.

But trade union activity in India received considerable momentum during World War I when workers were sufficiently awakened. Our national leaders also realised that unless the workers were organised freedom will remain far away. Even Lokmanya Tilak, Annie Besant and Gandhiji paid attention to the workers and Ahmedabad Textile Labour Union was organised by Gandhiji. In 1920 Indian National Trade Union Congress was founded. In 1923, the Government of India passed Indian Trade Union Act by which all recognised trade unions were given constitutional recognisation.

In 1926 the Communists entered trade union activities and controlled the movement which resulted in division of the movement. Those who did not subscribe to communist methods of working remained separate and aloof. In 1931 All India Red Trade Union Congress came into being, but the division of the movement between Congress and the Communists gave a setback to the cause of the workers. The unity in the movement however, came in 1940 but that too was short-lived.

During World War II M.N. Roy founded Indian Trade Union Labour Federation and worked parallel to Indian National Trade Union Congress. In 1948 INTUC was declared as the official body representing the interests of labour in India. The Communists and Congress parties had already organised trade unions in India. After independence the Socialist, Jan Sangh and several other political parties are engaged in the task of organising the workers in trade union to follow their own ideology and policies. Trade Union activity in the country is very brisk and the workers are now quite conscious of their rights and struggling to get these as well.

Indian Trade Union Act

It is an accepted fact that in the struggle between the employers and the employees, the labourers are always placed in a very disadvantageous position. It was therefore recognised that the labourers and the workers must come closer to each other and organise themselves so that they can have collective bargaining capacity. Since this adversely affected the interests of the employers therefore, they always stood against this move. It was quite clear to them that any attempt at paying them higher wages could be only at their cost. But it was in 1926 that in India Trade Union Act was passed which legal recognisation to trade unionism in India. This Act was amended in 1947. Main provisions of the Act were:

1. Each union will get itself registered with the Registrar, to be appointed by the Government.
2. Recognised trade unions have a right to protect their collective interests.
3. Each trade union must have clear aims and objects.
4. Account of the union will be furnished every year.

The Act of 1947 : Trade Union Act of 1926 was amended in 1947. By this Act the employers have been asked to give recognition to the unions and if they refuse to do so the matter can be taken to the labour courts. It has been said that the members of the trade union will not instigate their workers to go on strike. Those employers who are found guilty of indulging in unfair activities are to be fined. Thereafter several Acts have been passed about the trade unions which recognise the right of collective bargaining of the workers.

Definition and Functions : In India, Trade Union Act of 1926 gave legal recognition to trade unions in the country. Inspite of the fact that in the country the wages are very low and the working conditions very poor, yet the trade unions have not become very powerful.

Term Defined : But before we discuss the rise and growth of trade unionism in India, let us first define the term. In the words of Sidney and Beatrice Wibbs, It is *"a continuous association of wage earners for the purpose of maintaining and improving the conditions of their working and living"*. J Cunnison says, *"Trade union is a monopolistic association of wage earners,' who sell to the employers in relation to dependence for the sake of their labour and even for its production; and that the general purpose of association is in view of that dependence, to strengthen their power to bargain with their employers"*. Indian Trade Union Act 1926 says that a trade union is, *"any combination, whether temporary or permanent formed principally for the purpose of regulating the relation between workmen or employers or between employers and employees or for imposing restrictive conditions on the conduct of any trade or business and includes any federation of two or more trade unions"*. It will thus be observed that the main aim of trade collective bargaining in an organised way against the employer.

Role of Trade Unions

The functions of trade unions may be classified as militant, ministrant and positive. Militant functions include strike and boycott. Trade union tries to get for its members sufficient wage, better working conditions, adequate working hours, arranges for profit sharing, better treatment for employees and ensures that employer gives all possible facilities to the workers. It also tries to educate the workers and their children, creates spirit of cooperation among its workers, publishes material relating to welfare of worker, spreads feelings of brotherhood, initiates struggle for increase in wages and helps in improving efficiencies.

Reason for the Slow Growth of Trade Unionism in India: We have already said that growth rate of trade unionism in India is very slow. It is because workers lack education; due to low wages they cannot finance trade union activities. The workers are divided by race, religion, language and caste. They are not aware of their rights and legal protection is not given to them. Intermediaries try to create hostilities. Due to low wages and poverty workers cannot remain on strike for long. The employers are usually hostile towards trade union and the leadership is not very good in the country.

Thus the trade unions help in removing dissatisfaction among the members and train the workers so that they can improve their efficiency and proficiency. The number of small unions in the country is very large. The subscription paid by workers is very low because they cannot pay high subscriptions. The unions cannot afford to have whole time paid officers. Moreover, leadership in the trade unions is in the hands of political parties, who promote political rather than workers' interests. Trade unions in India have also not undertaken social welfare activities to the direct advantage of the workers.

Then another reason is that the labour in India is of migratory character. The labourers not only leave and migrate from one industry to another but also leave one city and migrate to another. Still another reason is that in India there are many industries which are not well organised and in such industries problem of organising trade unions becomes really very serious.

System of recruitment in the country is such that it is not conducive to the growth of trade unions. The workers are either employed on daily wages, or against temporary posts or only such workers come who are known to the employers or their trusted workers.

In this way there are really very serious problems in so far as growth of trade unions in the country is concerned. In a country like India, in fact there should be strong trade union system but on account of these difficulties, the system has not fully developed.

There is too much politicisation of trade union workers and the movement as a whole has political orientation. The employers have shown no interest in the betterment of workers and every demand for improvement is considered confrontation and very badly resented. In the country unemployment is so much widespread that the unemployed remain on the outlook to grab every opportunity with the strikes of trade union workers may create.

Criticism of Trade Unions

Trade unions can play a big role in industrial development of a country. These can also help the workers in improving their lot. In is however, unfortunate that some trade unions adopt negative rather that positive attitude. This has more particularly very much defamed the movement in the eyes of the employers.

Positive Point : When the workers organise themselves into trade unions they gain certain advantages namely:

> They help in maintaining industrial peace when the outlook is positive. Employers get a channel for negotiations and as such many problems are solved on the table without straining relations. The unions help in getting better working conditions for the members. These help in raising technical efficiency and living standard of the workers with the result that production increases. These help in creating a sense and spirit of brotherhood among the workers. Healthy relations can be maintained with the management.

Negative Points : But the trade unionism has its

disadvantages as well. Some such important disadvantages are:

> The workers try to become undisciplined. Selfish leaders gain in the name of the workers and get opportunity to gain personal ends. These help in developing an agitational approach to every problem. Since the employers and the employees usually do not agree on many points, therefore, workers do not put heart and soul in the work with the result that production goes down. The employees always go on putting one demand or the other with the result that dissatisfaction is always created.

What is the present role of trade unions in industries and everywhere else? Today the workers everywhere organise themselves in trade unions. Many trade unions are under the direct or indirect influence of political ideologies. Their leadership is obviously interested in bringing as many workers under its influence and control as possibly it can. The result of all this is that the workers are faced with the problem of joining one of many trade unions which are organised in the industry or offices. Usually industrial workers being illiterate do not know the implications of joining a particular union. Then another problem is that the trade unions, in quite a number of cases, have asserted their rights but have failed to realise their responsibilities or duties with the result that they have antagonised their employers. Thus employer-employee relations have become strained. Still another difficulty is that quite a good number of unions develop agitational approach to every problem. They resort to giving strike calls to the workers even on trivial grounds. Sometimes even the well paid employees go on strike dislocating national economy.

Trade union activities, as a matter of policy, are accepted as a right of workers in every industrial organisation. It is also accepted by the Government that the workers can only collectively bargain usefully with the employers. But it is also accepted that the workers trade unions should be very careful while dealing with the employers. It is however, unfortunate that in India the trade unions have shown more interests towards their rights rather than in the performance of their duties. They have always adopted agitational approach. Recently the attitude of the government towards trade unions is rather relaxed.

Value System of Society and Trade Union Activity : Trade unions today are very strong and powerful instruments of collective bargaining. In India due to various reasons it has not been possible to develop a very strong and powerful trade union system. But social system in each country interacts with the trade unions. It is because:

1. No trade union system can ever think of going against well-established social systems because any such radical change can be opposed by the society.
2. In case our social system has deep roots in non-violence or evolutionary pattern, then the people will turn to that system and in no case will be prepared to accept violent changes. Accordingly trade unions will also have to follow similar approach towards every problem. On the other hand, if the social system has roots in revolution, the whole trade union approach will be different. It will try to bring about change by using violent means and methods.
3. It is social system which decides whether we should have small or large scale production. In case, it is small scale production, trade union system may not be powerful, as against the system when there is large scale production. In the case of large scale production chances of developing a strong trade union system are very bright.
4. Again it depends on our social system, whether we like

industrialisation or not. In case social system does not like industrialisation, the chances of trade union system developing and growing become very remote. In case we favour industries will develop and number of industrial workers will increase and trade union system will grow. We know that in agricultural economy trade union activity pattern is quite different from what is in a society with industrial pattern.

5. Then another factor is that what is the position of a trade union leader in our social set up. In case he is socially respected and loved, then activity pattern will be different, as compared with a system in which he is considered useless or nuisance and a burden on society.
6. It also depends on our social system whether we like machine oriented or labour based industries. In case there is vast and man-power is available, the system will appreciate only labour based industry and *vice-versa*. Obviously the role of trade union in two types of industries is quite different.

System of Collaborative Bargaining

Since the coming of Karl Marx the workers have started realising their importance and they now organise themselves in trade unions etc. so that they can collectively bargain with their employers. Similarly the producers and owners also feel that collectively they can deal better with the trade unions of the workers or similar other organisation than otherwise. Accordingly a system under which the employers and employees as a body sit together and discuss their demands and arrive at some conclusion, that is called the system of collective bargaining. Such a bargaining has no legal force unless otherwise provided. It is just like a contract. It is an attempt to settle disputes without the intervention of third party. This sort of bargaining is done by the parties which are quite well organised. In some countries collective bargaining is statutory. It involves some governmental regulations. In some other countries however, there is no system of statutory bargaining, but only that of voluntary collective bargaining.

Elements of Collective Bargaining : Whether collective bargaining is statutory or voluntary it has certain elements namely:

1. Those issues which come up for bargaining should be such which relate to both the parties and in which both are interested.
2. There should be clear idea about the procedure to be followed.
3. What type of machinery will solve the problem, about this there should be clear indication.
4. Points of disputes should be clearly specified.
5. The type of agreement to be reached should be specified in the nature of settlement over the matter under dispute.

Issues Range : There are wide differences over the range of issues but usually for collective bargaining some issues which can be discussed are productivity, job evaluations, matters relating to living standard of the people, matters connected with technical and economic progress, wages, overtime payments, bonus, paid holidays, working hours, working conditions etc. There is however, no hard and fast list and the parties can mutually decide about the items to be placed for bargaining.

Positive Point of Collective Bargaining : Some of the main arguments put forth for collective bargaining are: It helps both the parties to come closer and nearer to each other and thus many problems are amicably solved. It develops sense of self reliance since third party is not involved in it. It encourages sense of responsibility. It develops a sort of industrial democracy in the industries. Since both the parties mutually agree therefore the settlement reached is permanent and lasting. The workers will come to know the limitations of their employers and the extent to which efforts are being made to improve their lot. It reduces tensions and spirit of hostility. Employer-employees relations become happy and harmonious.

Negative Points of Collective Bargaining : Collective bargaining has its own disadvantages as well. It can be a success when both the parties have equal bargaining capacity. But usually employer has an upper hand and as such bargaining cannot be equal. System can be successful when trade unionism is strong, but in India there is no strong trade union system. In India trade unions can't collectively bargain because these have internal disputes and no common platform of meeting and bargaining with employers. When bargaining fails, strike is the only alternative, for which no nation will be prepared because each strike means that system cannot work well.

Collaborative Bargaining in India: In India system of collective bargaining is yet to take off. Delhi Agreement was concluded in 1951. In 1956 Bonus Agreement for Plantation Workers was concluded. Some similar other collective bargains have also been concluded, but the system is yet to gain popularity. It is because trade unions in India are yet to develop their bargaining capacity. These are faction and friction ridden trade unions and their membership is not very impressive. As against this, the employers are comparatively better organised and in a better bargaining position. The system of Joint Consultative Machinery has been introduced but that is yet to give results.

Social Determinants and Impact : During the British days there was financial drain on India's wealth, destruction of indigenous industries and control of sources of production and distribution in just few hands. This resulted in the ruin of our economy and gap between the rich and the poor very much widened. The system of economy thus received the worst setback but did not altogether change. The result is that even today our economic system is the combination of tradition and modernity. The former is based on agricultural system whereas the latter on market economy and has bias towards industrial economy. The former is less scientifically managed, as compared with the latter. In India there has always been population explosion which has undone the effect of economic development with the result that it is not showing desired positive gains and signs.

In India the society is traditional yet on the whole it has not been very adverse to accept industrial changes and new technology. India has also decided to allow both public and private sectors go together in a planned way.

Since independence in 1947, in India there has been rapid economic development. This has been possible due to several reasons. Some of those being as under :

> In India leadership has always tried to provide sound capital base to the industry with the result that the country has very much economically advanced. New industries mean more chances of employment, more production, more consumption of goods etc. In the industrial field there has been increased economic activity. More and more natural resources have been exploited.

More Hands to put on the Wheels : In the agricultural field there have been brisk activities. The peasants and agriculturists who have been living since ages a life of poverty and misery, have now started living a life of prosperity. Due to more attention being paid to them and on account of better and more supply of fertilisers and agricultural equipments, agricultural produce has much increased. The agriculturist now gets better return of his produce. His produce can easily be sold in the market at reasonable rates. The result is that economic standard and economic conditions of rural India have much increased.

India has decided to work through plans. Planning Commission which has been set up for the purpose decides how to use limited economic resources for the best use of the country. There is thus planned economic development in India. With each plan efforts are made to raise living standard of the people, to provide them more employment, to raise national income and so on. Thus Planning Commission has helped in economic development of India.

Then another cause of economic development has been international trade. Since independence India has been trying to increase her international trade. Of course, in the beginning India had very unfavourable balance of trade, because we had to import everything for meeting both our consumption, production and defence needs. Now the situation has much changed. Now India is exporting her goods to many countries of the world. In the industrial field, India is one of the industrially advanced nations of the world. International trade has helped in the economic betterment of the people.

Indians have now got more and better opportunities to establish their industries abroad. Each Indian who establishes some industries abroad earns some profits, a part of which comes to India. This has also helped in economic betterment of the country.

Financial assistance from abroad both from international financial institutions and also foreign governments has helped a lot in economic betterment and development of the people. This assistance is both for planned and non planned projects. Similarly it is also for general and specific purposes. India has always tried to use financial assistance from abroad for capital formation and for strengthening nation's economic and industrial base rather than using that for consumer goods and similar other purposes. The money has also been used for breaking vicious circle of poverty, needs, consumption, increasing population and needs again. In this way money made available to India has helped in raising economic standard of the people.

After independence in economy price mechanism has developed and price of every commodity is now determined by supply and demand. There is competition in the market and artificial demand and supply situations are created. The industrialists take the maximum advantage of the helplessness of the workers with a view to earning maximum profits. Big business organisations are coming into existence. Private property is being protected. Due to industrialisation living standard of the workers has gone up. There is economic development and increased cultural activities. In addition there is also more economic freedom.

Financial Inequality

There has been and continues to be rapid economic development in India since independence. Country which was not producing anything is today producing much of what the nation today needs. But this has resulted in several economic problems. One such problem is that of increasing gap between the rich and the poor. Economic inequalities have much increased. In India even before independence there was wide economic gap. The Brahamins were supposed to live poor. They were not supposed to amass wealth, because it was felt that in case they too started economic activity, they will fail to discharge their main function of spreading of knowledge.

The so called Shudras were engaged in economically unrewarding professions. They were also poor. Wealth was therefore concentrated in two classes. There was therefore, economic inequality between the classes. But even then that did not had much impact because the classes which were without wealth did not much protest against poverty and secondly because those who possessed wealth did not use that for the purposes of naked exploitation of others.

As the time however passed the gulf between the classes began to increase. Under the Muslim rules, the Muslims became favourite sons of the land. They enjoyed power and prestige to enable them to earn wealth. Some of these rulers even tried to reduce non-Muslims to poverty. The gulf between classes due to possession of economic resources increased.

Economic inequality continued to increase under the Britishers. The English who came to India started naked exploitation of the Indians. Our cottage industries were ruined. The agriculturists were forced to pay even by selling their utensils. It was really during this period that difference in economic resources *i.e.* economic inequality was felt. The society was sharply divided between the rich and the poor. Vast majority of the population was reduced to poverty and the wealth which got concentrated in just a small section of society, was used for exploitation of the poor. Industrial and commercial activities which were started by the foreign rulers gave benefit to only small population of the country. But the nation on the whole was poor. Even those who had wealth, were not too wealthy, because economic activity was not brisk.

But whole process of economic inequality became active when India became free. As already said in free India there was economic activity, due to several reasons but it benefited only small section of population. Then was uneven distribution of wealth. Various plan projects which were undertaken benefited those who already had some wealth, because they could invest and undertake some responsibilities. Then another reason was that foreign money poured in the country. This money was to be spent all over the country for the welfare of the people. But dishonest bureaucrats and politicians collaborated to misappropriate money for themselves. They actually did not spend for the purpose for which it was allocated and showed that as spent. With their influence and knowledge of working of our legal institutions they could successfully keep a part of the money with themselves.

Moreover, when money was available, they set up new industries and undertook new projects. Each such enterprise helped them to earn more wealth. Thus the gap which already existed began to widen.

Not only this but with the help of their money they and their families could manage to occupy high jobs in the bureaucracy. This placed them in highly advantageous position. This also provided them an opportunity to earn more wealth, because they were in a position to earn from those who approached them.

Then another cause which became responsible for economic inequality was that with this wealth small section was in a position to enter into international trade. Thus all advantages of this trade also reached these sections of society.

How to Exploit?

Another social problem which economic activity created in India was that of exploitation. As long as the society was simple and economic activity slow, there was really no problem of exploitation. Since during ancient and medieval India cottage industries flourished, therefore, there was no question of exploitation. It started with the coming of East India Company in India, when the poor Indians were forced to work for the interest of Britishers in India. They were required to take British rather than Indian interests into consideration.

But this exploitation became more when India became free and put herself on the path of industrialisation. New industries were set up both in the public and private sectors. Whereas an attempt was made by public sector undertakings to provide all facilities to the workers and to exploit them as less as possible reverse was the case with the private sector. This sector followed the policy of exploitation. Since Indian economy was mixed one and in that private sector has considerable share, this sector did not hesitate to exploit any one.

The workers were less paid, substandard goods were produced and social needs ignored. Only those goods were produced which gave maximum return to them. The machine was used for selfish end. This sector tried to control the sources of both production and distribution. It created a lobby in political circles by which it could get such laws enacted which went in their favour. They created conditions of artificial scarcity at time of needs, by hoarding goods needed by the society.

Knowing fully well that the government is in need of their help, they forced the government from time to time to allow them to sell their commodities at prices suited to them. In the process they retained maximum with them and left much less for the workers.

They were in a position to weaken trade union activity in the industry. They realised that once the workers united they shall bargain with them and try to get maximum out of their share. They therefore, did not wish that their slice of profit be cut. They therefore, created division among the workers and by fair and foul means including giving them promotions, better wages, bribery etc. and kept a section of workers with themselves. They used their favourites to their advantage and thus avoided a situation under which the workers could take away a share of their profit.

But in India workers have been raising protests against their exploitation. They have always tried to organise themselves into trade unions. Again they have adopted the system of collective bargaining by which their representatives try to get maximum advantage from their employers. In order to make their grievances public, they organise demonstrations and processions. In extreme cases they even go on strike. In some cases strikes even get prolonged for months together.

In India exploitation by this sector, is not only of manual but also of natural and mineral resources. This sector controls these resources, fully exploits them and ensures that maximum advantage is taken out of these.

Exploitation in its worst form was that of begar and bonded labour. Under both these systems the owners forced the persons to do work for them without getting payment or any wages. Even the children and women used to do work which their health did not permit. They were exposed to dangerous machines without protection. The constitution has legally abolished begar and has provided that none will be forced to work under unhygienic and unhealthy circumstances. Employment of children below the age of 14 has been legally abolished. Bonded labour system was abolished in 1975. Thus exploitation of the poor has been considerably checked.

Exploitation in India is both direct as well as indirect. Keeping more profit and paying less wages is a well established system of exploitation of the workers. But there are indirect methods of exploitation as well. The workers are paid less whereas they are made to sign for more, thus showing on record that adequate wages are being paid to the workers. They are also forced to work long hours, without payment of any additional wages in any form. In addition, the industry produces substandard goods by purchasing defective raw material at cheap rates, thus cheating and exploiting the consumers and the society as a whole.

But exploitation is unavoidable in a society which has capitalist system of economy. In India of course, we have adopted socialistic pattern of society and the state from time to time, takes adequate steps to check exploitation of workers and resources by the private sector, but still we are to go a long way. Exploitation, as a social and political system, has come to stay in India and it will not end as long as drastic measures are not taken in this direction.

Existence of Corruption

Corruption is today a world-wide phenomenon. There is no country of the world which can claim to be free from this evil. Corruption in India became widespread during World War II when every law and rule was sacrificed for the sake of production of increased war material. Not only this but the government of the day poured in huge amounts in India. This provided an opportunity both to officials and non-officials to amass wealth by unfair and corrupt means. After independence again the situation of corruption continued because of availability of economic resources from abroad for economic development. Since then the evil of corruption is eating our society and today it is posing serious threat to our socio-economic and political system.

Corruption may briefly be defined as misuse of public office and position. It also means misuse of authority for personal ends. For this several causes are responsible.

Economic activity has created social problem of corruption. The people have the capacity to pay. They wish that without much wastage of time their work may be done. They can afford money but not the time. They know that the time which is wasted in coming and going to government offices will be saved and can be utilised for attending to business. Moreover they know that in a vast country like India where demands are many and supplies less only those will be in a position to take advantage who can grease the palm.

In bureaucracy the officials are badly paid and have temptation to earn money by underhand means.

The laws are flexible and in many cases can be interpreted to suit the convenience of the person concerned. This has provided the bureaucracy an opportunity to become corrupt and interpret law in a particular manner.

Corruption is rampant not only at bureaucratic level but at political level as well. It is because money is needed for contesting elections at hand and for the next elections. The politicians need compensation for the time they spend and business which they sacrifice for joining political life.

Since demands on limited resources are many, and scope for exploitation of available resources once available ample, those interested in getting resources adopt all means of corruption, both moral and material.

Corruption has got deep roots because of black money, which is operating in the country as parallel economy. This money of course, cannot be put into business and shown as white but can be used for corrupting those from whom work is to be extracted. Unfortunately in India black money is increasing day by day and with that corruption is also on the increase. This has in turn given rise to inflation and price spiral.

Allegations of corruption against highly placed officials are either hushed up or very slowly processed. Usually they go scot free and this encourages them to continue to follow corrupt practices.

Black money economy provides funds to bureaucrats and other resourceful people try to get national secrets.

Corruption in India is of several types. It can be by way of giving hard cash, real estate or favours and concessions. It can also be by giving employment, by supplying goods at cheap rates, by adding sleeping partners in running business and so on.

In fact this evil of economic system in India is assuming serious proportions. In case it is not checked immediately, it may become too late to check the evils and its ill-consequences.

Effect of Industrialisation

Path of industrialisation, occupational diversification, trade unions and human relations, market-economy and its social consequences, economic reforms liberalisation, privatisation and globalisation.

Industrial Growth

Industrialisation is a process whereby the path of economic development shifts from agricultural domain to industrial domain. Associated with this there is a sharp increase in the industrial share of GDP (Gross Domestic Product -National income calculated as money value of the goods and services produced in the country during one year) and of the labour force.

In the process of industrialisation a large number of labour force shifts from primary occupation to tertiary and secondary occupation.

Adoption of technologically superior techniques of production that help to transform basic raw materials and intermediate good into manufactured goods and application of modem techniques of management and organisation like economic calculations, accountancy and management techniques etc. become the characteristics of an industrialising country.

Industrialisation is one of the most important aspects of economic development taking place in most of the third world developing countries including India. Once a developing country chooses the path of industrialisation it gets confronted with a number of problems, some of which can be identified such as;

(i) the extent of industrialisation,

(ii) the nature of industries to be established

(iii) the order for the establishment of the industries,

(iv) the pace of industrialisation and

(v) establishment of small scale and large scale industries.

These issues are highlighted in the following ways.

The extent and pace of industrialisation available in a developing country is determined by the amount of resources available both domestic and foreign that the economy can mobilise.

A developing country is faced with different sets of choice *e.g.* choice between export and domestic industries, choice between consumer goods and capital goods industries. Export industries are required to finance the import needs of development that industrialisation entails. Resources may have to be distributed among export industries producing for domestic market. Similarly investment in consumer goods industries is required to meet the more immediate needs, whereas investment in capital goods industries help to raise the productive potentials of the economy.

Placement of Industry

In the case of extractive industries, the location is determined by unalterable natural conditions. In all other industries, efforts are generally made to secure a balanced regional development of the country.

Large industries are generally capital-intensive, whereas small industries are labour-intensive. A labour-surplus economy would prefer labour-intensive small industries. But it may not be feasible to set some core and basic industries on a small scale. Hence, a decision may be taken to make use of the complementary role of these industries by the developing countries.

Location of industries to be set up is important regarding raw materials, market facilities, transportation and also the protection of ecology of that region.

The process of industrialisation in the developing countries began to take place only after British colonialism in these regions. One of the most important economic exploitations that occurred in these regions is the extraction of raw materials from these region by the British. This has become an important factor for hindering the industrial development in these countries. India as a developing country is no exception to this. In developing countries economic factors are the most potent obstacles to economic development. First there is a scarcity of capital. This results in low level of per capita income and low productivity.

Scarcity of capital adversely affects investment in industry and infrastructure. Secondly, developing countries by their very nature do not possess adequate infrastructure facilities such as transport,, communications, water, power etc. Thirdly, the absence of the industries to use the by-product of existing industries results in waste and a bad economy.

Fourthly, in developing countries there are no proper institutions which can give education and train labourers to improve their skill. Fifthly, lack of repair facilities is another obstacle in a proper utilisation of machinery. Sixthly, the absence of specialised institutions to promote proper credit facilities, sound banking, insurance cover etc., acts as a deterrent to industrial investment and activity. Seventhly, industrialisation may also be hampered by a lack of appropriate technology.

Sophisticated technology is held to be appropriate on the ground that they are so productive that unit production costs are potentially lower than otherwise. The potential advantages, however, are never realised because of the lack of higher level of technical managerial skills that must accompany sophisticated technology.

Finally, in many a situation, industry in a developing country may be confronted with a very small size of market which is inadequate to absorb production at an economically viable level which is mainly due to lack of purchasing power because of low level of saving among the people.

Among the demographic factors that hinder industrialisation is the fast rising population. First, a fast-rising population implies a sharp rise in the level of consumption in the economy. Given the fact that productivity in these economies is low, as well as it grows only at a very slow rate, a rising consumption level hardly leaves any surplus in the saving. Inadequate saving makes investment impossible. Secondly, as the population rises, the size of the labour force also increases. In the absence of alternative employment opportunities a large part of the increased labour force finds work for itself in already overcrowded agricultural sector which tends to affect adversely the productivity in this sector.

As regards to social factors, the social organisation and social attitudes in developing countries are such as to hinder the growth of industrial production. These act through influencing the supply of productive factors like labour, capital and entrepreneurial ability and also other factors like caste, kinship etc.

Various social customs and attitudes exercise a check on the mobility of labour which tends to get glued down to their hometowns, more generally in villages. The industrial labour tends to get back to land at any early opportunity. This flux of labour between industry and agriculture affects the stability of industrial labour.

The caste system in developing countries is such that people hesitate to take many types of jobs because of the monopoly of a particular caste. It restricts the mobility of labour leading to an inefficient and wasteful use of labour.

As regards the supply of capital, social factors reduce the accumulation of capital in developing countries. Conspicuous consumption and wasteful expenditure on luxuries accounts for a large current income. The propensity to consume is generally high. This restricts the level of saving and adversely affects capital accumulation and thus investment.

Entrepreneurial ability also suffers on account of social rigidities and attitudes. Due to these social evils it is very difficult to get people who can unite and cooperate undertakings and be loyal to society and government. The same factors also create personnel recruitment and industrial management.

Various administrative factors also adversely affect the productivity and output in the industrial sector in developing countries. Frequent changes in tax policy, inefficiency of administration generally leads to mismanagement and loss in public sector undertakings.

There is fluctuation in foreign exchange rates, in customs and excise, in trade controls and licensing policies etc., which create uncertainty in the mind of investors who may be reluctant to undertake new investment and improper and faulty labour legislation is another element of public administration which causes tension in these countries.

Industrialisation in these developing countries confront with many pressures and challenges posed by the developed, industrialised countries such as competition from the imported goods, imposition of custom barriers, high costs of imports of source raw materials, technical know how etc. High rate of taxes are to be borne by the people partly to meet the defects suffered in industrial sectors.

Growth of industrialisation in India can be summed up in the following phases. The first phase was the pre-independence phase of imported good; the second phase was a phase of import substitution. This has been a phase of wide-ranging quantitative capabilities with qualitative weaknesses. The country has now entered a third phase, the phase of upgradation of the quality of Indian goods and services before the county enters the fourth phase of major exports. In the present third phase the primary need is to upgrade the quality of products, so that they become exportable in the fourth phase.

For the improvement in industrial development, structural reforms are required which demand adjustment with new changes. The ongoing structural adjustment programme and the accompanying economic reforms aim at making Indian industry more competitive by encouraging foreign competition. This essentially implies that the industry must withstand competition from liberal imports and that too at reduced rates of tariffs. Industry must also achieve higher level of exports.

Accelerated industrial growth is possible with restructuring and overhauling. There is an overriding need to reduce capital-output ratio in the manufacturing sector. To achieve this, a major policy initiative is required to improve enterprise efficiency and reduce investment costs. The policies need to encourage modernisation, technology upgradation and production with calculation.

Various measures can be undertaken in order to improve industrial productivity. One of the factors responsible for high cost is low scales of production. It may become necessary to resort to merger or amalgamation to meet competition from outside and also to increase scales of production.

Input costs are high by international standards in India. Many of the basic inputs are produced in the public sector which are inefficiently managed and that too by bureaucrats. Public sector units must be managed professionally and commercial considerations must be the only guiding criteria. Development of entrepreneurial skills is a must for increase in productivity.

Industrial Relations

India's labour legislation is over-protective and management has no right to manage. This has hampered productivity of labour, quality of products and made Indian products costly despite low wages. To minimise cost, the management must possess the full authority to reorganise its human resources. The present system of wage payment discount productivity. In most countries where productivity is high wages are linked to productivity. The countries in which wages are linked to cost of living, the productivity has generally suffered, and industry lost its competitiveness.

With capital markets emerging as a major source of funding and the expanding role of mutual funds and foreign financial institutions, for Indian companies which wish to grow, significant institutional shareholding may be unavoidable. Therefore, instead of trying to reduce the institutional holding it is necessary to ensure that a healthy practice of committing support to managements so long as they perform well. Institutional holding will thus become a matter of anxiety only for entrepreneurs who cannot perform. The confidence needs to be built up by avoiding either purposeless or motivated destabilisation of management.

Managerial skills is important for successful industrial undertaking. Conducive environment, motivating factors such as reward system, harmonious relationship between the labourers and managers, flexibilities and democratic relationship between the two must exist in industrial units.

Economic reforms is an essential element for a society undergoing transformation. In the aftermath of India's independence till recently, India gave importance to both public and private sector which is called mixed economy. However soon after taking over as Prime Minister in 1985, late Mr. Rajiv Gandhi outlined the new trends in economic policy to the Government. The recipe suggested by him was improvement in productivity, absorption of modern technology; and fuller utilisation of capacity which must acquire the status of a national campaign. The basic thrust of the New Economic Policy was a greater role for the private sector.

To provide larger scope to the private sector a number of policy changes were introduced with regard to industrial licensing, export-import policy, technology upgradation, fiscal policy, foreign equity capital, removal of controls and restrictions, rationalising and simplifying the system of fiscal and administrative regulation. All these changes were directed towards creating an uninhibited climate of private sector so that private sector investment could get a big boost to modernise the economy and usher in rapid growth. Professor K.N. Raj rightly sums up the focus of new economic policy. "There has been however a general agreement that a very distinctive feature of these policy changes taken as a whole is the greater scope for unfettered expansion they offer to the private sector, particularly in the corporate segment of manufacturing industry and the opportunities opened up to multinational enterprises."

Consequently, the New Economic Policy focused its attention on dismantling the edifice of controls so as to remove unnecessary hurdles in securing licenses, in adjusting output to administered prices and in denying industrial licensing to MRTP companies.

Although economic reforms were introduced under late Rajiv Gandhi regime, they did not yield the desired result. After resumption of power by Congress in 1991, the Government adopted a number of stabilisation measures that were designed to restore internal and external confidence. Monetary policy was tightened further through increase in interest rates, the exchange rate of the rupee was adjusted by 22 per cent and major simplification and liberalisation of trade policy was announced. The Government adopted as the centrepiece of the economic strategy a programme to bring about reduction in fiscal imbalance to be supported by reforms in economic policy that were essential to impart a new element of dynamism to the growth process in the economy. The thrust was to increase the efficiency and international competitiveness of industrial production, to utilise foreign investment and technology to a much greater degree than in the past, to improve the performance and rationalise the scope of the public sector so that it can more efficiently serve the needs of the economy.

Economic Transformation

The Liberalisation : In India liberalisation began in the mid-seventies. In 1975, a scheme was introduced which provided for an increase in licensed capacity up to a maximum of 25 percent in a five-year period. Other measures included regularisation of capacities in excess of authorised capacities for certain industries, some liberalisation from controls for units which exported 100 percent of their production, and a more general scheme of re-endorsement of capacities introduced in 1982. The main emphasis during the seventies was on reducing the restrictive and complex features of the licensing policy.

However the system seemed to have acquired a momentum and only attempt to reduce its procedural rigours or to make peripheral improvements. The whole system was caught in a vicious cycle of scarcity, contrasts and low productivity. The government looked into the matter by setting up several committees to examine its fiscal, monetary, industrial and trade policies. The general outcome of their findings and recommendations can perhaps be simply expressed in two sets of interrelated propositions.

Economic growth depends on several factors such as :

(i) Increased imports, increased exports to pay for increased imports.

(ii) To increase exports it is necessary to enhance the competitive advantage of ex-portables.

(iii) The competitive advantage for ex-portables requires changes in industrial and trade and fiscal policies.

(iv) The Government budget should no longer be a source of finance for investment.

(v) Reducing defence expenditure should no longer be an option available to Government as usual.

(vi) Subsidies can be reduced only gradually to avoid major social and political upsets.

(vii) The only way to raise additional resources is to make the tax system more responsive and to make the public sector enterprises generate resources through greater efficiency.

Some domestic controls simply fail to achieve their stated objectives.

In view of these a number of policy initiatives have been taken since 1985 with a view to:

(i) Limiting the role of licensing, by raising the exemption limit, since June 1988, from Rs. 5 crore to Rs. 25 crore for those units that are set up in the non-backward areas and to Rs. 75 crore for those units that are set up in the backward areas.

(ii) Expanding the scope for contribution to growth by large houses.

(iii) Encouraging modernisation.

(iv) Raising the investment limits for the promotion of the small-scale sector.

(v) Providing fiscal incentives for the same, and

(vi) Encouraging existing industrial undertakings in certain industries to achieve economic levels of operations.

The process of liberalisation got a fillip with the announcement of the New Industrial Policy (NIP) in July 1991. The New Industrial Policy had the following major provisions.

(i) Industrial licensing will be abolished for all projects for a short list of industries related to security and strategic concerns, social reasons, hazardous chemicals and overriding environmental reasons and items of elitist consumption.

(ii) Existing units will be provided with a new broad banding facility to enable them to produce any article without additional investment.

(iii) The exemption from licensing will apply to all substantial expansions of existing units.

(iv) All existing registration schemes will be abolished.

(v) Entrepreneurs will henceforth only be required to file an information memorandum on new projects and substantial expansions.

(vi) The mandatory convertibility clause will no longer be applicable for term loans from the financial institution for new projects.

A significant development has been the introduction of a measure of stability to the policy framework via long-term fiscal policy and medium-term trade policy commitments. There has also been move away from extensive physical controls and an increase in the role of financial incentives in channelling investments in the desired areas. This, plus the lowering of the tax rates combined with better administration of the revenue collecting system, should help in attracting a lot of economic activity which had strayed away from the mainstream back into the fold. The role of financial institutions becomes very important in the new development.

The policy issues described above for improving industrial performance involve a considerable measure of deregulation and therefore may be called economic liberalisation. There is considerable internal deregulation aimed at strengthening the more efficient domestic firms and encouraging them to invest and expand. The internal liberalisation has been accompanied by a policy of maintaining a sufficiently open access to imports to permit modernisation and technological upgrading in Indian industry which again will reduce costs and promote international competition.

As for as trade liberalisation is concerned, a broad direction has been given about the desirability of switching from quantitative controls of tariffs, but the movement in this area is limited and certainly does not include imports of final consumer goods. However, significant tariff rationalisation measures have been implemented in several sectors.

The aim of economic policy changes is to evolve an integrated economic package that can be implemented to create an appropriate environment to facilitate higher productivity and faster industrial growth.

Accelerated growth of manufacturing accompanied by radical restructuring and induction of sunrise industries within a suitable modified policy frame would bring about a significant transformation of India's industrial economy. Apart from basic industries the major thrust in the liberalisation phase and the programme of accelerated industrialisation is towards mass consumption goods and export oriented industries.

Although it is too early to evaluate the impact of these policy changes, it can nevertheless be established that the industrial climate is in for changes. A recent study by the All India Management Association notes the following trends in the post-liberalisation phase: In the aftermath of economic liberalisation, the following trends were developed.

(i) Almost 32 percent of the respondent entities opted for doing away with their not so profitable businesses after July 1991, as against 6 per cent before July 1991.

(ii) More ambitious players have been consolidating themselves in the last three years by way of mergers and acquisitions in comparison to a mere 14 per cent before.

(iii) Economic reforms have influenced the industry into directing its efforts towards the world market.

(iv) The work culture has improved tremendously following systematic recruitment and professional training. The workers have become more quality and cost conscious as well.

(v) Reliance on automation when labour power is insufficient.

(vi) A high percentage of trade unions and the workers have responded positively in the economic reforms. Their open-minded approach towards adoption of new technologies and productivity linked wage agreements would go a long way in consolidating the future of Indian industry.

(vii) Liberalisation has altered the investment pattern of Indian entrepreneurs. Industrialists have realised the role of scale economies, rapid technological growth and increased productivity. Indian companies are now going in for world-size plants. This will enable them to meet the competitive challenge of forces imposed by globalisation and multinational corporations.

The number of manufactures in many sectors of industry has increased, shortages have given way to surpluses, competition is becoming a way of business life in which only the fittest will survive. Protection both against potential domestic competition and foreign competition was the right approach in the initial stage of industrialisation in a developing economy which was struggling to come over of the stronghold posed by two-centuries of old colonial domination.

The industrial landscape underwent a dramatic change within a period of about four decades. But the major failure of the policy of protection was that it did not have a built-in-mechanism that could prompt the industry to adapt itself to the fast changing technological scene to which a large part of the developing world was responding with zeal and enthusiasm. The industrial structure of India, under the burden of protection turned out to be high-cost and low-quality that lacked the basic ingredients of international competitiveness. The resultant external imbalances and fiscal deficits led to a reappraisal of the industrial policy culminating in recent policy changes.

Simultaneously it also suffers from various disadvantages. These are :

> Hundreds of small-scale units have closed down due to absence of market for their products. Growth in some significant sectors of the India industry (*e.g.* Chemical industry) has dipped down; the large players are putting their planned investments on hold. This is because there has been large-scale dumping of raw material feedstock from abroad at cheaper rates. Non-transparent export incentives like the Value Based license Scheme for promoting growth of exports back fired as people imported items that fetched a premium in India, more than they needed, and dumped them in the market. Liberalisaiton has altered the industrial structure in favour of goods in demand from the better-off sections of society. These sections have benefited from inflation, high interest rates on financial savings and the growth of high paid jobs with lavish perks. Pattern of investment continues to favour the use of sophisticated plants and equipment at the expenses of labour. Job growth is inadequate in both the urban and rural area. Industry's profitability has slumped and demand is sluggish for the capital goods. Even the large industrial houses have felt the impact of liberalisation.

PATTERN OF PRIVATISATION

Privatisation literally means the assignment of a business or service to private domains as distinct from state control or ownership. In a broader sense it implies the induction of private ownership in publicly owned enterprises. It connotes besides private ownership (or even without change of ownership) the induction of private management and control in the public sector enterprises. "Privatisation is the general process of involving the private sector in the ownership of operation of a state owned enterprise.

The above most appropriate definition of privatisation was presented by Barbara Lee and John Nell's.

Privatisation processes the following features :

(i) Total denationalisation of public enterprise to private sectors.

(ii) Partial introduction of private ownership ranging from 25 to 50 per cent or more depending upon the nature of the enterprise and state policy.

(iii) Management buy out *i.e.* the sale of assets to the employees. Loans from banks are provided to enable the individuals to take over ownership.

Public sector enterprises are to be restructured in order to regulate it under the market discipline.

(a) Financial restructuring can be effected in the sense that accumulated loses are written and capital composition is rationalised in respect of debt-equity ratio.

(b) Basic restructuring may be effected by redefining the set of commercial activities which the enterprise will undertake henceforth.

Operational measures are intended to improve efficiency of the organisation even when full denationalisation has not been undertaken. They infact inject the spirit of commercialisation in public enterprises. The measures include grant of economy to public enterprises in decision making. Provision of incentives to blue-collar as well as white-collar consistent with increase in efficiency or productivity, freedom to acquire certain inputs from the market by a system of "contracting" instead of producing them within the enterprise and development of proper investment criteria, etc. The basic purpose of these measures of operational privatisation is to bring about a drastic reform to reduce government control over the enterprise.

In India it was geared up only after Rajiv Gandhi took his prime ministerial office. A sudden shift in economic policy faced a lot of problem of management adjustment and restructuring of the different institutions within the economic domain.

In the presence of strong trade unions, privatisation in the sense of denationalisation is not considered possible. Statements regarding denationalisation of banks, insurance companies, power generation companies, coal mines, unvailable public sector units, postal services, were issued but they have aroused spontaneous and violent reactions from trade unions which are highly organised. Even the INTUC which is affiliated to the Congress-I has to fall in line with the CTTU, HMS, AITUC and BMC in opposing all moves against denationalisation. Consequently, the Government in order to assuage the feelings of the trade unions declared that it does not intend to denationalise any of the public sector undertakings.

One hurdle that one faces in implementing the aim of privatisation through the transfer of ownership of PSUs into private is that of finances. If it is outright sale, the amount involved will be very large indeed. Over and above this the money comes from the public financial institutions including banks (in the form of loans of the private sector). It will amount to the transfer of ownership from one public institution to another. The alternative to the outright sale is the sale of shares to the general public.

Another serious problem is that the private sector which is supposed to improve upon the performance of PSUs, may not come up to the mark. This apprehension arises from the fact that the private sector too has not performed satisfactorily in a large measure. Many units in the private sector are lying sick. There are many with large overdues. All these units are seeking, financial help from the public sector to bail them out. Efficiency in the private sector is not that high. Further, this sector, despite some modernisation in a few fields, is still technologically far behind. Same is with the cost-price and the quality of products.

The policy of privatisation is also faced with difficulties of a type which is not easy to overcome. One such difficulty could be associated with the behaviour of the employers/owners/ capitalists towards the labour. But in many private enterprises particularly many small sized ones, as also in the unorganised sector, there is gross exploitation of labour. The wages are low and there are no amenities and benefits for labour. The women and child-suffer the most.

THE UNIVERSALISATION

Since the dawn of civilisation, no nation state has been independent. Different nation states are thus interdependent on each other politically, economically and above all there has been cultural exchange between and among nations. Today it becomes so difficult for any nation to remain isolated, irrespective of their different political set ups, economic policies and cultural diversities. These nation states have become a global community.

The world market place and the entire global economic environment are today at one of the most profound points of change. This has been due to several dramatic developments that have taken place in the recent past. These include the formation of United Germany—a powerful economic and political entity—which came into being in October 1990, the collapse of the communist regimes in Eastern Europe and the opening of their markets, reorganisation of USSR and the formation of Commonwealth of former Soviet Republics, rise of Japan as a world technological leader, emergence of four tigers in East Asia namely Republic of Korea, Hong Kong, Singapore and Taiwan in addition to Thailand, Malaysia and Philippines as successful and leading exporters and the last but not the least is the efforts being made by China to modernise its economy and double its GNP by the year 2000.

The policy of globalisation in brief, means the followings. Export sector has to form an important ingredient of the national macro economic aggregates. When exports form an important economic aggregate, the industrial growth to a substantial extent becomes dependent upon the export sector.

When industrial production is attached to the export sector, indirectly the other sectors of the economy specially banking and services sector are also integrated with the export sector. Finally, since exports are themselves dependent on the GDP growth of the major trading partners, the growth of the domestic economy inextricably gets linked up with the global economies.

Therefore for globalisation to be successful it is necessary to have a strong, sound domestic economy which is uniformly spread all over the regions within a country which becomes a big challenge for the developing countries in which the domestic economy has been left naked through exploitation by the colonialists. Integration of the global economy as one unit is one important feature of globalisation.

The proponents of globalisation of developing countries have argues that such integration will improve the allocative efficiency of resources, reduce the capital output ratio and increase the labour productivity, help to develop the export spheres and the export culture, increase the inflow of the capital and updated technology into the country, increase the degree of competition in the domestic economy, reduce the relative prices of industrial and manufactured goods, improve the terms of trade in agriculture, and in general, give a boost to the average growth rate of the economy in the years to come. Globalisation will help to restructure the production and trade pattern in a capital-scarce labour abundant economy in favour of labour intensive goods and labour-intensive techniques. As a result, the over-all resource-productivity will go up.

The export trade will be geared more to the relatively labour-intensive products and processes. Foreign capital will be attracted to exploit the professional export opportunities along the above lines. With the entry of foreign capital, updated technology will also enter into the country. It is contended that the existence of relatively lower wages and the abundance of labour supply will imply larger profits. With the entry of foreign competition and the removal of import tariff barriers, domestic industry will be subject to price-reducing and quality-improving effects in the domestic economy.

Uneconomic import substitution will slowly disappear and cheaper import, particularly of capital goods, will reduce the capital-output ratio in manufacturing. Lower prices of manufactured goods will improve the terms of trade in favour of agriculture. With the entry of foreign capital the aggregate and net investment proportions to GDP will go up, and with a reduced capital output ratio the growth rate will go up. It is also believed that the main effect of integration will be felt in the industrial and related sectors; and cheaper and high quality consumer good will be manufactured at home. And as there is a large domestic market for these goods employment opportunities would expand and over a period of time, the trickle effect will operate and the proportion of people below the poverty line will go down. It is also believed that the efficiency of banking and financial sectors will increase with the opening up of these areas to foreign capital and foreign banks.

Many economic analysts and sociologists even have examined the impact of globalisation on developing countries in anticipation and many were for it as well as against it.

Those who stood for globalisation maintain the argument that these countries cannot remain in isolation and hence its economic domain is to be influenced by the world economy as well. When globalisation comes into the picture, it all depends on how widely we open our windows to let the foreign capital come in and to what extent we restrict such entry. These things much depends on the policies of the government. Their basic argument is thus that the developing countries cannot remain untouched by globalisation.

The globalisation offers both challenges a well as opportunities to the developing countries. Already, they have lost a lot of time in preparing for the global competitiveness. A higher level of world prices, continuiting devaluation of the currencies and increase in the quantum of their imports are further adding new complexities to their international marketing efforts.

The opportunities that are opening for global marketing are further dampened by rising protectionism, notwithstanding the successful conclusion of the Uruguay Round of GATE negotiations, discriminatory government procurement policies, offset requirements, force technology transfers, local content requirements and other mechanisms used and the growing trend towards bilateralism instead of multilateral trade agreements.

The current system of world trade and finance was constructed in the 1940s using one of the Bretton Woods institutions, the International Monetary Fund and the General

Agreement on Traffic and Trade (GATT). This liberal multilateral trading system spurred the growth of international trade and allowed both developed and developing countries to achieve rapid growth. However the global system is now at risk. The Uruguay Round is being touted as an opportunity for all to participate in what will be dynamic, open and rapidly evolving global economy. There is no safe middle way between heroic success and dismal failure.

The increasing trend towards globalisation of markets is one of the contributing factors for the formation of different regional trading blocs. The European Community (EC) aims at unifying Europe. EC is the largest single world trading bloc accounting for approximately 20 per cent of the world trade and consisting of 320 million consumers. The assurance has been given by EC that the single market will not result in a fortress.

Europe : The developing nations fear that their share of trade with EC will decline especially in the content of major changes that are taking place in East European countries with whom the EC would prefer to increase their share of trade in the coming years.

Another major challenge and the most disturbing one is the international debt problem. According to a recent study by OECD, the total debt of the developing countries remained roughly unchanged for the fourth successive year at the beginning of 1994 at $1365 billion. India's long term debt at the beginning of 1994 stood at $80.8 billion and the short-term debt was $9.2 billion of which 79 billion were owed to international banks.

Unless developing countries are given preferential treatment and they are helped to increase their export earnings the problem of external debt cannot be solved. The increasing debt burden of developing nations will in turn adversely affect the growth rate of developed nations.

Many developing countries have improved their export performance by reforming domestic economic policies. Countries like South Korea, Taiwan, Hong Kong and Singapore achieved faster growth in both exports and income because of their outward oriented development strategies. By entering the global market, they have been able to achieve economies of scale that their domestic markets would not have allowed.

Faced with a precarious foreign exchange situation, adverse balance of payments and huge external debt, the Government of India adopted a number of stabilisation measures beginning from June 1991 and initiated far-reaching trade, fiscal and industrial policy reform measures with a major thrust on improvement of competitive efficiency of Indian industries by utilising foreign investment and technology to a much greater degree than in the past. The new reform measures ended the regime of licensing and controls and made the industry virtually independent. Liberalisation of economic policy is intended to promote the integration of Indian economy with the global economy. This has brought before the Indian business and industry a tremendous challenge to compete aggressively in world markets and push up our exports.

Despite the fact that India has a large domestic market, a broad-based industrial infrastructure, a large pool of trained manpower, abundant supply of cheap labour and adequate natural resources, in terms of competitiveness, it is far behind several other Asian countries including Korea, Singapore, Taiwan, Malaysia, Hong Kong, Indonesia and Thailand. Its share in the world market is hardly 0.5 per cent.

Even though India has not been able to catch up with her counterparts. India, with every effort should not miss the opportunity to utilise any opportunity offered by globalisation.

India has the skills and investments which make it the lowest cost producer in the world. These investment can easily obtain a share of the world market.

It is of crucial importance for Indian corporation to go into world markets and to become India's multinationals abroad with markets and later, production centres spread across the globe. Here again India has national advantage in certain sector such as the knowledge-led services sector and wide range of agricultural, industrial and fashion products. This can be done by creating India's own Soggoshoshas, who can operate as the marketing arm of India.

To attract foreign investors to make India their home for their world markets we must recognise that Latin America, Eastern Europe, the former Soviet Union and China are also making a determined effort to attract foreign investment. We

5

Role of Social Welfare

Social welfare aims at the well-being and improvement of the life of individuals in general, and alleviating the sufferings and ameliorating the lot of the destitute, deprived disadvantaged and underprivileged sections of society in particular. In other words Social Welfare comprises income maintenance and support programmes together with the wide range of social services that have been developed to meet human needs and respond to social problems. Though social welfare has come to acquire an identity of its own, it has to be considered in relation to social development, a term in wide use internationally. In the international context, social development is linked with economic development, the latter dealing with the technological and material aspects of growth, and the former with the human aspects. In this context social development includes the services of health and nutrition, education and training, social protection and shelter needed to improve the human condition.

Social and welfare services of a country are the product of its social policies which reflect the social goals and objectives it aspires to achieve. Social work aims at enhancing, restoring or modifying the psycho-social functioning of individuals, families, groups and communities. Thus social welfare encompasses social services, social legislation, social work, social security and its two approaches—social insurance and social assistance.

To achieve the aims and objectives of social welfare, the Government formulates social policies, and in pursuance thereof enacts social legislation, delineates various projects, schemes and programmes, makes financial allocations and provides organisational structure and administrative apparatus in the form of ministries, departments, corporations, agencies and solicits the support and cooperation of non-government organisations (voluntary agencies) for the implementation of various programmes. The administration of all the activities undertaken in the sphere of social services, social work, social legislation, etc. would be considered to belong to the realm of social welfare administration.

The discipline of social and welfare services as an area of systematic study is comparatively new. Its main concern is to diagnose the social problems, identify social inequities and social injustice and to resolve and redress them. In this task it has to depend upon the knowledge derived from other disciplines such as sociology, psychology, philosophy, political science, economics and other social sciences. K.M. Slack is of the view that social administration is not one more social science with its own theory and body of knowledge. It makes use of the findings of any of the social sciences which are relevant to its sphere, which includes the solving of social problems, the implementation of social policy and the promotion of social welfare.

But its distinctive character is that it combines and benefits from any of the conclusions of the social sciences which assist it and uses them as tools in the performance of the functions which are its particular concern. Social problems which constitute the core of this discipline are constantly changing and assuming different concepts and complexions in various societies and so are the respective societies' perception and response to them, this discipline, therefore, cannot be static and has to be dynamic. Consequently it is not easy to define it.

Shri T.N. Chaturvedi gives it the shortest definition of two words only when he designates it as "problem centred" discipline and "as an approach to solve social problems", V.M. Kulkarni describes it as the "administration of social welfare programmes" and states that the administration of social services and social welfare programmes should fall in the sub-area of social administration.

Narrowly defined, social administration, is the study of development, structure and practices of the social services, encompassing every activity of transforming social policy into social service. Forder holds the view that social administration is concerned with the study of welfare system and particularly the government sponsored social services. According to Professor Titmus, social administration may be defined as the study of social services whose object is the improvement of the conditions of life of the individual in the setting of family and group relations. It is concerned with the development of these services, both statutory and voluntary, the moral values implicit in social action, the roles and functions of the services, their economic aspects and the part they play in meeting certain needs in the social process—all these are important and need to be explored in social service administration.

Kidneigh also defines social welfare administration as 'the process of transforming social policy into social services—a two-way process : transforming policy into concrete social services, and the use of experience in recommending modification of policy. This definition, of course, encompasses the idea that administration is the process of implementation of translating policies into action programmes.

According to Dunhan, "Administration is the process of supporting or facilitating activities which are necessary and incidental to the giving of direct service by a social agency. Administrative activities range from the determination of function and policies, and executive leadership to routine operations such as keeping records and accounts and carrying on maintenance services."

Arthur Kruse states that the administrative process seeks to mobilise the total resources of the agency to the end that its purposes are translated into efficient and effective service.

A comprehensive definition of Social Welfare Administration, however, is given in the curriculum study of the American Council of Social Work Education in the following words :

> "Administration is the process of transforming community resources into a programme of community service, in accordance with goals, policies and standards which have been agreed by those involved in the enterprise. It is creative in that it structures roles and relationships in such a way as to alter and enhance the total product. It involves the problem-solving process of study, diagnosis and treatment solution, or action and evaluation of results".

As discussed earlier the argument given against social welfare administration claiming to be a distinct discipline centres round the fact that it has to draw heavily on other social services. But this argument is not valid as all subjects these days are essentially interdisciplinary because of the very nature of society and man and social administration cannot therefore be an exception to this general rule. All social sciences are 'hybrid' disciplines and newer the discipline, greater would be its mixed origin. As a matter of fact, various disciplines through the findings in their respective fields add new vistas to social administration as a new discipline and lend vitality and realism to this evolving discipline.

That social welfare administration is a new discipline is further substantiated by the fact that it was only in 1946 that the American National Conference on Social Work sponsored a section on administration for the first time in its twenty-two years and included for its consideration such subjects as process of administration, dynamics of leadership, job satisfaction, public relations, civil service, programme development, etc. Earlier in 1914, a course of social welfare administration was established in some of the Schools of Social Work and the interest in administrative process had begun to grow in the wake of World War, the Great Depression and World War II due to the numerous problems and tensions created by them, it had come to be realised that administrative process is the very heart of social work education and process. Consequently some graduate schools of social work were designated as Schools of Social Service Administration, at the University of Chicago and Arizna State University.

In Britain which is rightly credited to be the model welfare state, fullfledged faculties of Social Administration in the various universities have been existing since early twentieth century. Social welfare administration has been a conspicuous constituent of the curriculum of graduate and post-graduate courses of Social Work in University Departments and colleges in India. Tata Institute of Social Sciences, Bombay, the pioneer institute imparting instruction in social work set up in 1936 has recently introduced graduate courses in social welfare administration exclusively.

Departments of Social Work in Universities and colleges which have since multiplied, of late, have also embarked upon diploma and degree courses in this discipline in view of specialised knowledge and techniques required for its practitioners and the avenues and potentialities for employment it offers in various fields of social welfare in the government departments and in the activities undertaken by voluntary organisations. Similarly most of the developed and developing countries are seized of the significance of social administration as a discipline with its own identity and provide for its education in their post-graduate educational institutions for theoretical knowledge and professional training in its various fields.

The discipline of social welfare has received due recognition at the regional, international and global levels also. The United Nations emphasises on the best possible use of human resources, and to this end, gives special attention to the problems of rising population and increasing shift of families from country- side to cities with an accompanying need for housing, urban facilities and social services. It offers aid in community development, in improving living conditions both in rural and urban areas, in land reform programmes and in efforts to deal more effectively with youth problems, delinquency and crime.

The United Nations through its various specialised agencies like WHO, UNESCO and UNICEF and regional commissions such as the Economic and Social Commission for Asia and Pacific (ESCAP) conducts studies on social welfare administration, social welfare planning, policy trends concerning youth, the handicapped and the aging with the assistance of consultants from all over the world and undertakes research on world social situation and training of social welfare personnel not only at its headquarters at the Centre for Social Development and Humanitarian Affairs and the Department of Technical Cooperation for Development but also at the United Nations Institute for Social Development (Geneva) and institutions such as Social Welfare and Development Centre for Asia and Pacific (Manila), the Asia and Pacific Development Centre (Kualalampur) and European Centre for Social Welfare Training and Research (Vienna).

The United Nations Secretariat disseminates information

on specific topics relating to social welfare administration and findings of researchers to the member nations thus helping in the evolution of the discipline of social welfare administration both in theoretical and practical areas.

The Extent

It is evident from the definitions of the discipline of social welfare administration attempted above that its scope is very wide, and the areas constituting the subject matter of its study are increasing every day due to the emergence of new social problems in the dynamic society such as population explosion, relief and rehabilitation of migrants on account of militants' activities, gas leak accidents, dowry deaths and drug addiction etc. and the consequent increasing responsibilities of the governmental and voluntary agencies in finding solutions for them.

The contents of social welfare administration are of variegated nature and its tasks are numerous. It is primarily concerned with

(i) social problems—the diagnosis of their causes and their treatment through social reform and social legislation; detection of the reasons for the ineffectiveness of laws enacted for combating social evils and vices and suggesting measures to make them effective mainly through the creation of public consciousness and opinion in regard to the social problems ;

(ii) Social Services aiming at the well being of the general public through the provision of health, education, housing, etc. and the upliftment of the disadvantaged and underprivileged and vulnerable sections of society such as women and children, the old and the infirm, the disabled and the handicapped ;

(iii) Social Security to compensate for the loss of income due to unemployment, disability, or death caused by accident and old age through social insurance and social assistance ;

(iv) Social work helping people to solve their personal, family and community problems through enhancing social functioning by methods of case work, group work and community organisation and enabling processes of research and administration ;

(v) Social policy delineating the aims and objectives, and the goals to be achieved for the welfare of the clientele concerned through social action.

Social Welfare Discipline : administration being of interdisciplinary nature has to include in its scope the knowledge of other social sciences as well especially of philosophy, psychology, sociology, political science and economics in order to understand society and man in their totality and to make use of the knowledge gained through these sciences to help solve problems of individuals, families and groups.

The Organisational and Administrative Structure : of social services and social welfare programmes at various levels of government at Federal (central), State and local levels.

Voluntary Agencies Role : (non-government organisations) in supplementing the efforts of governmental agencies in providing social services and social welfare services on their own or on being sponsored by the government to implement its schemes through grants-in-aid, and to study their organisation and effectiveness in carrying out their functions.

Role of International Social Welfare Agencies : United Nations Economic and Social Council, Regional Commissions, and its specialised agencies like ILO, WHO, UNESCO, UNICEF, etc. and International non-governmental agencies like the Red Cross, OXFAM, CARE, Regional Associations like SAARC and individual government organisations such as United States Agency for International Development (USAID),

Norwegian Agency for International Development (NORAD); Overseas Development Agency (ODA) etc. all interested in the promotion of social welfare in developing countries by providing financial and technical assistance for their various welfare programmes.

Administer Financial Matter : includes all the processes involved in collecting, budgeting, appropriating and expending public moneys ; accounting and auditing. A welfare state has to undertake numerous activities for the welfare of its people for which it has to spend large amounts of money. Financial management is to ensure that public funds are properly utilised and there is no wastage. This is all the more essential in the course of social welfare administration which has limited financial resources to cater to its multiplying responsibilities and functions of welfare.

Personnel Management : involves recruitment policies, job specification, job classification, caderisation, training programmes, career development, security of service, fixing professional standards, retirement plans, right to form associations and unions to bargain collectively with the management, staff evaluation etc.

Relations with General People : for dissemination of information among the people through press, radio and television about the social services and social welfare programmes being carried on by the government and voluntary agencies and to project their favourable image, and to get a feedback of the reactions and responses of the public and beneficiaries to enable necessary modifications in the welfare policies and programmes to serve the clientele in better ways.

Participation of People : the involvement of people and their representatives is essential for the success of any welfare programme. The confidence and trust of the people have to be won over by associating them with the planning and implementation of policies and programmes intended for their welfare.

Administrative Tasks : Functional aspects of administration as reflected in Luther Gulick's terminology "POSDCORB" representing the activities of Planning, Organisation, Staffing, Directing, Coordination, Reporting and Budgeting.

Research and Evaluation : Research and evaluation studies provide useful information on different dimensions of social problems to facilitate effective planning, policy formulation and implementation of programmes. Effective social welfare work demands a good knowledge of the structure, life, work and values of the local communities. This knowledge has to be precise in context and needs to be based on proper scientific analysis and interpretation if it is to be applied to teaching or to helping social workers in their social work with local communities. This knowledge cannot be gathered without well-conducted social research. Realising the need of social re search, Ministry of Welfare sponsors schemes for research and provides financial assistance to universities, organisations, and social sciences research institutes for conducting action oriented research relating to development of scheduled Castes. It has also set up thirteen Tribal Research Institutes in different parts of the country.

These institutes substantially contribute to development efforts and provide professional input in the preparation of Tribal Sub-plan document. The Ministry gives priority to research projects of applied nature keeping in view the plan, policies and emerging social problems requiring urgent public attention such as destitution, child labour, drug abuse, needs of the aged etc. A standing Research Advisory Committee approves the research projects for sponsoring.

The Third Five Year Plan made particular reference to the need for evaluation of welfare services in these words, "inevitably, extension in a field of activity as varied and dispersed as social welfare brings its own problems and these cell for systematic review from time to time of what has been achieved and of the measures needed to improve the quality of welfare services". Evaluation is also essential to identify the problems such as "benefits not going to the target groups, operating costs being much higher than anticipated, interest in the schemes beginning to decrease, unexpected sociological consequences, and so on" and to suggest remedial measures for them. Among other things Evaluation should not be a mere post-mortem of the past but should be forward looking to enable the government to use the findings for understanding the future course and prospect of achievement. Evaluation of Social Welfare programmes has accordingly been carried on as a regular exercise.

Programme Evaluation Organisation (PEO) set up in 1952 under the auspices of the Planning Commission is the principal national organisation charged with the responsibility of evaluating development programmes. Ministries at the Centre as well as in the states have their own evaluation cells or monitoring units for review of progress of various programmes. But social welfare programmes constitute a very small fraction of their study and research.

The Department of Social Welfare of Government of India had initiated in 1973 the scheme of grants to universities and research institutes for undertaking research and investigation into different areas of social welfare. Indian Council of Social Science Research, University Grants Commission and professional bodies also sponsor research and evaluation studies on social welfare programmes. Schools of Social Work, Departments of Economics, Sociology and Public Administration offer topics relating to social welfare for M. Phil and doctoral candidates.

Ministry of Welfare, provides financial assistance to universities, organisations and Social Sciences Research Institutes for conducting action oriented research and evaluative studies relating to development of scheduled castes/tribes, and in the fields of social welfare, social policy and social development to facilitate planning, policy formulation and programme implementation. During 1987-88, the Ministry sanctioned Rs.15 lakhs to 36 organisations for studies relating to scheduled castes, Rs. 65 lakhs to 12 tribal Research Institutes, Rs. 60 lakhs to 20 doctoral and 2 post-doctoral fellowships for research relating to scheduled tribes and Rs. 10 lakhs for Research on 11 continuing projects and 5 new projects. Similarly, the Department of Women and Child Development, Ministry of Human Resource Development, Government of India had sanctioned Rs. 15 lakhs for 6 children and 8 women research projects for 1988-89.

Social Welfare Administrative Principles : The term 'administration' in social welfare is used in several different meanings. It is sometimes used so broadly as to be virtually synonymous with operation as in the administration of social welfare, in other cases it is restricted to the 'executive function or management'.

But actually it should be used broadly in the sense of supporting or facilitating activities which are necessary and incidental to the giving of direct service by a social agency. The administrative activities of a social welfare organisation would thus range all the way from the determination of function and policies, over all planning, executive leadership and professional supervision to routine operations such as dictating letters, keeping records and accounts, and carrying on 'house-keeping' and maintenance services.

Social Welfare administration as a matter of fact is the art and science of those governmental and non-governmental activities which are directed towards the relief of distress, the care of dependent and neglected children, the treatment of criminals and delinquents, and the care and treatment of the mentally ill. It is social welfare organisation in operation.

Administration might also be thought as the life processes of the social welfare structure. It is the application of knowledge and skill of case work, law, medicine, management, public relations, and statistics—to the solution or mitigation of social problems of individuals and groups. Once legislation is adopted providing social welfare services and directing the appropriate authorities to set up an organisation, administration has its beginning. In other words administration comes in after the services have been organised. It may be good administration or poor administration ; that depends upon the knowledge, the ability and the sincerity of purpose of those responsible for taking the first steps towards organisation of social welfare agency. Matters of major importance in administration are :

(i) Personnel-selection, classification and management;
(ii) Management of funds ;
(iii) Communication
(iv) records;
(v) Public relations;
(vi) Professional services ; and
(vii) planning. These constitute the contents and scope of administration of social welfare services.

Social welfare administration suffers from the lack of any authoritative or officially established set of administrative yardsticks for all social agencies. Nevertheless following principles are generally recognised as being in accordance with social welfare practice and experience and are observed by well administered social agencies :

(i) The objectives and functions of a social welfare agency should be clearly defined.
(ii) Its programme should be based upon actual needs ; it should be limited in scope and territory to a field in which it can operate effectively ; it should be related to social welfare needs, patterns and resources of the community ; it should be regarded as dynamic rather

than static and the programme should change to meet changing needs.

(iii) The agency should be soundly organised ; it should have a clear cut distinction between policy making and execution ; unity of command, that is, administrative direction by a single executive, logical allocation of functions in accordance with a general plan of administration; clear and definite assignment of authority and responsibility ; and effective coordination of all organisation units and staff members.

(iv) The agency should operate on the basis of sound personnel policies and good working conditions. Personnel should be employed on the basis of qualifications for their jobs ; paid adequate salaries and they should be adequate in quantity and quality of the needs of the agency.

(v) The work of the agency should be characterised by a basic desire to serve human beings ; an understanding of the individuals whom it seeks to serve, and of their needs ; and a spirit of freedom, unity and democratic.

(vi) All those who are connected with the agency in any capacity should develop attitudes and methods of work which will build sound public relations.

(vii) The agency should operate on the basis of an annual budget; it should have an adequate accounting system and its accounts should be audited annually by a competent disinterested professional authority.

(viii) It should maintain its records in an accurate and comprehensive but simple manner to be easily accessible when needed.

(ix) Its clerical and maintenance services and facilities should also be adequate in quantity and quality and efficient in operation.

(x) The agency should put itself to the test of a

self- appraisal at appropriate intervals to take stock of its successes and failures in the past year, its present status and programmes, its performance as measured by objectives and established criteria, its strength and weaknesses, its current problems and the next steps it ought to take to achieve better performance in the service of its clientele.

Tasks of Social Welfare Administration: In addition to the elementary principles of social welfare administration as mentioned above, the functional aspects or tasks of administration as contained in the concept of POSTCORB are also considered to be the basic postulates of the discipline of social welfare administration. These are discussed as follows:

(i) *Proper Planning :* is the formulation of intended future action. It involves the appraisal of current conditions, identification of the problems and needs of the society, determination of objectives and goals to be achieved on short-term or long term basis, and the delineation of programmes to be implemented to reach the desired ends.

Ever since the establishment of Planning Commission in India and the introduction of planning process in 1951 social welfare policies, programmes and the administration machinery to implement them though had not been given initially the consideration they merited but they have been given the place they deserved subsequently in the various Five Year Plans documents. During the last four decades of planned development, social welfare as a plan component has acquired significance as is reflected in the plans.

The First Plan, for example called upon the state to play an increasing role in providing services for the welfare of the people. The Second Plan drew attention to the factors responsible for the slow delivery of social welfare services to the vulnerable groups of society. The Third Plan stressed on women and child welfare, social defence, welfare of the handicapped and grants-in-aid to voluntary organisations. The Fourth Plan laid emphasis on the needs of destitute children. The Fifth Plan aimed at a proper integration of welfare and development services.

The Sixth Plan accorded high priority to the children welfare within the overall frame of social welfare. The Seventh Plan designed the social welfare programmes essentially to supplement the efforts directed towards human resource development. The Eighth Plan when finalised is expected to include the extension of the existing welfare programmes and inclusion of new programmes.

(ii) *Organisational Arrangements:* is essentially the conscious integration of human effort for a definite purpose. It is the systemic bringing together of interdependent parts to form a unified whole through which authority, coordination and control may be exercised to achieve a given purpose. In the past social welfare was more or less a sporadic and adhoc relief activity which could be administered without elaborate organisational structures. Whatever action was to be initiated could be managed through simple, ad hoc, informal mechanism operating at the level of the community or the clientele. Another factor which contributed to the non-formal, unorganised nature of social welfare was its reliance on non-governmental and voluntary action. Unlike governmental operations which assumed massive bureaucratic proportions demanding equally elaborate organisational structure, non-governmental action remained the mainstay of social welfare and which by its very nature tended to be less reliant on highly formal organised mechanism. But with the expansion of social welfare programmes, the number of persons affected and the amount of money spent, the best organisation has become indispensable.

Organisation can be formal and informal. A formal organisation implies a planned system of cooperative effort in which each participant has a recognised role to play and duties and tasks to perform. But informal relationship among the persons engaged in social welfare is equally important to develop feelings of good will and mutual trust among themselves to ensure the best possible implementation of social welfare programmes.

An organisation insists upon certain principles for its effective functioning. It divides work among its members ; it establishes standard practices by working out detailed procedures ; it provides a communication system. It has a hierarchical or scalar process with lines of authority and responsibility running up and downwards through several levels with a broad base at the bottom and a single head at the top ; it provides for unity of command which means that no individual employee should be subject to the orders of more than one immediate superior to avoid confusion and blurring of responsibility and it should recognise the distinction between line and staff as a working principle.

A sound organisation for social welfare manifests itself in the organisation of Ministry of Welfare with a Minister as its political head and a secretary as its administrative chief, with various Divisions for administration of different schemes, subordinate organisations like the National Institute of Social Defence and the Four National Institutes for the Handicapped, and National Commission for Scheduled Castes and Scheduled Tribes and the Minorities Commission, at the Central level; organisation of Social Welfare Departments in the states and union territories, corporations for welfare of different groups of society such as women, children, scheduled castes/tribes, ex- servicemen both at the central and state levels ; and organisation of voluntary agencies such as Indian Council of Child Welfare etc. The Ministry of Welfare grants organisational assistance to voluntary organisations primarily and predominantly engaged in the field of welfare activities and whose scale of operation warrants a central office for coordination of its various activities. The organisation of welfare services at the local level, however, continues to be weak in comparison to their counterparts in foreign countries.

(iii) *Regulating Staffs* : Assuming that a good organisation exists, the quality and efficiency of administration are conditioned by the suitability of personnel correctly placed in the organisation. Even poorly devised machinery may be made to work if it is manned with well trained, intelligent, imaginative and devoted staff. On the other hand, the best planned organisation may produce unsatisfactory results if it is operated by mediocre or disgruntled people. Staff thus constitutes an integral part of the social welfare organisation, both governmental and non- governmental. Their problems of recruitment, selection and certification for appointment, classification, training, determination of pay scales and other conditions of service, motivation and morale, promotion, conduct and discipline, superannuation, their right to form associations and trade unions need to be taken proper care so that they devote themselves heart and soul in their respective assignments and build the image of the organisation they serve.

(iv) *Direction:* implies the issuing of necessary guidelines and instructions for the implementation of the programmes of an organisation, and the removal of any difficulties which may arise in their execution. The directions relating to the execution of a programme also prescribe the rules of procedure to ensure efficient and smooth working of the organisation for the achievement of its appointed purpose. Rules of procedure also determine steps to be taken in the processing of a request or an enquiry in regard to a particular activity of an agency. In social welfare administration, directions are indispensable as these provide guidelines to the officials in the delivery of welfare services to the beneficiaries and also enlighten the latter about the procedure to be followed for applying for a specific kind of benefit they are eligible for. But a rigid adherence to the procedure and 'red-tapism' flowing there from causes unnecessary harassment and results in prolonged delays in granting the deserved benefits to the needy people. The tendency on the part of social welfare administration personnel to avoid taking any decision on their own responsibility and 'passing on the buck' is a malady of welfare administration hampering effective service to individuals and communities and needs to be guarded against.

(v) *Coordination Work:* Every organisation is characterised by divisions of work and specialisation. Its employees are assigned their respective duties and they are not supposed to interfere in the work of their colleagues. Thus in every organisation an effort is made to avoid overlapping and duplication of functions and to achieve maximum team work among the various personnel of the organisation in order to achieve its objectives. This arrangement of ensuring cooperation and team work among the employees is termed as coordination. Its purpose is to achieve harmony, unity of action and avoidance of conflict. In view of its importance, Mooney and Reiley consider coordination as the first principle of organisation because it expresses the principles of organisation in toto, and all other principles of organisation are subordinate to it. According to Charlesworth, "Coordination is the integration of several parts into an orderly whole to achieve the purpose of the undertaking". Newman describes coordination 'as the orderly synchronisation of efforts to provide the proper amount, timing and direction of execution resulting in harmonious and unified actions to a stated objective'.

Coordination is of crucial significance in social welfare as numerous ministries, departments and agencies are engaged in the delivery of social welfare programmes which suffer from the maladies of overlapping and duplication resulting in the wastage of resources and human effort. There are at present half a dozen ministries engaged in welfare services at the centre and the pattern of welfare administration is marked by the dispersal of subjects, a multiplicity of grants giving bodies, delays in communication and indifference to concerted action. Similarly at the state level as many as seven to seventeen departments in different states are dealing with welfare matters and programmes of welfare services suffer from a lack of unity in approach, uniformity in organisation and harmony in operation. The voluntary organisations are also engaged in identical services and the problems of coordination among them as also with the government departments is getting more complicated with the emergence of their ever increasing number, motivated by the liberal scheme of grants-in-aid.

Coordination among various ministries and departments and voluntary organisations concerned with social welfare can be achieved through inter-departmental and intra-departmental conferences to which non-officials representing various interests may also be involved for consultation. Ministry of Welfare, accordingly, holds annual conferences of Ministers of Social Welfare of State governments and union territories administrations and those of secretaries to discuss the various issues and programmes of social welfare to avoid duplication and ensure their effective implementation.

Coordination may also be secured through institutional or organisational devices such as inter-departmental committees and coordination officers, standardisation of procedures and methods, decentralisation of activities etc. The Central Social Welfare Board established in 1953 consisting of officials and non-official social workers was designed to provide a mechanism of proper coordination between the voluntary organisations and the government organisations engaged in social welfare programmes. The state Social Welfare Advisory Boards were also assigned, interalia, the function of coordinating welfare and developmental activities of the state government and the Central Social Welfare Board to avoid duplication. But despite these institutional arrangements to achieve coordination, the welfare programmes continue to suffer from overlapping and duplication both in the government and voluntary organisations jurisdictions. A clear cut demarcation of the spheres of activities of both governmental and voluntary agencies, a policy on the integrated development of welfare services and above all a stimulating leadership would go a long way in ensuring proper coordination for the maximum achievement of welfare objectives.

(vi) *Reporting* : means keeping both the superiors and subordinates informed of what is going on and arranging for the collection of such information through inspection, research and records. Every social welfare programme has certain targets and objectives to achieve. In a hierarchical system of organisation, the Chief Executive informs the persons at the lower levels about the policy, financial outlays and the timeframe for achieving the fixed objectives. The subordinates report to the higher authorities periodically monthly, quarterly or yearly, the progress achieved vis-a-vis the targets, the amount spent, and the problems confronted if any and seek their guidance in combating the problems. Reports are also made in regard to the discussions and conferences held within the agency and on inter- agency basis from time to time to sort out various issues. The higher authorities inspect periodically the subordinate offices to apprise themselves of their functioning and to detect irregularities committed if any and to suggest steps to avoid their recurrences. Sometimes enquiries have to be conducted in the working of social welfare agencies on receipt of complaints and findings reported to authorities concerned for necessary action. Research is also carried on by some welfare organisations and its conclusions and suggestions are reported for modifications in policies and programmes or for use in the formulation of new programmes. All social welfare agencies, without any exception, submit their annual reports to the Ministry/Department concerned and the latter to the Head of the State for information of the legislature. The public gets informed about the activities of the welfare agencies through all these different types of reports. Reporting thus constitutes an important ingredient of any social welfare organisation.

(vii) *Funding* : Budgeting denotes the process by which the financial policy of a public agency is formulated, enacted and carried out. In the days of laissez-faire, Budget was a simple statement of estimated income and expenditure. But in a modern welfare state, the activities of the government are fast extending and they tend to cover almost all aspects of social life. Government is now an agency for promoting general welfare of the citizens by positive acts. Budgeting is, therefore, now conceived as one of the major processes by which the use of public resources is planned and controlled. Budget making is a prominent component of financial management and is followed by the formal act of appropriations, executive supervision of expenditure, the control of the accounting and reporting system, treasury management and audit.

Budgets of the central government reflect the provisions

made for the Ministry of Welfare and Department of Women and Child Development in the Ministry of Human Resource Development and other Ministries like Ministry of Health and Family Welfare, Ministry of Home Affairs etc. in regard to the social welfare programmes to be undertaken by them and the grants-in-aid to be made available to the voluntary organisations through the Central Social Welfare Board. Similarly the state governments in their respective budgets provide for financial allocation for their departments of social welfare, in addition, United Nations and its specialised agencies like UNESCO, WHO, etc., and International Non-governmental Organisations also provide financial assistance for various welfare programmes.

Voluntary agencies arrange their finances through government grants, donations, subscriptions and foreign aid. Government of India, state governments and Union Territory administrations in their concern for social welfare have been progressively increasing financial allocations for welfare programmes in the successive five year plans but they are too inadequate to meet the evergrowing needs of the increasing number of people deserving welfare services and benefits. As a matter of fact, they touch only a tip of the iceberg. There is thus the need for tapping additional sources of mobilisation of finances for augmenting the revenues for welfare programmes. Voluntary organisations suffer from a chronic shortage of funds. They need to explore various sources to collect funds commensurate with their needs of providing welfare services in different areas.

Financial management also includes the mechanism and methods to ensure that the funds provided for welfare programmes are used faithfully, economically and intelligently; proper accounts are maintained and audit is conducted to ensure that there have been no misappropriation, misuse or embezzlement of funds, it has been observed that a major portion of appropriation is pocketed by middle men and very little of them reaches the beneficiaries for whom these are primarily intended. Misappropriations and corruption were also reported in the case of voluntary organisations. Fiscal administration, therefore, needs to be streamlined to ensure that the funds earmarked for various programmes are properly and honestly utilised.

As an Occupation

In early times, social welfare functions were performed by a few individuals or groups of individuals motivated by compassion and concern for the poor, the needy and the destitute. They were lay men, embodiment of the qualities of humanism and selfless service to the community. But in modern times the concept of welfare state has made the governments ail over the world conscious of their obligation to provide maximum social welfare services to their people with a view to provide remedies to social problems and to secure social justice. It is no longer accepted that any normally intelligent person with good intentions can do welfare work. Social Welfare departments and voluntary organisations now require properly qualified and trained social welfare personnel to perform social welfare functions of various types in different fields, from the field to the highest echelon of administration. It is argued that for serving the people efficiently and effectively it is necessary to professionalise ; once professionalisation can increase the ability of social welfare personnel to solve the pressing social problems confronting our society.

Definitions : A profession has been defined in several ways. According to Carr-Saunders and Wilson, "A profession is defined as the possession of an intellectual technique acquired by special training, which can be applied to some sphere of everyday life" Talcoot Parsons considers a profession as performance of certain functions valued in society in general and earning a living as a full time job by these activities. Howard Galdstein held that the final measure of a profession's identity lay in the explicit character of what it does in the fulfilment of a social need.

Main Features

A profession is generally characterised by the following distinguishing marks and criteria :

(i) A profession is expected to be responsive to public interest and contribute through its services to the advancement of social well-being and to be accountable to the public for the manner and standards with which it conducts its activities.

(ii) It should possess a relatively coherent, systematic and transmissible body of knowledge rooted in scientific theories which enables the practitioners of the profession to utilise concepts and principles and to apply them to specified situations.

(iii) The professional practitioner must adhere to an identificable body of values and display attitudes which stem from these values and which determine the relationship of the professional person with his colleagues, the recipients of his advice and the community.

(iv) A profession must have a body of skills which reflect the application of general concepts and principles to attain the goals of the profession.

(v) The members of the profession must be organised and consider themselves as members of a group where knowledge, skills, attitudes and norms of conduct they share and to whose achievement they are dedicated. According to Greenwood, distinguishing attributes of a profession are systematic theory (body of knowledge), authority (building confidence in trie clients), community sanction and approval and respect by the society ; ethical codes and professional culture (focus on certain values and norms), dedication and interest in mankind and society.

Judged by the criteria of a profession mentioned above, Abraham Flexner (1915) was not inclined to grant social welfare the status of a fullfledged profession. He felt that it was not founded on a body of scientific knowledge. Though it has considerably developed as a profession since then, yet it is granted at the most the status of a "semi-profession" as it has inter alia, underdeveloped theoretical knowledge ; it has within itself conflicts over concepts, objectives and techniques, it has not been fully able to convince the community that those who possess the professional skill deliver a superior service than those who do not, and that it does not enjoy an image and prestige comparable to other established professions like medicine or law.

On the other hand, it is asserted that social work is a profession, as it has come to acquire a systematic body of knowledge to serve as its foundation ; a social worker is respected by clients who come for help and also by the society as is evident from their employment in large numbers both by the public and private agencies ; provisions made for their training ; the adoption of code of ethics, and the existence of professional organisations to reflect professional culture as exhibited in the values and norms of social work and the stress it lays on social work as a career and on the necessity of dedication and interest in mankind and society as personal requisites for the individual who plans to go into this field.

This view is supported by Brown who asserts that social welfare/social work fulfills all the requirements of a profession. Greenwood also was of the opinion that social work is already a profession, it has many points of congruence with the model to be classifiable otherwise. Social work is however, seeking to rise within the professional hierarchy, so that it too might enjoy maximum prestige, authority and monopoly, which presently belong to a few top professions.

The claim of social welfare to a profession is further strengthened by the fact that the trained, qualified social welfare personnel are in great demand in America, Canada, Britain and other developed countries and job opportunities are available to them in variety of settings and agencies. Research, publications and private practice all point to an outgoing profession of social welfare. Above all, the profession has received recognition at the international level. United Nations, on its own, and through its specialised agencies and regional commissions sponsors seminars, conferences and consultancy on various themes of social welfare and arranges training for social welfare personnel.

There also exist three main social welfare bodies at the international level :

(i) The International Conference of Social Work organised in 1926, which later became the International Council on Social Welfare (1928) aims at bringing together representatives from various countries of the world to share knowledge, plans and activities which would strengthen social work on a global basis to facilitate and promote cooperation between international organisations related to social welfare and to make the views of the social welfare field known to the United Nations ;

(ii) the International Association of Schools of Social work focuses particularly on educational (patters of international importance ;

(iii) the International Federation of Social Workers founded in 1932, aims at developing a coordinated method for the exchange of ideas, the encouragement and maintenance in every country of high professional standards and the expression on an international scale of the viewpoint of professional social service. All these associations corroborate in publishing the quarterly journal International Social Work.

Indian Review : Social Welfare scenario in India does not admit it to be a profession in the true sense of the word, notwithstanding the fact that certain elements of professionalism are discernible in it.

It is argued that social welfare functionaries are rendering welfare services in numerous fields like Health and Family Welfare and Welfare of child, youth, women, the aged, handicapped, scheduled castes, scheduled tribes and backward classes sponsored both by the government and voluntary organisations and they are thus fulfilling the social needs ; that instruction and training in social welfare is provided at a number of schools of Social Work and the institutions run by voluntary agencies ; that the social welfare personnel have come to acquire an identity of their own as is evidenced by the floating of their professional organisations like the Indian Council of Social Welfare, the Association of Trained Social Workers, the Association of Schools of Social Work in India and the publication of newsletters and journals by them. Social Welfare therefore deserves to be considered as a profession.

On the contrary, it is alleged that social work/welfare is not entitled to the status of a profession since it is borrowed from the west and its theoretical framework, practice, methodology are not drawn from Indian context, that the curriculum and training imparted at schools of social work are not geared toward actual social work practice.

Moreover, they suffer from the paucity of indigenous literature and dearth of suitable teaching staff resulting in the erosion of the credibility of social work education suitable for social demands ; that the social welfare organisations are not so far in a position to exercise control over the maintenance of standards of the profession or over the conduct of professionals as do the other organisations in their respective fields ; that the publications of these organisations—"Social Work Forum" of the Indian Association of Trained Social

Workers and the Indian Journal of Social Work do not adequately serve the purpose of organs for professional communication; that it has obtained neither social recognition nor developed a code of ethics grounded in a philosophy of social work and social welfare, that some of the important characteristics like licensing, certification, registration and regulation of professional practice especially in private agencies have not been given due consideration. In view of these deficiencies of the practice of social welfare, it can be designated as a new and emerging profession which has still to go a long way to be recognised and accepted as a fullfledged profession in India.

The entitlement of social welfare as a profession can also be determined by the administration of personnel engaged in it. An attempt is therefore made to examine social welfare personnel administration.

Personnel Administration of Social Welfare : All states irrespective of their political ideologies, and form of government provide for social welfare services for their people on a scale to be determined by the financial resources at their disposal. The success of the various welfare programmes would however, depend on how effectively and efficiently these are implemented, executed by the personnel who are entrusted with the task of administering them. Well thought out and well considered policies, plans and programmes fail to succeed, the best organisations based on sound principles break down if the available human material is not competent to manage the public affairs. A.E. Gorwale observes, "It shall be understood that the mere laying down of right policies and programmes is not enough, the test is performance and implementation. It is by this test of performance that the work of individual officials of all grades should be judged and praise or criticism given".

The enormous growth in social services and delivery system

makes incumbent upon on the part of the government to devise special measures for ensuring adequate and appropriate personnel system to meet the increasing demand in social welfare administration. There are no more important administrative problems than those connected with personnel. The quality of the agency's service is related directly to the number and competence of the employed personnel.

The agency's basic personnel relationship are defined in its personnel policies concerning such matters as employment, salaries, tenure, vacations, grievance procedure, retirement and so forth. It is a sound practice for an agency to formulate comprehensive personnel policies. According to Pfiffner and Presthus, personnel policy of an organisation and its major activities in the area of 'Personnel Administration' should include:

(i) Job analysis and position classification : the description of the work to be performed in a given job which becomes the basis for effective recruitment.

(ii) Recruitment and Placement : the process of individual skills and aptitudes with job or class specifications.

(iii) Evaluation, promotion and transfer: the procedures used to recognise accomplishment and to use individual abilities to greatest advantage.

(iv) Compensation scales Plan for assuring equal pay for equal work, with salary gradation based on individual skills required by the job.

(v) Training, counselling and improvement of working conditions : the most important of a variety of services designed to motivate employees.

(vi) Relations with employees' organisations and unions : handling relationships with these groups.

(vii) Disciplinary action : The Supervision of individual suspension and dismissal cases.

(viii) Personnel records : maintaining such employees records as rosters, time records, sick and vacation leave records eligible lists, pay roles.

These methods and their underlying assumptions are however, likely to change from country to country in the context of changing circumstances and conditions and the new insights into organisational behaviour afforded by research and experience.

In the United States of America great advances have been made in personnel administration. A carefully worked out set of standard personnel policies has been formulated by the American Association of Social Workers.

Progress has been made towards adequate salaries, staff security had increased, there has been considerable headway in establishing the principles that a worker is not to be dismissed from his job at the whim of his employer or without due cause; that a worker is entitled to appeal ; job specifications and job classifications have come into wide use ; and retirement plans have been set up for at least some employees of social agencies; the desirability of staff evaluation has been established in progressive agencies and progress is being made in working out sound concepts and methods of evaluation ; the right of employees of social agencies to organise and to bargain collectively with management has been established ; and the Union has emerged as an important factor in social welfare administration and increasing interest is manifested in such subjects as democratic administration, group dynamics, creative leadership, participation and morale.

Personnel Policy and Administration in India : It is alleged that no attempt has been made to evolve a social welfare manpower policy, and personnel administration leaves much to be desired in practising the principles of welfare administration as compared to western countries as substantiated by the following observations :

The Appointments

A host of agencies employing social welfare personnel such as various "ministries of Government of India, Departments of State governments, voluntary organisations have their own categories and classes of positions and cadres and use different recruitment policies, methods and techniques. The primary ingredient of a sound recruitment policy is that the candidates competing for welfare services should be equipped with knowledge and techniques of social welfare services as imparted to them at schools of social work but the recruitment agencies many a time select candidates possessing degree in any of social sciences ignoring those having educational qualifications in social work and social welfare.

The civil service merit system which is designed to secure and retain qualified personnel in the public service, generally provides for job and salary classification, security of tenure during continued efficiency upto the age of retirement and insulation of members of the classified service from political activity and political pressure, does not operate in social welfare personnel administration. Only some of the executive positions are filled through Public Service Commissions and sometimes these are also taken out of their purview and are filled on adhoc basis on political considerations. Voluntary organisations do not observe any principles of personnel administration in recruiting their personnel, which is solely guided by their whims, they do not insist on qualifications and training despite the instructions of the Central Social Welfare Board—the grants giving agency—that they should employ qualified and trained persons.

Their plea is that suffer as they do from a chronic shortage of funds, they are unable to employ suitable trained staff having an aptitude for this kind of work at reasonable salaries. This confirms that there is no Central agency entrusted with the task of formulating personnel policies and coordinating the recruitment practices of different welfare agencies. It is high time that Ministry of Welfare, the nodal agency should act as a coordinating agency, capable of taking a total view of personnel problems and perspectives inclusive of recruitment, promotion, discipline, manpower planning etc. in social welfare administration.

Staff Training

Social welfare programmes need qualified and trained personnel for their successful implementation. Training of social welfare personnel has therefore assumed substantial significance.

The Sixth Plan document while highlighting the importance of voluntary organisations in the implementation of welfare programmes and services had observed that their personnel needed orientation training so that the standard of services rendered by them could be improved. Accordingly a number of training institutions have been set up in various fields of social welfare administration to cater for variety of personnel belonging to different areas of social welfare. The social welfare personnel were categorised by the Study Team on Social Welfare and Backward Classes (chaired by Renuka Ray, 1959) into three categories :

(a) *Administrative and Senior Supervisory* : category at the headquarters for supervisory duties, research and planning comprising directors and research officers trainers, field work supervisors in training institutions; superintendents, medical and psychiatric social workers and probation officers in large institutions.

(b) *Intermediate Supervisory Category* : Superintendents, community organisers in urban areas and in medium and small size institutions ; and social education organisers, chief welfare organisers (Mukhya Sewikas) in rural areas for the direction and supervision of field staff in project centres.

(c) *Workers of Field Level :* such as gram sevikas in rural areas and welfare workers, recreation leaders and assistants in welfare institutions in urban areas.

The Indian Institute of Public Administration and the National Institute of Public Cooperation and Child Development organise general development courses whereas specialised training courses are conducted by the National Institute of Social Defence, National Institutes for the Handicapped, Centrally sponsored Tribal Training Institutes, Family and Child Welfare Training Centres sponsored by the Central Social Welfare Board and Balsevika Training Centres instituted by the Indian Council of Child Welfare. These training programmes are conducted mostly in collaboration with national level voluntary organisations, schools of social work and/State governments.

The training facilities available are inadequate to cope with the needs of the increasing number of welfare personnel due to expansion of welfare programmes. Moreover, the training institutes are concentrated at a few places. These need to be dispersed in different parts of the country to enable the maximum number of personnel to be benefited. The present training programme also need to be so designed as to provide for the training of senior personnel as well. Some of them are deputed for training at the institutions existing at the regional and international levels but these cannot be availed of by all the high ups as only a limited number of them can be sponsored for training abroad.

Training of social welfare personnel has been a major area in the United Nations social welfare programmes, in the earlier years, the emphasis was on the training of social workers based predominantly on western model. But in recent years the emphasis has shifted to include personnel working in the broader areas of social welfare, including those working under health, education, nutrition, rural development and similar other fields. The other important aspects of United Nations programme on social welfare training comprise publication of periodic global and regional surveys of social welfare training, convening of inter-regional and regional meetings on aspects of social welfare training, training of social welfare administrators and planners, training of field level personnel, the development of indigenous teaching material, exchange of social welfare educators between countries in a given region and fellowships for education abroad.

Skill Development

In order that the social welfare system achieves its objectives and fulfils its mission, it is essential that all the members of the staff are involved and informed. Staff Development should be an administrative priority as it enhances and upgrades staff skill and knowledge through exposure to new techniques and ideas and fosters improved communication and Work-group cohesion. The objectives of staff development can be achieved through the mechanism of in-service training of the staff in which administrators at the higher echelon of the organisation should also participate to convince the employees that they are as much concerned about the achievement of the goals of the organisation, holding of professional conferences and seminars for discussion of various issues, arising in the execution of programmes, and exchange of views on the basis of experience gained through practice and execution of programmes and to encourage the employees for participation by providing them facilities of leave, reimbursement of expenses etc. and giving grants for personal professional libraries, subscriptions to professional journals and research in their respective fields of activities. These measures for staff development would not only enhance their prospects for career development and promotion possibilities but also contribute to efficiency in the execution of welfare programmes.

The Inspiration

A creative, well planned staff development programme can also lead to improved staff morale and motivation. Morale is the single most important factor in determining overall service quality. If staff feels that their personal needs for participation and their professional needs for growth are recognised and rewarded, they will bring a great degree of enthusiasm and activities to the work. Motivation constitutes one of the major tasks of the Chief Executive. He is to ensure that his staff is motivated by adequate incentives, appreciation and encouragement to use their knowledge, skill and ability to achieve best results.

Motivation and morale are somehow lacking in social welfare administration due to lack of effective and inspiring administrative leadership and their elitist attitude, poor communication, lack of adequate information or the presence of misinformation, inadequacy of manpower planning, spoils system in recruitment, scarcity of promotion avenues, interference of politicians in postings, transfers and disciplinary actions ; appropriate mechanism for periodic evaluation of staff in the context of performance standards and finally lack of proper appreciation and recognition of good work. Government has established National awards for best voluntary workers and institutions in the field of child welfare to be distributed every year. It shall contribute to the morale boosting of employees of government departments and agencies of social welfare if similar awards are instituted for them as well.

Administration is defined as 'The Organisation and use of men and materials to accomplish a purpose". Public Administration is a particular sector of the broader field of administration and it connotes the administration of government affairs which are undertaken for public good. It consists of all those operations having for their purpose the fulfilment or enforcement of public policy. In the past, the

State was responsible merely for the enforcement of law and order, dispensation of justice, protection of property and lives of people. But in the modern age, the negative aspect of "Police State" has been replaced by the positive welfare concept of the state and with the advent and emergence of welfare states like Britain, USA, Canada, Germany, Sweden etc. and the welfare oriented states in the developing countries including India, governments have been called upon to perform important public and social welfare functions.

Consequently administration has ceased to be merely regulatory and is increasingly being involved in the formulation of policies and programmes of tasks concerned with social welfare and economic growth. Science and technology and resulting industrialisation have given rise to new social problems. Thus the sphere of activities of administration in the field of finding solution of social problems, providing social services and social welfare services has increased on an unprecedented scale making it expedient to evolve organisations and agencies exclusively concerned with the implementation of welfare policies and programmes. This has resulted in the emergence of Social Administration as an integral part of total administrative system. Social services and social welfare administration form important constituent of social administration.

Social welfare administration is thus a branch of Public Administration ; it is subdivision of the broader field of Public Administration or general governmental administration ; it constitutes a sub set of public administration. It is concerned with the administration of social sciences which include in its purview health, social security (payment to those in need) and the personal social services (the provision of help, social care and support in the community for individuals and groups who appear to be in need of it) in Britain ; and refer to provision to enhance individual and group development and well- being and to aid, rehabilitate or treat those in difficulty or in need, in USA and welfare benefits to disadvantaged and underprivileged sections of society in India.

Though Social Welfare administration is in the process of establishing an identity of its own as a separate discipline and profession, yet it shares certain technical processes with all other administrative enterprises reflecting eventually their organisational requirements. To a greater or less degree, it also shares some structural and political dynamics. All undertakings require planning organisation, command, coordination and control and in order to function properly, all must observe the same general principles. Public Administration and Social Welfare Administration have these common features. Again, all subjects, these days are interdisciplinary, have to depend on one another for proper study of man and society. Both Public Administration and Social Welfare Administration share this character also.

Public vs. Social Welfare Administration : Despite Social Welfare Administration being a branch or subdivision of public administration, *M* has come to possess certain specific and distinctive features and characteristics of its own as mentioned below :

(i) Just as Social Welfare administration is a branch of public administration, the latter was also once a division of Political Science. It was continued to be treated as such for long and it was taught as such, not as a separate discipline but as a constituent of Political Science or even Economics and History in the Universities.

(ii) Public Administration is a new discipline and Social Welfare Administration a newer one. As a field of systematic study, the development of public administration has been only receipt. The credit for making a beginning of the academic study of public administration goes to Woodrow Wilson who had published his article "The Study of Public Administration" in 1857. Prof. Waldo has rightly called him the "Founding Father of Public Administration as a discipline".

Social Welfare Administration had its beginning as late as 1946 when American National Conference on Social Work sponsored a section on administration and thereafter Social Welfare administration began to be included as one of the basic courses for training students.

Independent courses in Public Administration in India started in 1950 only with Nagpur University giving the lead. Now the discipline has carved out a place for itself in many university departments and colleges. But social welfare administration continues to form a part of courses of Social Work and it is only at the Tata Institute of Social Sciences, Bombay that it has been granted independent status as a discipline.

(iii) Public Administration has been able to establish itself by and large, as a profession though the controversy still goes on whether it deserves this title or not. Anyhow, it is agreed by all that it is a profession in the making. But social welfare administration is yet to go a long way to acquire the status of a profession attractive monetarily or elevating socially.

(iv) Public Administration has a number of institutes for training of in-service administrative personnel and for research, Indian Institute of Public Administration, New Delhi is the pioneer institution founded in 1954 under the Presidentship of Shri Jawaharlal Nehru. Lal Bahadur Shastri National Academy of Administration, Mussorie, Administrative Staff College, Hyderabad and State Institutes of Public Administration in various states are other prominent institutes. But social welfare administration is yet to have an institute catering exclusively to social welfare administration personnel on the pattern of Public Administration institutes.

(v) Social welfare administration differs from Public Administration in the quality of persons needed for their respective services. The personnel of the former are expected to be imbibed with the qualities of dedication, devotion, discipline, integrity, compassion, belief in dignity and worth of human beings. They require mastery of a body of knowledge and skills gained through professional education and experience. But Public Administration personnel can do without such qualities and specialisation.

(vi) The code of ethics for social welfare personnel embodies certain standards of behaviour in their professional relationships with those they serve, with their colleagues, with other professions and with the community. They choose a course of action consistent with the Code's spirit and interest. But the public administration personnel observe their code of conduct more in breach than in compliance. The instances of serving their own interest at the cost of their obligations to the society and nation are numerous. Some of them are politically committed and they would not hesitate to do anything to please their political masters to serve their personal ends.

(vii) Administrative leadership required in social welfare administration is of a unique type as compared to that of Pubic Administration. An administrator in social welfare is to possess an intimate and technical knowledge of delivery of social welfare services to inspire and guide his subordinates ; social welfare administration need not be authoritarian in tone, it is concerned fundamentally with enlisting willing participation in a cooperative enterprise. Public Administration, on the other hand, is alien to the public because of its bureaucratic attitude and is, therefore, unable to get the public cooperation required for the success of a programme.

(viii) The role of voluntary agencies in social welfare administration is commendable and is duly recognised as such by the government as is evident by the tremendous amount of money given in grants-in-aid to more than 12000 voluntary agencies. A partnership has developed between government and voluntary agencies so that each supplements and supports the other. But in no other field of public administration such an appreciable role is being played by voluntary agencies and too many in number working on their own or with government aid. Mobilisation of voluntary effort is a facet of social administration that transcends the traditional boundaries of public administration. As a function, it is as old as the British rule, though the discipline of public administration grew only after independence.

(ix) Social welfare administration is an activity which is carried on entirely with the noble objective of rendering services to the deserving people based on 'all expenditure and no income' and 'no-profit' whereas in Public Administration activities in other fields do bring to the government enormous revenues. Moreover, welfare administration is supposed to ensure that services reach the beneficiaries and no wastage is permitted. But in Public Administration activities, corruption, misuse of funds, extravagance and wastage are unavoidable.

Social welfare administration is a unique profession and it is hoped that it will be able to establish itself as such in due course of time.

Social welfare administration constitutes a branch, a

subdivision, a subset or a specified subsystem of Public Administration. Its scope extends from the diagnosis of the emergence of social problems in all times, initiating measures to eradicate them through social legislation and the creation of public awareness, to the provisions of social welfare services for the deprived, disadvantaged and underprivileged sections of society with a view to alleviate their sufferings and to ameliorate their lot. It has come to acquire a systematic body of knowledge, specialised skills and unique methods and techniques to deserve entitlement to a distinct discipline and profession.

But it has not yet been able to acquire the status of an independent discipline with its own identity and individuality because its own knowledge base is not sufficiently developed, it has to heavily depend on other social sciences for its subject matter, it is based on interdisciplinary approach, it continues to form a part of the curriculum of other social sciences especially sociology and social work and instruction in it is imparted as one of the majors in these subjects at universities and colleges ; and only very few of them have come to possess Departments exclusively of Social Welfare administration even in the advanced countries. It is, therefore, a comparatively new, evolving discipline and it will have to go a Song way to get recognition as an independent discipline.

The status of social welfare administration as a profession is also disputed. Those who are inclined to accept it as a profession are convinced that it has its knowledge base, specialised skills, fields of application, policy concerns, preoccupation with the delivery of social services to a delineated clientele ; code of ethics ; professional associations, research publications and private practice, elaborate training programmes both preserves and in service, and employment of large numbers of workers in various social welfare programmes. But those who do not concede it the position of a profession are of the view that it is not wounded on a body of scientific knowledge and it does not enjoy the some prestige in the society as other fullfledged and developed professions like medicine, engineering and law enjoy.

They would grant it the status of a semi-profession, though it is accepted as a profession at the international level as is substantiated by the fact that United Nations, its specialised agencies and Regional Commissions in their effort to enrich the knowledge, skills and techniques of social welfare convene regional and international conferences, hold seminars and organise training programmes for administrators and personnel employed in social welfare agencies, and international organisations like International Council of Social Welfare, International Association of Schools of Social Work and International Federation of Social Workers also help in the promotion of social welfare administration as a discipline and a profession.

Social welfare administration both as a discipline and a profession is as yet in its nascent stage. But it is expected to grow gradually with the ever increasing demand of qualified and skilled personnel to man social welfare agencies and the social recognition that it is going to earn in view of the unique services that it renders for the wellbeing and improvement of various sections of society. The Government is required to evolve a sound personnel policy and personnel administration system so as to attract qualified persons and to retain them in the vocation they opt to choose to serve the people in need, in a spirit of dedication and devotion.

A partnership has developed between government and voluntary agencies so that each supplements and supports the other. Administration, of course, relates to both of them, and many administrative problems, principles and methods are common to both. It is therefore imperative that voluntary agencies also develop sound personnel administration policies and methods with a view to make themselves more effective and efficient instruments of service to society.

Public Administration has taken sufficiently long time to be accepted as a profession, though it is still known as a profession in the making by some. But it has definitely established itself as a discipline as is borne out by the fact that it is taught in numerous universities and colleges and is accepted as such for competitive examination by the Union Public Service Commission and various State Public Service Commissions.

It is admitted in the western model welfare states also that of the many aspects of social welfare practices, the least developed conceptually is administration. The literature is sparse, and the research embryonic. There is little that one can identity as useful theory or even as thoughtful theoretical perspective. In India, literature on the subject of social welfare administration is scarce because social administration as a branch of public administration is comparatively new and requires to be explored more and more.

Social welfare administration, it is hoped, will emerge as a popular discipline and a unique profession in due course of time as people become aware and convinced of its validity and utility.

6

Role of Social Uplift

The Meaning

The use of the concept of system has the merit of eliminating some misleading dichotomies and of including crucial social factors in one model. Structure and process, concord and conflict are viewed in the same general perspective. Stability and change, norm and deviance can be examined together. There need be no treatment of social control apart from social conformity. The system is the social control; the feedback of counterchange is as integral as is the expected interchange. A people's main values are expressed in the kind of systemic order they seek and maintain.

Social structure is here taken as one aspect of social system. The concept of structure focuses on the component groups and their interrelations at a particular time. The concept of system adds the processes of counterchange among the groups and the systemic changes that they produce overtime.

A social system is kept constantly in motion and can be adoptively changed. As an adaptive means, people use their systems, not merely to cope with their world, but also to elaborate their lives and to create new ways of life. The concept of system guides us to see a society as more than the sum of its parts, to try to understand it—in Redfield's rather paradoxical phrase—as an "analysed whole." My own use of the concept has been informed by the writings of Homans (1950), Nadel (1951), Redfield (1955), Vogt (1960), Parsons (1961), and by the more recent syntheses by Buckley (1967).

Yet any concept that purports to embrace so much can explain correspondingly little specifically. It is a potent means of departure, not of arrival. Moreover, its use entails some lingering questions.

Whose concept is it? Is it only in the eye and mind of the professional beholder or is it a verity of human life, part of the people's truth? As we use the concept here, it is both. The people whose society we study have quite lively ideas (not necessarily accurate ones) about the systemic nature of their society, which influence, if they do not determine, their social relations. Their ideas are important elements in our analysis.

Another question is about the boundaries of a system. A family, is a component of a larger system of kinship. But kinship is also one of the subsystems of the larger society. If we focus on family relations, each family should be viewed as part of a general system of family relations. Similarly, religious, economic, and political activities can be considered as separate systems for certain purposes and as subsystems in other contexts of analysis. On this question, too, we are guided by how the people whom we study perceive various contexts of action and how they differentiate among them, though we must separate their notions of ideal conduct from that which they expect and that which is actually realised.

Finally, there is always some question about the application of any guiding concept, no matter how cogent or sound it may be. We tend to focus on the evidence that fits more neatly into the system concept and look past that which does not fit so well. Because we postulate counterchange, we produce the real evidence of counterchange.

Because we postulate that there are systemic social relations, we do not test the utility of the concept at every step of the exposition. Because we postulate a general human preference for orderly relations and for a return to order, we may slight disorder and disarray in social relations, or interpret them as a means of attaining some new and more satisfactory order—which they may or may not be. However, the general test of the usefulness of a concept is whether it helps to clarify, explain, and assess probabilities, not whether its use surmounts all questions about it and gaps in it.

The subject of social stratification is more in the background than in the foreground of this enquiry. We are dealing with the classic instance of stratification as frame and focus for a civilisation, yet we must also recognise that ideas about stratification are being changed in India in ways similar to those in which other peoples throughout the world are shifting ideas about social divisions. These grand changes are close to the nerve and bone of most modern nations. Hence intellectuals and political activists everywhere are apt to be absorbed with one or another aspect of the subject of social strata and the proper rights and rewards pertaining to each grouping.

Stratification is considered to be the main distributive arrangement of a society accounting for who gets what, how, and why (Gould 1960a; Tumin 1967, p. 12; Lenski 1966, pp. 1-23). So it is no wonder, as Melvin Tumin comments in his survey of the subject, that the study of stratification has come to assume a central place in modern sociology. He notes that it has become a "dominant pursuit" of sociologists and is likely to continue to be, so long as inequalities are critical for the life-chances and life-patterns of people in different strata of a society (1967, pp. 10-11). Anthropologists have not been so heavily engrossed with this subject as have sociologists, but they well recognise its importance.

Some of the writings on stratification stress the objective criteria and the material forces that impel social divisions. Others emphasise the subjective views that the participants hold. Karl Marx set off great consequences with his testament of the technological causes and the objective criteria for social classes and his analysis of the inevitable conflict between classes. More recent sociological writers, Lloyd Warner and Talcott Parsons among them, have noted that a major factor is how people understand the nature of their society and how they consequently class themselves. Parsons points out that social relations inevitably involve value choices and moral judgments, and the way in which stratification is carried out depends on the moral evaluations made by the people (1953; 1961, pp. 42-44).

A much debated issue is between those who emphasise that stratification supports stability and those who view stratification as an inherent source of conflict. The former tend to dwell on order, rewards, interdependence, subjective satisfactions, the latter on power, exploitation, strain, objective causes for dissatisfaction (cf. Lenski 1966, pp. 22-23, 441-443; Dahrendorf 1966, pp. 714-718). The manner in which this issue has been debated seems less apposite for an understanding of Indian society than for other societies. Social divisions in India most clearly follow both objective and subjective criteria; they involve both stability and strain, both cooperation and conflict. The problem is not whether the one kind or the other kind of influence prevails but how much of each exists and under what circumstances.

Another debated issue is whether highly stratified societies outside of South Asia can usefully be labelled caste societies, with the implication that they share important characteristics with the Indian systems. This idea has been explored by Barth (1960), by Bailey (1963a), and especially by Gerald Berreman, who has strongly maintained that they do, drawing his evidence mainly from a comparison of India and the American South in the mid-twentieth century.

DEFINITION OF CASTE SYSTEM

A caste system, as Berreman discusses the concept, is one that is composed of ranked groups. Membership in a group is only through birth. The groups are exhaustive, exclusive, and discrete; that is, every person is a member of such a group and of only one; he is clearly recognised by others as a member of his separate group. Membership in his group influences most of his roles and activities; there is a high degree of "role summation." No one should try to change his inherited membership and any attempts by individuals to shift themselves to a higher group are strongly disapproved (Berreman 1966, pp. 275, 285; 1967a, p. 48; 1967b, p. 355).

Relative rank affects almost all social relations. Most interaction among people of different groups involves considerations of superiority and inferiority, and superiority means greater privileges, precedence, and a larger share of the good things in life. Each group is a firm entity, named, bounded, self-aware, culturally homogeneous. Because interaction between people of different groups is limited and that within a group is more intense, the members of a group tend to share distinctive cultural characteristics. A caste system is therefore one of cultural pluralism (Berreman 1967a, pp. 46, 55; 1967b, p. 354).

The groups are interdependent; each needs the services or goods provided by others. But they are held together less by agreement about mutual needs and purposes than by the coercive power wielded by the superior groups. (Other students of caste systems recognise the importance of coercive power but do not consider it to be the sole cement of such a system.) The inferior groups conform in their actions, not necessarily in their ideas about the reasons for subservient behaviour (Berreman 1966, p. 289; 1967b, pp. 352-357).

A general concomitant of such a system, Berreman notes, is that the higher groups explain their superiority in terms of a moral evaluation that shows why they are intrinsically more worthy. They take a paternalistic attitude toward the lower people, considering them to be childlike, irresponsible, incapable of finer feelings or higher achievements. The lower do not share these views but adjust to the superior power by avoiding conflict, by apathy and psychic withdrawal, or by over compliance. Other concomitants are the restrictions on relations between people of different groups. Eating and sitting together, marriage and sex relations are rigidly controlled or are forbidden (Berreman 1966, p. 308; 1967a, pp. 59, 64).

The higher, privileged groups hold that the social order is static; the lower strive to improve their status. Any system of marked stratification is itself a source of mobility motivation as Veblen, Bendix and Lipset, and others have noted. Such mobility striving is a constant dynamic force in a caste system. Berreman discerns a difference between India and the U.S.

South in that a lower group in India is usually more interested in achieving superiority for the group rather than equality in the society, whereas Southern Negroes, because the society of the deep South has two main divisions rather than multiple groups, have objected to the system as well as to their position in it. In this way there is more consensus about the proper nature of the social system in India than in the South, though Berreman stresses that in neither place do the lower groups accept the concept of their inferiority (1966, pp. 298, 308, 318; 1967a, p. 66).

The principal functions of a caste system, as Berreman sees them, are to perpetuate social and cultural diversities, and to enforce and articulate them. Privilege is protected through power. These functions, his discussion notes, are highly disfunctional in the modern world, irrelevant to human welfare and sources of unnecessary conflict and suffering (1967b, pp. 352, 356-366).

The critics of such definitions of "caste system" question whether the category is a useful one. Certain groups, such as the low-ranking groups in Japan, do not fit readily into the general definition (cf. DeVos 1967). These critics point out, moreover, that specialisation is essential in all modern societies and leads to some degree of stratification and ranking. Social and cultural diversities have to be articulated in all societies; each separate group tends to seek some privileges and power for its members.

These processes are inherent in a complex society and, as processes, can scarcely be called disfunctional. The trend in most contemporary societies is certainly away from the inclusive, invidious distinctions of caste divisions but also it is away from cultural pluralism and toward a cultural conformity, which some deplore. Those critics add that the discussions of caste systems in general have done little to advance an understanding of caste organisation in Indian civilisation (Leach 1960, 1967; Dumont 1967; S. Sinha 1967; Cohn 1968, p. 196).

But at least these discussions of what is meant by a "caste system" help us to understand the systems of Indian society as part of the human continuum, as special phrasings and configurations of social processes common among much of mankind. It is especially important to understand the dynamic nature of the Indian systems, because they have so often been depicted as static in Hindu scripture and in villagers' concepts, as well as in much of the writing on the subject.

THE DIVISION

In their interrelationships, people tend to classify each other within higher or lower positions. Society is thus segmented—consisting of various strata in accordance with the system of hierarchy that prevails. The powerful and privileged occupy the topmost stratum and usually receive preferential treatment. Whatever the criteria for allotment of position at various levels of the social structure, and however idealistic the sentiments of a "need for classlessness and equality", the fact of stratification in rural society is a reality that must be faced objectively as a universal tendency in societies all over the world. Students of Rural Sociology should not question the justification or rightness or wrongness, for such sentiments are irrelevant to the study of rural society. Recognise their existence, understand and appreciate their relevance and influence on behaviour. Attempt to recognise and understand the forces that are generated from within and outside of the system. Consider your own reactions if you belonged to a lower or higher class of society, or if you lived in a rural village. You will begin to understand at least some of the forces at play and their impact and influence on the stratification system of rural society in the area.

The various forms of the segmentation of the social structure, based on ease of vertical mobility from one strata of society to the other, have been represented on continuum. At one end exists a rigidity of divisions between strata which presents mobility and at the other, complete freedom of movement. A position on the continuum, however is subject to change in time, in response to the various societal forces both within and external to the stratification system that exists.

All societies exhibit some system of hierarchy whereby its members are placed in positions that are higher or lower, superior or inferior, in relations to each other. The term stratification is taken from the geologist who refers to different layers of soil or rock as stratum-the earth's surface consisting of various strata, each of which are distinct from the others. Society similarly consists of several layers of certain criteria according to which they have been categorised. Each society hence constructs a vertical evaluative scale in terms of specific criteria according to it and places its population in various layers or strata at different classified levels on this scale—some in higher, others in lower and still others at various levels between the highest and lowest strata.

Those in the top stratum have more prestige, power, preferential treatment than those below and each succeeding stratum possesses less of these attributes than the one above.

There is thus a universal tendency for societies all over the world to evaluate differences that are socially significant among people, and that arise from cultural or biological variations. These variations are ranked on a scale involving differential social status carrying different prestige and social worth or value. Social status refers to social standing or position of an individual or group in relation to others as ranked by society in accordance with criteria which are considered of social worth or value by society.

Thus in some societies occupation, income and wealth may be the most important criteria that determine social status; in others, caste, creed, family name and background may be most important; in still others education and ownership of material possessions may be the uppermost criteria. Whatever may be these socially defined criteria, they serve to place individuals and groups within some stratum of society.

Various Divisions

Two concepts have been developed in respect of such classification and placement in society. One is differentiation and the second is stratification. In differentiation society bases on a certain kind of trait which may be :

(a) physical, such as colour of skin,

(b) social, such as differences in etiquette and manners which set apart groups who vary in their conformity (or lack of it) with competence and grace to certain codes of "refined" behaviour. Thus, there may be exclusive organisations that restrict their membership to members of only certain levels of society, and

(c) cultural, such as status ascribed to individuals and groups from a foreign culture who are conspicuous by their cultural differences. Differentiation hence serves as a sorting process to analyse people into groups on the basis of roles and status.

Stratification tends to perpetuate these differences in status so that through this process they are fixed in the structure of society. Status may in some cases be so fixed in social stratification as to become hereditary, as in the case of caste membership. Differentiation may be considered the first stage preceding stratification in society in which people are differentiated one from another, sorted, and classified into groups. To the extent that the differences tend to become fixed, is the extent that society becomes stratified. It does not necessarily follow that all differentiation leads to stratification in society, however, for there exist forces in society both to fix and to eliminate differences among people.

Social stratification is "the division of a population into two or more layers, each of which is relatively homogeneous and between which there are differences in privileges, restrictions, rewards and obligations" [Lundberg, 1968, p. 361]. Stratification involves rank differentiation and constitutes an order of ranking on the basis of relative position within the rating system operating in society. Each stratum of society is only relatively homogeneous as distinct from other strata. Further, privileges and rewards enjoyed or restrictions imposed may or may not be related to needs of society. Another definition will aid to further clarify the concept. Social stratification has also been defined as "a pattern of superimposed categories of differential privilege" [Cuber, 1954, p. 11]. Three features of this definition need to be emphasised for greater comprehension:

(a) Social stratification is a socially accepted cultural pattern that assigns members of society a general position in the structure of society;

(b) Social stratification is superimposed by members of society by tradition and, without either, the will or conscious knowledge of the majority; and

(c) Social stratification involves a system of differential privilege unequal distribution of privileges, goods, power services, etc. among members belonging to different social strata.

Social stratification emerges from interaction of members in society. When people in society interact with one another over a prolonged period of time they tend to compare and rank individuals and groups who differ from one another. Their relative worth is judged in terms of specific criteria. Roles are evolved, ascribed and evaluated differentially. Some roles are regarded more important, with greater esteem and social value than others, and individuals filling these roles thereby receive preferential treatment and greater reward than others. Groups thus ranked with some degree of performance are said to be stratified. When society divides its population into a large number of such groups, a highly stratified society is the result.

Role of Stratification

The following functions of stratification are identified:

A Means of Accomplishing Essential Jobs in Society : Stratification in society constitutes a means of society's getting some of its essential jobs done by distributing different amounts of prestige and privilege to various strata. An army is an example of stratification with clearly defined strata, each marked with visible symbols denoting rank, specific roles and role expectations, norms and prescribed standards of behaviour and interrelationships—all clearly organised to do a job. Armies are within the structure of society and societies as a whole are also stratified although more often with less clarity and demarcation between various strata than in an army.

As society moves from the primitive, with little differentiation except on such bases as sex and age, toward greater size and, with technological advances, greater complexity, its system of distributing privileges, prestige and rewards and punishment becomes increasingly elaborate. The rewards society gives serve as incentives to get the various essential jobs accomplished; hence, rewards must be commensurate with the job to be done or at least adequate to attract individuals to do the job. These rewards may be economic, aesthetic or symbolic and give material and/or psychological satisfactions.

Regulation and Control of Individual and Group Relationships and Participation : Stratification regulates and controls human relationships in society. Prescribed roles and role expectation, norms and standards of behaviour are involved in relationships within each stratum and in interstratum relationships.

Stratification tends to regulate participation of groups and individuals in the total life of society, giving them access to certain areas and restricting them to others. Inequality of opportunity or nonavailability of facilities gives advantages to those in higher strata and deprives those belonging to lower strata thus, regulating participation. In pre-independence India, for instance, certain clubs and organisations and areas of social life and experience are inaccessible to participation by members of higher strata in society. A member of high class urban society cannot have intimate knowledge and experience of the intimacies of life in the poverty-stricken slums. Whatever an individual's position, whether high or low, stratification regulates his or her participation in certain areas of social life.

Contribution to Social Integration and Structure : Stratification in society has a strong integrative function, serving to coordinate and harmonise units within the social structure. A vivid illustration is the Indian Caste System, which consists of an elaborate complex of castes (over 10,000) involving specific occupations, roles and functions—all coordinated and organised under four major castes or Varnas. There is functional inter-dependence and interchange of services that together with other factors serve to integrate and harmonise its various units within the total social structure.

Stratification further serves to influence the function of various units of social strata. Each may develop its own voluntary organisations to serve recreational (and some other) needs, the nature of such organisations varying from stratum to stratum. Thus members of a particular stratum will have clubs, teams and perhaps a recreational centre distinct from those of other strata in society.

Simplification : Stratification of society categorises people into different strata, thus simplifying man's world in respect to his relations with other people. While within primary groups it is no problem to know how one should behave toward other individuals because of intimate knowledge of each other, to know how to react in various situations involving several people outside of primary groups is extremely difficult without such classification. For example, the criterion of age as an identification of adulthood, while not always valid in specific instances, does serve a desired purpose when dealing with the entire population. There is hence practical justification in the practice of categorising of people and responding to each category differently, but responding identically to all persons within a category.

Dysfunctions of Social Stratification : Several dysfunctional effects of social stratification have been identified.

1. Status and role in stratified society carry with them duties, rights and expectation. It has been observed that the individuals who have been accorded status and roles by nature of their placement in various strata in society often lack the capabilities and competence necessary to effectively fill these roles and perform the expected functions. Since others who may be more competent and capable of filling such roles are not prescribed these roles because of the stratification system that precludes them, the net result is wastage of social resources. This situation is particularly so in the case of a rigid system stratification such as hereditary aristocracies, where status positions and responsibilities are inherited. The Roman Empire, and the French Empire immediately prior to its revolution in 1789, are illustrations in which the last rulers proved incapable to meet the requirements of the monarchy. The traditional caste system in India contains illustrations of wastage of social resources due to restrictions of the stratification system.
2. Essential roles of society are sometimes neglected or made subordinate when status is ascribed, not to them, but to some other roles that are less important to the essential interests of society. Essential effort and resources are thus diverted to functions that are of less social importance. The elaborate and somewhat ostentatious observance of feasting by certain stratified groups may reflect their high status, but contributes little and is functionally unimportant to effective performance of prescribed roles.
3. Social stratification may "set the stage" for interstratum rivalry and conflict. Such conflict may take various

forms but in general results from an upthrust from lower strata to share equal rights with the upper strata and a downthrust from upper strata to keep lower strata in their place. Such conflict frequently occurs when stratification systems are weakening, or in the process of disintegration being subjected to a variety of influential forces within society such as new ideologies, pressure groups, collective frustration of lower strata, and/or political and other interest groups. Examples of this phenomenon in operation are in the Caste System in India, and in racial conflicts in the USA, South Africa and countries newly independent or immediately prior to achievement of independence from colonialism.

4. Stratification may be linked with various types of deviant behaviour. A stratification system involves ascribing of roles to individuals and enforcement of conformity according to roles, expectations and prescribed norms and standards of behaviour. For some, particularly members of lower strata of society who have less rights and privileges than those belonging to higher strata, conformity is difficult. They therefore deviate from normative behaviour and may even withdraw from society to become vagabonds, drug addicts, drunkards; seek devious means to avoid normal social behaviour; resort to crime, or rebel in some way or other.
5. Concentration of power by controlling a lower class group may result in the monopoly of the assets of society for personal gain and benefit at the expense of the dominated class. Thus, a privileged few may prosper while the lower classes are deprived. Such inequitable distribution of power usually sows seeds of revolutions, which often has been the only way to destroy such imbalances.

6. Each class tends to develop its own sub-culture, which may or may not fit into the cultural whole of society. In some cases where stratification is rigid, social integration is impeded and inter-communication between various strata may be difficult, concern for the whole may be lacking as stratum tends to function as a subculture.
7. Unless a member of a lower class is supported by a basic philosophy that explains position in society and enables him to adjust to it, his personality will be adversely affected as will his own perception of himself as a "nobody" and one who does not count. Stratification in society can hence impede normal development of personality of members of lower classes so that realisation of potential is never achieved.

Foundations of Stratification

Differential position, or status of members of society in its system of stratification is to be found in human societies all over the world, from the most primitive to the most modern. Members differ in the roles and status ascribed to them by society whether they belong to a band of hunting tribes, a gigantic modern economic corporation, or a professional group of surgeons. All are placed, however, in various strata of society according to specially prescribed criteria. The dreams of Utopia and Classless state seem doomed by the very nature of society which involves inevitable stratification. Despite political ideologies which may claim a classless society and equal opportunities for all, the fact of inequality in actual practice cannot be avoided. For in practice the structure of society is divided into various strata ranked in hierarchical order with preferential treatment and different opportunities given to individuals and groups belonging to various strata.

There appear to be two different sources from which stratification in society has developed, either Ethnic or Social.

Ethnic stratification occurs in society in which two ethnic or racial groups exist and one dominates the other over a long period of time. Illustrations are numerous, found in history and anthropology in various countries, and include ethnic stratification resulting from the Aryan invasion in India, the enslavement of Israelites by the Egyptians in Biblical times, and the importation of Negroes from Africa as slaves in the USA before the abolition of slavery.

The social basis for stratification in society involves the growth of a system of ranked strata within society. Members of society are ascribed status at some level on the basis of purely "social" factors that are prescribed by society. The social factors that give status to individuals or groups are criteria socially determined, based on the value system and social values of society. The presence of the factors which are considered of social worth contribute to one's prestige and high status and may vary from society to society. In some societies, occupation, income and wealth, education are considered; in other societies, ownership of landed property, ancestry and family name may be most important; in still others education are considered; in other societies, ownership of landed property, ancestry and family name may be most important; in still others education, caste, creed, and power or influence with authorities may rank high as social values.

Despite the variation, certain universal criteria of approval, disapproval, esteem and disesteem are common in societies throughout the world, and can be broken down into what may be considered determinants or factors that are present in some form, degree or combination whenever society exists. These universal criteria or determinants of status are listed as follows:

1. *Wealth* : in some form as recognised by society—measured in quantity or assessed in quality. Living standards displayed and the source of wealth is also significant.

2. *Ancestry* : referring to the family reputation, length of residence in the area, legitimacy or illegitimacy, racial or ethnic background and nationality.
3. *Functional Utility of the Individual* : his occupation as executive, teacher, scientist, unskilled labourer, skilled craftsman.
4. *Religion* : the kind and degree of religion professed and practiced. All societies include some attitude towards the supernatural expressed in the form of a religion with sets of beliefs and rituals.
5. *Biological Characteristics* : including both age and sex. Adulthood is valued more than infancy and childhood in most of the societies, and males are accorded higher status than females in many societies. Closely related to both age and sex is physical beauty according to standards defined by the society.

Each system of ranking, classification and placement of individuals and groups in various strata of society, then, will be built with these universal criteria as a base and will together constitute the social stratification system of that particular society. This will happen irrespective of what may be the dimensions of stratification in society-power, prestige, caste, creed, wealth, knowledge, education, skills, etc.—that are important criteria for allocation of position in the social structure.

Of the two different bases for social stratification described above, only one, the social base, is functional in as much as the basic functions of society are furthered by its presence. It serves a definite purpose in society and has been described as having an inevitable place in the social structure. Ethnic or racial stratification on the other hand has no such functional value. It does, in fact, appear to have a dysfunctional effect in society particularly where waste of human resources results from deprivation of opportunities for development, participation and contribution to society by certain "deprived" sections of society who possess great potential abilities that remain undeveloped and unrealised. [Merill, 1965, p. 280-282]

Certain general conditions have been identified as giving rise to stratification in society. These are listed below and have in part been included in the preceding discussion:

Conquest **:** Stratification has resulted from conquest wherein the conquerors have ascribed the best positions, for rights, privileges, power, status for themselves and reduced the conquered to an inferior status of subordination in the social order to serve the needs of the conquered.

Race and Cultural Differences **:** Dissimilarities of biological characteristics such as colour of skin, ethnic and cultural background has led to stratification in society under conditions of domination by one group of similar ethnic and cultural background over others which are dissimilar. Illustrations are domination of South America by the Spanish, Africa by the English and French Asia and Islands of the Pacific by English, Dutch and Portuguese.

Division of Labour **:** Most societies have developed a degree of complexity sufficient to have a division of essential tasks into a system of specialisation. Positions within this specialisation include differential power and functions and stratification of the social order emerges. Stratification evolves from allocation of privileges and powers which are scarce. Shortage or scarcity is created whenever society differentiates positions, terms of power and functions, and assigns at the same time rights and privileges. Such positions available are scarce and, because of the rights and privileges and rights among people in society results and creates stratification.

Different Types

From the foregoing it is evident that basic similarities and differences in various systems of stratification exist in societies all over the world. In summary, the underlying facts of basic similarities are that, in any society, the stratification system depends on such criteria of evaluation as are inherent to its culture and considered significant by most members of the society. The major values and goals of society and these criteria are closely related, and high or low status is ascribed to individuals in accordance with the extent of legitimate control that society recognises them to exert over attainment of the goals defined by existing values. It follows that societies sharing similar values and goals will tend to utilise similar criteria in evaluation and consequent stratification.

Cultural differences produce differences in the stratification systems of certain societies. In the USA, differences in sub-cultures, for instance, make for variation in stratification systems. Thus, rural farm communities and urban communities use different stratification systems and criteria to evaluate individuals and ascribe status. Differences in status evaluations depend to some extent on the value oriented goals of sub-cultures associated with religious, racial or ethnic sub-groups in American society.

Systems of stratification exhibit wide variance in different societies of the world. This variation may be in the criteria utilised for placing individuals and groups in various social strata of the system, or in the number of strata in the system, with some having two broad strata such as feudal lords and serfs, or nobility and commoners, and others having more. They may further vary in rigidity or flexibility and the sharpness with which each strata are demarcated. In some systems different strata are easily identifiable, while in others the boundaries are hard to locate. Considering the various societies that have existed and do exist in the world, certain recurrent forms of social stratification generally can be identified. Three forms or types are described briefly below:

Caste Systems : The term "caste" was derived from the Portuguese word Casta [meaning lineage or race], although in India, the term Varna [meaning colour] is used to apply to caste. "A caste is a social category whose members are assigned a permanent status within a given social hierarchy and whose contacts are restricted accordingly". [Lundberg, 1968, p. 374] It is the most rigid and clearly graded type of social stratification and has been often referred to as the extreme form of closed class system. An individual is born into the caste of his parent and can rise no further. With few exceptions he cannot fall to a lower caste, but if he does violate taboos and other mores of his caste he may be ostracised and expelled from his caste group. Personal qualities or ability have no part whatever in determining the caste of an individual, with lineage being the only criterion. The system is supposedly justified and explained by custom and religion.

The following have been identified as the characteristic features of a rigid caste system:

1. Deference to higher caste members by those of lower caste is enforced with implementation of strict punishment and disciplinary measures for violators.
2. Lower castes are so repeatedly impressed of their inherent inferiority that such castes remain subordinate to higher castes.
3. Lower castes are alleged to have compensatory gains, but such gains are cited more often by higher castes than by members of lower castes.
4. The past is repeatedly and persistently perceived and looked back upon as a "golden age"—a time of inter-caste harmony—when the entire caste system worked as an efficiently operating machine that has now been spoiled by external agitation and interference resulting in resentment and unrest among lower castes.
5. Men of higher castes have access in sexual relationships

with women of their own caste as well as lower castes. Lower caste men however do not have similar access and are confined in this respect to women of their own caste.

6. Lower caste members implicitly deny the legitimacy of their inferior position.

The Hindu Caste System of India is a striking illustration of stratification in society on the basis of caste. Within the four major castes of Brahmin, Kshatriya, Vaishya and Sudra and the additional caste of Harijan formed by Mahatma Gandhi to include all "outcastes", is a complex stratified social structure consisting of thousands of sub-castes. It is reported that in a small state with 350,000 population there were in the early 1930s almost 400 sub castes belonging to the Brahmin major sub-caste. Present estimates report over 10,000 caste groups. 1931 figures indicated that 6 per cent of India's Hindu population were Brahmins, a little over 70 per cent belonged to other castes and over 20 per cent were "outcastes".

Class System : Sharply contrasted with the caste system, the open class system can be placed at the opposite end of a continuum. A social class has been defined as an "abstract category of persons arranged in levels according to the social status they possess. There are no firm lines dividing one category from another" [Rogers, 1960, p.97]. "A social class consists of a number of individuals who share similar status often ascribed at birth but capable of being altered [Woods, 1966, p. 298].

Class, therefore, does not consist of organised, closed groups defined by law or religion as does caste, nor are the various strata in the system as rigid and easily identifiable. Movement of groups and individuals to other strata is possible. Social class, not a lineal or familial inheritance, hence can be acquired and changed according to one's achievement and efforts, although the extent of such mobility varies from one society to another. Further, the socially defined criteria that ascribe an individual a position in the class system of a society are not irrevocable. Efforts to bring about change in the value system of society emphasising certain factors and de-emphasising others may often prove successful and may facilitate change of status in the class system. Such change is much easier in the class system than in the caste system. Value definitions that are used to justify class differences are much less rigid than those used for the same purpose in the caste system. These differences are further more attributable to human than to supernatural factors in the former than in the latter system.

Justification for non-change in the caste system must be incorporated into the value system of the society, on the other hand in a class system the justification for change must be incorporated into the system of social values.

The following table summarises a comparison between the class and, caste system of society:

Characteristic	*Class Pattern*	*Caste Pattern*
Value definition of inferiority-superiority	Applied to any characteristic	Usually applied to biological aspect
Relevancy in norm-role definitions	Less than in caste system	More than in class system
Self definitions	Labels and awareness may be vague	Rigid labels and awareness
Change and mobility	Provided for and expected	Neither provided for nor expected
Material objects	Possession of valued objects increases as class position increases	Possession of valued objects increases as caste position increases
Justification of system (value definitions)	Pragmatic "this worldly" justification	Strong religious endorsement
	Status achieved	Status ascribed

Contd...

[Vernon, 1965, p. 2301

Illustrations of the class system are to be found in various societies of the world. For instance, the class system of the USA is said to contain the following general classes:

Upper-Upper class–1%

Lower-Upper class–1.5%

Upper-Middle class–10%

Lower-Middle class–28%

Upper-Lower class–34%

Lower-Lower class–25%

[Biesanz, 1964, p. 193]

Further illustrations of class systems in society are to be found in Latin-American countries and in some near-east Asian societies which have a five-fold classification: (1) The elite, (2) Moderate size land holders, (3) Non-agricultural labour, (4) Small-land operators and, (5) The ordinary fellahin.

In the USSR, "classless society" actually contained the following major classes, identified in 1950 by Alex Inkeles. (1) The ruling elite, (2) The superior intelligentsia, (3) The general intelligentsia, and (4) The white collar group.

The working class was also differentiated into (1) The working class aristocracy, (2) The rank and file workers and (3) The disadvantaged workers.

The peasantry in rural areas although relatively homogeneous was also subdivided into distinguished groups: (1) The well-to-do peasants, and (2) The average peasant [Inkeles, 1950, quoted in Chinoy, p. 186]

Sociologists seem to favour five classes in American Society- namely:

Upper

Upper Middle

Middle

Lower Middle

Lower

Other research (Fussell) indicates that there are as many as nine—namely:

"Top out-of-sight

Upper

Middle

High Proletarian

Mid Proletarian

Low Proletarian

Destitute

Bottom out-of-sight"

It has been pointed out that in the above it is not riches alone that defines these classes in American Society.

Another pattern of stratification identified in American society has been referred to as five subjective classes:

Poor

Working

Middle

Upper Middle

Upper

Social Conditions Influencing Class Structure : Class structure in society is influenced by many different social conditions:

Philosophy of the Society : The general philosophy of a society exerts influence on the type of class system that is developed within it. Where equalitarian ideas and concepts prevail, society evolves a system in which an individual can move from one stratum to another through his initiative and ability. Such society stimulates effort to move upward believing that social welfare and societal advantage will accrue as a result. On the other hand, a society may develop a more closed system, based on hereditary placement of individuals and groups in various strata of society, because it believes that inherent differences exist among people, and certain individuals and groups are inferior and subordinate to others.

Cultural Antecedent : Prior class structure leaves an influence on the development of new systems: The class structure of society evolves within a background of different societies. Class systems in certain newly established countries tend to follow the class structure prevalent for years during the period of existence as a foreign colonial entity.

Homogeneity and Heterogeneity of Population : The homogeneity and heterogeneity of population composition influence the type of class structure evolved.

Predominant Economic System : Land ownership and land control have been important influencing factors in the development of class structure in predominantly agricultural countries. For instance, in Leba non and Egypt, ownership of land ranked high as a social value and prestige giving factor. Max Weber, Engels and Marx have emphasised the influence of economic systems in determination of classes in society.

Occupation : Occupation, an aspect of the economic system, often influences the structure of the social class system. In the USA for example, occupation has been considered the most important criteria of class status.

The above are some of the important conditions or factors that influence class structure. There are others. However many may be such factors, it is essential to recognise that they rarely are responsible for class structure by themselves. Classes evolve from the inter-relationship of several of these factors [Anderson, 1964, pp. 364-366].

Estate System : Under the estate system a person's social position depends on his hereditary relationship to the land. In Medieval Europe, for instance, land tenure was related to military service. The highest strata was occupied by nobility—the royal family, and dukes, barons and lords who constituted the landed military aristocracy. The clergy were the intellectual elite, serving also as administrators, and were considered at par with the nobility. Within the nobility and the clergy (the church) there existed a system of hierarchy based on position in the church and land ownership.

The next layer of social strata was occupied by merchants and craftsmen, and lowest of all were low income village people. Inter-dependence and bondage in various degrees existed between strata which, like the Caste System, were clearly defined and rigid, although some mobility was possible. A low income villager or serf could be freed by his lord. He could render outstanding military or other service and be given a title with landed property by the king. He could enter priesthood and sometimes rise to the status of a noble through marriage.

The above forms of social stratification have considered sharply contrasting types such as, the class and caste systems. These various forms may be considered as occupying positions along a continuum of systems of social stratification with caste and open-class systems at opposite extremes. Systems in societies all over the world are distributed at various points on this continuum differing from each other in terms of two factors:

(a) The comparative ease with which an individual can move or change his social status in the system; if he possesses the necessary attributes, and

(b) the extent to which he secures his position or status by virtue of his own ability and attributes or through predetermined factors of lineage and family.

It is well to recognise that these systems of stratification are not static but constantly in the process of modification and change.

Classification of Caste and Class

Identification of caste and class is essential for study and analysis of systems of stratification. Caste identification, because of its clear-cut, rigid nature and commonly known criteria for evolution, presents no particular problem. Simple questioning of those involved in the system will reveal the details.of caste structure without much difficulty.

Class identification is not as readily discemable or determined. Three major methods are used for this purpose:

1. *Self Identification :* An approach often referred to as the "subjective" approach consists of asking members of society to identify social class to which they feel they belong. What is sought in this approach is self-definitions of identification with a particular class in society.
2. *Reputational Approach :* Also subjective, the reputational approach asks persons to rank someone else on a social status scale. This method is restricted to smaller communities where people know each other. Both in the reputational and self-identification approach, respondents are permitted to use criteria in ranking and the interview does not specify any particular criteria.
3. *Objective Approach :* The objective approach directs attention to objective characteristics, which are considered to reflect prevailing values or are used as measures or indicators of class structure. These objectives are those such as income, education, occupations and type of home, upon which researchers evidence high consensus. These objective class criteria permit the researcher to divide his area of study into any number of categories. Thus, income can be used

as a criterion of class and divisions into income-groups can be conveniently made at the researcher's discretion.

Whatever may be the approach followed or the methodology adopted in studying systems of stratification, such analysis calls for consideration of at least the following conditions:

1. The number and size of classes and status groups.
2. The amount of movement of individuals and groups from one stratum to another (social mobility).
3. The sharpness of the lines between groups as seen in apparent differences in behaviour or style of life, and the extent of class consciousness.
4. The specific bases for division-the kind and amount of property owned, occupations followed and values which determine status.
5. The distribution of power among the several classes and status groups.

Transformation in Society

The term social mobility usually refers to the movement of individuals or groups from one strata of society to another or vertical mobility. However, three types of social mobility have been identified: 1. vertical. 2. horizontal, and 3. geographic.

Vertical Social Mobility is usually implied when one speaks of social mobility and refers to the two-way movement-up or down-of individuals and groups from one stratum in society to another.

Horizontal Social Mobility refers to movement of individuals and groups between positions in society which are roughly of the same social status. In other words, it is movement within the same stratum of society. Certain occupations for example, may be ranked or rated as associated with the same social class such as a college professor and a research scientist or a lawyer (assuming the society classifies all three at par with another). Movement from one to another would be referred to as social mobility of the horizontal type. If on the other hand an individual moved from the position of college professor to vice chancellor of a university or to clerk in a business firm vertical social mobility would be involved—upwards in the former and downwards in the latter instances (provided the positions of vice chancellor and clerk are considered superior and inferior respectively to that of college professor).

Geographical Social Mobility differs from both vertical and horizontal mobility and refers to movement of a group from one geographic area to another. Such migration may also involve vertical or horizontal movement. Thus a newly immigrated member of society may be ascribed social status that is higher or lower than he had in the society from which he immigrated or he may maintain the same status but may move horizontally to an occupation of equal social rating. Further comments on social mobility in this writing will be confined to vertical social mobility unless otherwise specified.

Societies differ in the extent to which individuals and groups can move from one stratum to another. In societies that have an open-class system of stratification, movement up and down the social ladder is by and large unrestricted. In societies with a closed system of stratification there is no upward or downward movement of individuals and groups except by default or illegitimate manipulation. This is the basic difference between class and caste. Whereas in the more open class system upward movement of individuals and groups is possible, in the closed class or caste system such vertical movement is not possible. Under the latter system there are restrictions also on horizontal movement.

Transforming Elements

Several factors serve to restrict social mobility. Some of the more important are as follows:

1. Racial differences and religious beliefs in respect of status in society are important factors and make for a closed class or caste system of stratification. Hindu religious beliefs established and supported the Caste System in Hindu Society. While different from the Hindu Caste System, in the U.S.A., racial differences between Negroes and White Americans gave rise to what closely approached a caste or closed class system in society.
2. Class discrimination in an open class system serves as a barrier to upward mobility, as evidenced by restricted membership to certain organisations. Such discrimination may be conscious and/or unconscious and exercised in rather subtle ways, nonetheless, its presence cannot be denied.
3. The fact that social classes act as sub-cultures within which individuals are reared from infancy and socialised, serves as an important obstacle or deterrent to upward mobility. A middle class child has been brought up to "fit" into his class with known roles, role expectations, values and norms. This process of learning and socialisation tends to hold him in his class position.
4. Taken in its negative aspect, the lack of wealth may restrict opportunities for the individual to develop and acquire the materials necessary for social advancement.
5. Sexes differ in various societies in prestige, power, social status, and opportunities. They also differ in social mobility. In most societies, man is dominant and tends to be socially more mobile than a woman. However, woman takes on the social status of her husband when she marries, but in general, the reverse is not the case. Marriage thus serves, among other purposes, a means for social mobility for women rather than for men.

There are several other factors that condition social mobility in various ways. Some of the more important of these are:

1. *Changing Social Conditions :* The class or caste structure in societies may itself change under the impact and influence of external and internal forces of change. The rapid advance of technology, and the urbanisation of rural areas are two such conditions which increase mobility and may cause ideological changes in society itself, giving rise to a new system or stratification. Frequently, changes in the class structure or stratification system in society are brought about when societies are disturbed by economic, social and political revolution. Such conditions provide fertile ground for reorganisation or replacement of an old system of social stratification with one that is different or entirely new.

   Static conditions in society, on the other hand, impede social mobility and serve to crystallise the existing class structure. When such conditions persist over long periods, status positions tend to become fixed and rigid and to be transmitted from generation to generation, moving increasingly towards the closed-class or caste type end of the continuum of stratification.

2. *Territorial Expansion and Population Movement :* Conditions of rapid territorial expansion-where population moved into "new territories" on a reasonably large basis-have proved conducive to flexibility of the stratification structure and social mobility.

3. *Limitation of Communication :* Any situation that limits communication between various strata of society, preventing interchange of knowledge and experience between them, will serve to strengthen inter strata dividing lines and discourage social mobility. Free and effective communication and education, which cut

across all strata boundaries, will serve to stimulate social mobility and weaken class barriers.

4. *Division of Labour* : The extent of social mobility will be negatively influenced by the degree of division of labour that exists in society. If the division of labour is high and specialised involving specific well trained skills, social mobility will be low, for it will be difficult for individuals to move easily from one strata to another.
5. *Differential Fertility Rates* : High reproduction rates of lower classes serve to restrict and hamper opportunities for family members to rise socially because of economic stringency and consequent low levels of living. The lower classes appear to have a scarcity of everything except children. High fertility rates of low income classes deprive family members from a higher level of living, development and opportunities for moving upward in the social scale in most societies.

On the other hand, upper classes tend to have fewer children and hence do not reproduce themselves in society. "The upper classes create what Professor Pitirim Sorokin terms a 'social vacuum' within society when they do not reproduce themselves. People from lower strata have an opportunity to move their positions and advance in the social scale" [Anderson, 1964, p. 374].

Bibliography

Alderson, J. : *Law and Disorder,* Hamish Hamilton, London, 1984.

Berhard, Davies : *The Use of Groups in Social Work Practice,* Routledge and Kegan Paul, London, 1975.

Brown, R.G.S. : *The Management of Welfare: A Study of British Social Service Administration,* Collern London, 1975.

Bruce Maurice : *The Coming of the Welfare State,* B.T. Batsford, London, 1961.

Carr, G. : *The Angry Brigade: the Cause and the Case,* Gollancz, London, 1975.

Clarke, R. V. and Hough, J. M. : *The Effectiveness of Policing,* Gower Publications, Farnborough, 1980.

Dubey, S.N. : *Administration of Social Welfare Programmes in India,* Somaliya, Bombay, 1973.

Durkheim, E. , *The Rules of Sociological Method,* The Free Press, Glencoe, 1958.

Gangrade, K.D. : *Social Legislation in India,* Concept Publishers, New Delhi, 1978.

George, V.N. : *Social Security,* Routledge, London, 1971.

Goel, S.L. and Jain, R.K : *Social Welfare Administration,* Deep and Deep Publications, New Delhi, 1988:

Gokhale, S.D. : *Social Welfare : Legend and Legacy,* Popular Prakashan, Bombay, 1975.

Gupta, B.B : *The Welfare State in India*, Central Book Depot, Allahabad 1966.

Hall, S. : *Policing the Crisis: Mugging, the State, and Law and Order*, MacMillan, London, 1978.

Hart, H. L. A. : *The Concept of Law*, Clarendon Press, Oxford, 1961.

Ionescu, G. : *Politics and the Pursuit of Happiness*, Longman, London, 1984.

Jagannadham, V. : *Social Welfare Organisation*, Indian Institute of Public Administration, New Delhi, 1967.

Jocob, K. K. : *Methods and Field of Social Work in India*, Asia Publication, Bombay, 1965.

Kulkarni, P.D. : *Social Policy and Social Development in India*, Association of Schools of Social Work in India, Madras, 1979.

———— : *The Central Social Welfare Board*, Indian Institute of Public Administration, New Delhi, 1961.

Lyons D. : *Ethics and the Rule of Law*, Cambridge, University Press, Cambridge, 1984.

Madan, G. R. : *Indian Social Problems*, Allied Publishers, New York, 1970.

Mamoria C.A. : *Labour Welfare, Social Security and Industrial Peace in India*, Kitab Mahal, Allahabad, 1983.

Mathur, A.S. and Gupta, A.S. : *Prostitutes and Prostitution*, Ram Prasad and Sons, Agra, 1965.

Miller, D. : *The Use and Abuse of Political Violence* Oxford University Press, Oxford, 1984.

Minhas, B. S. : *Planning and the Poor*, S. Chand & Co, New Delhi, 1974.

Packer, H. L. : *The Limits of the Criminal Sanction*, Oxford University Press, Oxford,1969.

Paul, Chowdhry, D. : *Voluntary Social Welfare in India*, Sterling Publishers Delhi, 1971.

Pfiffner, John M. and Sherwood Frank, P. : *Administrative Organisation,* Prentice Hall of India New Delhi, 1968.

Platt T. and Takagi P. : *Crime and Social Justice,* Macmillan, London, 1981.

Radzinowicz, L. : *Ideology and Crime: a Study of Crime in its Social and Historical Context,* Heinemann, London, 1966.

Reed, E.W. : *Social Welfare Administrative,* Columbia University Press, New York, 1961.

Selznick, P. : *Law, Society, and Industrial Justice,* Russell Sage, New York, 1969.

Singer, P. : *Democracy and Disobedience,* Clarendon Press, Oxford, 1973.

Sinha, S.N. and Basu, N.K : *History of Prostitution in India,* The Bengal Social Hygiene Association, Calcutta, 1933.

Srivastavia, S.P. : *Public Participation in Social Defence,* Lucknow University, Lucknow, 1978.

Taylor, I. P. Walton and J. Young : *The New Criminology: for a Social Theory of Defiance,* Routledge and Kegan Paul, London, 1973.

Taylor, I. : *Law and Order: Arguments for Socialism,* Macmillan, London, 1981.

William : *Evidence for Voluntary Action,* Allen and Unwin, London, 1949.

INDEX

J

K

L

M

N

O

P

R

S

T

U

V

Z

❑❑❑